Liberal Beginnings

Making a Republic for the Moderns

Liberal Beginnings examines the origins and development of the modern liberal tradition and explores the relationship between republicanism and liberalism between 1750 and 1830. Andreas Kalyvas and Ira Katznelson consider the diverse settings of Scotland, the American colonies, the new United States, and France and examine the writings of six leading thinkers of this period: Adam Smith, Adam Ferguson, James Madison, Thomas Paine, Germaine de Staël, and Benjamin Constant. The book traces the process by which these thinkers transformed and advanced the republican project, both from within and by introducing new elements from without. Without compromising civic principles or abandoning republican language, they came to see that, unrevised, the republican tradition could not grapple successfully with the political problems of their time. By investing new meanings, arguments, and justifications into existing republican ideas and political forms, these innovators fashioned a doctrine for a modern republic, the core of which was surprisingly liberal.

Andreas Kalyvas is Assistant Professor in the Department of Politics at The New School for Social Research and the Eugene Lang College for Liberal Arts. He is the recipient of the 2002 Leo Strauss Award for the best doctoral dissertation in the field of political philosophy and the author of *Democracy and the Politics of the Extraordinary: Max Weber, Carl Schmitt, and Hannah Arendt* (2008).

Ira Katznelson is Ruggles Professor of Political Science and History, Columbia University. His most recent books are *When Affirmative Action Was White* (2005) and *Desolation and Enlightenment: Political Knowledge after Total War, Totalitarianism, and the Holocaust* (2003), which received the David and Helene Spitz Prize and the David Easton Award.

For our families

Liberal Beginnings

Making a Republic for the Moderns

ANDREAS KALYVAS

The New School for Social Research

IRA KATZNELSON

Columbia University

CAMBRIDGE UNIVERSITY PRESS

CAMBRIDGE UNIVERSITY PRESS
Cambridge, New York, Melbourne, Madrid, Cape Town, Singapore, São Paulo, Delhi

Cambridge University Press
32 Avenue of the Americas, New York, NY 10013–2473, USA

www.cambridge.org
Information on this title: www.cambridge.org/9780521728287

First published 2008

Printed in the United States of America

A catalog record for this publication is available from the British Library.

Library of Congress Cataloging in Publication Data

Kalyvas, Andreas.
Liberal beginnings : making a republic for the moderns / Andreas Kalyvas,
Ira Katznelson.
p. cm.
Includes bibliographical references and index.
ISBN 978-0-521-89946-8 (hardback)
ISBN 978-0-521-72828-7 (pbk.)
1. Liberalism – History – 18th century. 2. Liberalism – History – 19th century.
3. Republicanism – History – 18th century. 4. Republicanism – History – 19th
century. I. Katznelson, Ira, 1944– II. Title
JC421.K36 2008
320.51092′2 – dc22 2007051569

ISBN 978-0-521-89946-8 hardback
ISBN 978-0-521-72828-7 paperback

Contents

Acknowledgments

When authors labor over the course of some years on a manuscript, they come to owe debts more extensive than can be specifically recognized. During this period, we have profited enormously from the lively intellectual communities where we have been fortunate to teach: at Columbia University, the University of Michigan, and The New School for Social Research. We are grateful for the rich comments we received when we presented parts of this book at conferences, seminars, and colloquia, including the American Political Science Association annual meeting, the Columbia Colloquium in Political Theory, the New School's Political Theory Seminar, and a conference on Benjamin Constant at the University of California, Riverside. Along the way, Jeffrey Isaac, David Kettler, and Melissa Schwartzberg read the entire manuscript and offered exceptionally helpful observations and suggestions. Additionally, Stephen Holmes, David Johnston, Nadia Urbinati, and Jeremy Waldron, having read sections, provided incisive criticisms that we have tried to take into account. We also warmly appreciate how Lewis Bateman, our editor at Cambridge University Press, has helped conduct this book to publication.

Various chapters appeared in earlier versions. We thank the following for their permission to base our revisions on these publications:

"Adam Ferguson Returns: Liberalism through a Glass Darkly," *Political Theory*, 26 (April 1998), pp. 173–197.

"'We Are Modern Men': Benjamin Constant and the Discovery of Immanent Liberalism," *Constellations*, 5 (December 1999), pp. 513–539.

"The Rhetoric of the Market: Adam Smith on Recognition, Speech, and Exchange," *Review of Politics*, 63 (Summer 2001), pp. 549–580.

"Embracing Liberalism: Germaine de Staël's Farewell to Republicanism," in *From Republican Polity to National Community: Reconsiderations of Enlightenment Political Thought*, ed. Paschalis Kitromilides, Oxford: Voltaire Foundation, 2003, pp. 167–190.

"The Republic of the Moderns: Paine's and Madison's Novel Liberalism," *Polity*, 38 (October 2006), pp. 447–477.

New York, November 2007

1

Beginnings

At a challenging time marked by global transformations and political uncertainty, and at a moment when modern liberalism has discredited one enemy and is embattled with another, its history, character, and prospects have become ever more urgent. The relationship between republicanism and liberalism, which emerged as a central issue for historians of modern political thought some decades ago, presently can aid such a consideration.

At first, this subject defined an important axis of debate among political historians, especially as they discovered republicanism as an alternative to the liberal tradition in colonial America and the early republic.[1] Studies of the links joining liberalism to an older republicanism

[1] See, for instance, Bernard Bailyn, *The Ideological Origins of the American Revolution*, Cambridge, Mass.: Belknap Press of Harvard University Press, 1992; Gordon S. Wood, *The Creation of the American Republic, 1776–1787*, Chapel Hill, N.C.: University of North Carolina Press, 1998; J. G. A. Pocock, "Civic Humanism and Its Role in Anglo-American Thought," in *Politics, Language, and Time: Essays on Political Thought and History*, Chicago: University of Chicago Press, 1989, pp. 80–103; J. G. A. Pocock, *The Machiavellian Moment: Florentine Political Thought and the Atlantic Republican Tradition*, Princeton, N.J.: Princeton University Press, 1975; Robert E. Shalhope, "Toward a Republican Synthesis: The Emergence of an Understanding of Republicanism in American Historiography," *William and Mary Quarterly*, 29 (1972), pp. 49–80; Robert E. Shalhope, "Republicanism and Early American Historiography," *William and Mary Quarterly*, 29 (1982), pp. 334–356; Joyce Appleby, "Liberalism and the American Revolution," *New England Quarterly*, 49:1 (1976), pp. 3–26; Joyce Appleby, "The Social Origins of American Revolutionary Ideology," *Journal of American History*, 64:4 (1978), pp. 935–958; Joyce Appleby,

then migrated to political theory and to comparative, cross-national investigations. Animated by strong normative motivations, these works have taken what is, by now, a familiar form, where one or the other is endorsed as the superior doctrine and as a better guide to contemporary politics and society.[2] Speaking directly to the standing

Liberalism and Republicanism in Historical Imagination, Cambridge, Mass.: Harvard University Press, 1992; Dorothy Ross, "The Liberal Tradition Revisited and the Republican Tradition Addressed," in *New Directions in American Intellectual History*, ed. John Higham and Paul K. Conkin, Baltimore: Johns Hopkins University Press, 1979, pp. 116–131; Isaac Kramnick, "Republican Revisionism Revisited," *American Historical Review*, 87:3 (1982), pp. 629–664; Isaac Kramnick, "The 'Great National Discussion': The Discourse of Politics in 1787," *William and Mary Quarterly*, 45:1 (1988), pp. 3–32; John P. Diggins, *The Lost Soul of American Politics: Virtue, Self-Interest, and the Foundations of Liberalism*, Chicago: University of Chicago Press, 1986; James Oakes, "From Republicanism to Liberalism: Ideological Change and the Crisis of the Old South," *American Quarterly*, 37:4 (1985), pp. 551–571; Linda K. Kerber, "The Republican Ideology of the Revolutionary Generation," *American Quarterly*, 37:4 (1985), pp. 474–495; Lance Banning, "Jeffersonian Ideology Revised: Liberal and Classical Ideas in the New American Republic," *William and Mary Quarterly*, 43:1 (1986), pp. 3–19; Richard C. Sinopoli, "Liberalism, Republicanism, and the Constitution," *Polity*, 19 (1987), pp. 331–352; Morton Horwitz, "Republicanism and Liberalism in American Constitutional Thought," *William and Mary Law Review*, 29 (1987), pp. 57–74; Thomas L. Pangle, *The Spirit of Modern Republicanism: The Moral Vision of the American Founders and the Philosophy of Locke*, Chicago: University of Chicago Press, 1988; Daniel T. Rodgers, "Republicanism: The Career of a Concept," *Journal of American History*, 79:1 (1992), pp. 11–38; Milton M. Klein, Richard D. Brown, and John B. Hench, eds., *The Republican Synthesis Revisited: Essays in Honor of George Athan Billias*, Worcester: American Antiquarian Society, 1992; Michael P. Zuckert, *The Natural Rights Republic: Studies in the Foundation of the American Political Tradition*, Notre Dame, Ind.: University of Notre Dame Press, 1996; James T. Kloppenberg, *The Virtues of Liberalism*, Oxford: Oxford University Press, 1998; Quinter Skinner, *Liberty before Liberalism*, Cambridge: Cambridge University Press, 1998.

2 Jeffrey Isaac, "Republicanism vs. Liberalism? A Reconsideration," *History of Political Thought*, 9 (1988), pp. 349–377; Frank Michelman, "Law's Republic," *Yale Law Journal*, 97:8 (1988), pp. 1493–1537; Cass R. Sunstein, "Beyond the Republican Revival," *Yale Law Journal*, 97:8 (1988), pp. 1539–1590; Philip Pettit, "Liberalism and Republicanism," *Australian Journal of Political Science*, 28 (1993), pp. 162–189; Philip Pettit, *Republicanism: A Theory of Freedom and Government*, Oxford: Oxford University Press, 1999; Jürgen Habermas, "Three Normative Models of Democracy," in *Democracy and Difference: Contesting the Boundaries of the Political*, ed. Seyla Benhabib, Princeton, N.J.: Princeton University Press, 1996, pp. 21–30; Michael P. Zuckert, *Natural Rights and the New Republicanism*, Princeton, N.J.: Princeton University Press, 1994; M. N. S. Sellers, *The Sacred Fire of Liberty: Republicanism, Liberalism and the Law*, New York: New York University Press, 1998; Stéphane Chauvier, *Libéralisme et Républicanisme*, Cahiers de Philosophie de l'Université

and possibilities of liberalism today, such discussions consider a range of issues that include tensions joining virtue and self-interest, the common and the personal, sovereignty and representation, authority and freedom, law and ethics.

We contribute to this ongoing conversation by way of a historical and textual strategy. In coming to terms with liberal beginnings, we examine the association – or is it a bond? – connecting liberalism and republicanism. We revisit the origins and development of liberal thought to think about how it ascended, despite many challenges, to today's leading position. In so doing, we distance ourselves from an important strand in Anglo-American political theory stressing the disagreements, even the antagonism, dividing republicanism from liberalism.

This literature proceeds along conceptual, methodological, and normative lines based on the assumption of two distinct paradigms. Whereas one is identified by strong notions of citizenship, tight connections between law and ethics, military valor, a sacrificial logic, civic religion, and the priority of collective life, the other is portrayed as devoted to the protection of individual rights, religious liberty, limited government, rule by consent, a division between the right and the good, the heterogeneity of interests, and the centrality of legislative representation. The conceptual line compares and contrasts the two, identifying such distinctions as freedom as noninterference from freedom as nondomination.[3] The methodological weighs up the balance between continuity and rupture in the history of political thought.[4] The normative asks us to evaluate and choose.[5]

de Caen, Caen: Centre de Philosophie de l'Université de Caen, 2000. For a fine comparative assessment of liberalism in the age of revolution, see Mark Hulliung, *Citizens and Citoyens: Republicans and Liberals in America and France*, Cambridge, Mass.: Harvard University Press, 2002.

3 Pettit, *Republicanism*, pp. 51–80, 297–298; Philip Pettit, *A Theory of Freedom: From Psychology to a Politics of Agency*, New York: Polity Press, 2001.

4 Quentin Skinner provides a clear defense on the benefits of the study of discontinuities in the history of modern political thought. Skinner, *Liberty before Liberalism*, p. 111. But see also Pettit, who refers to the "displacement" of the republican concept of freedom in favor of the liberal one as a "*coup d'état*," a "usurpation." Pettit, *Republicanism*, pp. 41–50.

5 Skinner, *Liberty before Liberalism*, p. 120; Maurizio Viroli, *Republicanism*, trans. Antony Shugaar, New York: Hill and Wang, 2002, pp. 12, 64, 95, 102–103.

Presented as mutually exclusive repertoires of ideas, with the one precluding the other, many scholars line up in opposed camps.[6] Republicanism and liberalism are said to have emerged from particular wellsprings, each isolated and insulated from the other, as two "incommensurate" vocabularies.[7] Their historical relations are constructed as a zero-sum game. The victory of the one must imply the defeat of the other.

We reject this false antagonism. We refuse the tendency to read history backward. It is a mistake, we show, to stylize the past as if each tradition possessed a wholly distinct genealogy, thus constituting entirely separate paradigms. By contrast, our burden is to demonstrate that liberalism is not external to the history of republicanism. Rather, we argue, liberalism as we know it was born from the spirit of republicanism, from attempts to adapt republicanism to the political, economic, and social revolutions of the eighteenth century and the first decades of the nineteenth.

Between 1750 and 1830 – not earlier or later – liberalism took a doctrinal and institutional form that has endured. Liberalism first became conscious of itself as a particular political and constitutional doctrine when the most promising and viable alternative to monarchy was republicanism. Over the course of this period, antimonarchical discourse was predominantly republican.[8] Yet, paradoxically, just as republicans were presented with an unprecedented possibility to limit or even replace the monarchical order on both sides of the Atlantic, a dramatic form of innovation was initiated that soon transcended established republican boundaries.

A close look at this pivotal moment reveals a rich, complex interpenetration joining the two and suggests that underscoring the enclosed individuality of each is far too limited. Instead of simply thinking of republican and liberal ideas as rival, external each to the other, we demonstrate that what we recognize today as liberalism in fact was

[6] Of course, as we discuss in this chapter, we are not alone in examining the close ties often connecting the two traditions.

[7] J. G. A. Pocock, "Virtues, Rights, and Manners: A Model for Historians of Political Thought," in *Virtue, Commerce, History*, Cambridge: Cambridge University Press, 1985, p. 47.

[8] Franco Venturi, *Utopia and Reform in the Enlightenment*, Cambridge: Cambridge University Press, 1971, pp. 22–23.

constituted as a conceptual hybrid both against and within republican terminology, ideas, and aspirations. In tracing this process, we show how republicanism was transformed radically from inside and by introducing new elements from without. Republican discourse, concepts, and motivations were not abandoned but were adapted. By investing new meanings, arguments, and justifications into existing ideas and political forms, a doctrine for a modern republic was fashioned, the core of which was surprisingly liberal.

Without compromising republican principles or abandoning republican language, this tradition unrevised could not have grappled successfully with a series of pressing problems. To remedy this circumstance, contemporary thinkers transformed existing republican resources and, where necessary, supplemented from outside republicanism's conceptual and institutional boundaries, introducing new principles and arguments drawn from other intellectual and philosophical currents, especially those inspired by John Locke and natural-law thinking. These amendments and synergies produced constitutional liberalism, not as an external alternative to classical republicanism, but, in significant measure, as a doctrine incubated within it. Political liberalism burst from the shell of a republican chrysalis.

The more republicanism sought to retrofit itself for modern conditions, the more liberal it became. The more liberal republicanism became, the more its relevance was lost. From the middle of the nineteenth century, in a complex process, liberalism's entanglement with republican thought began to bring their relationship to an end. Liberalism subsumed and transformed key elements of what previously had been a distinct doctrine of government. As a freestanding model, republicanism disappeared.

I

The eighteenth and early nineteenth centuries witnessed momentous transformations, not just in large-scale economic, social, and political structures, but in the ideas and values that could be utilized to make sense of this new world. Even before the American and French revolutions, the western and northern parts of Europe, as well as North America, wrestled with unprecedented conditions – centralized states, formalized law, commercial capitalism and a new middle class, religious pluralism, a distinct sphere of civil society, global warfare, colonial conquest, and monarchical insecurity. Concurrently, the West experienced the emergence of innovative currents of thought, including secularism or at least limitations to the sphere of religion, an enlarged status for individual persons, and universal natural rights, and, more broadly, systematic rationality, critical thinking, and scientific methods. This constellation generated a powerful, anxious political question: could a free republic be fashioned and sustained under these circumstances?

This question was double-edged. For just as humankind was developing new capacities to think and act freely and to control, perhaps master, the environment, it also had to come to terms with profound losses. A remarkable efflorescence of expectations went hand in hand with the palpable demise of beliefs, manners, and behaviors that had been thought necessary to underpin the growth of liberty. The more modern the world, the more individuals might become free. Yet the same modernity was generating contrary forces threatening this very prospect.

A wide array of thinkers confronted this predicament. How they did so is our subject. From this group, we closely study Adam Smith, Adam Ferguson, James Madison, Thomas Paine, Germaine de Staël, and Benjamin Constant. Writing in the diverse settings of Scotland, the American colonies and the new United States, and France, they combined in their profound reflections originality with influence in tackling the vexing and rapidly changing features of the modern world. Their texts considered a breathtaking range of themes – literature, moral philosophy, aesthetics, political economy, history, law, and geography. The quest to understand the conditions required for the exercise of freedom in a viable republic unified their different explorations. Of course, they were hardly the only figures searching for answers. Other important intellectuals, including Thomas Reid and Dugald Stewart, Thomas Jefferson and Alexander Hamilton, Baron de Montesquieu, Marquis de Condorcet, and Emmanuel Sieyès, also merit detailed examination.

The group we consider, however, was selected for three principal reasons. Even at the time, these persons stood out as preeminent guides to modern politics and policy. Their writings were explicitly motivated to understand the prospects of republican institutions and orientations in rapidly changing circumstances. Each of their interventions in public life powerfully shaped the content, terms, and vectors of political discussion and debate in that period.

In addition to the here and now, they pursued a more general analytical, normative, and abstract question. What, they wished to know, can republicanism be? Though motivated primarily by the most pressing contemporary questions, they offered broader theoretical reflections regarding the nature of republicanism as a type of regime. They sought to identify constitutive norms and arrangements according to which it might be possible to distinguish republicanism from other types of rule, and between genuine and inauthentic republics.

Our selection further was guided by the way the work of the six authors has been considered by historians of ideas. There are two divergent, even stylized readings. For some, each should be read as a staunch republican, situated within civic humanism. Yet for others, indeed for the majority, they are treated as canonical, even foundational, liberal thinkers.[9]

In focusing on these writers, we began by wishing to explore the meaning and implications of such apparently contradictory characterizations. Soon we discerned that these competing interpretations capture real but only partial truths. We came to realize that they are symptomatic of a deeper and more integral association. As we will see in each chapter, the republican and liberal readings find much textual justification. Close attention to each author reveals a republican language of virtue, corruption, patriotism, and political ethics. Each elaborated characteristically republican themes, seeking to discern what constitutes a good polity. But these thinkers also significantly transcended the bounds of republicanism. Thus, it also is right to call them liberals, a term, of course, not then in use. Unlike classical republicans, they stressed individual interests, freedoms and rights, government by consent, the contingent sources of political activity, a wish to protect citizens from potentially predatory rulers, and skepticism toward organized political authority.

[9] We discuss these assignments in each of the substantive chapters that follow. For alternative analytical narratives of the liberal tradition, see Gertrude Himmelfarb, *The Roads to Modernity: The British, French, and American Enlightenments*, New York: Knopf, 2004; and Paul Starr, *Freedom's Power: The True Force of Liberalism*, New York: Perseus, 2007.

Tracking these concerns, they invented institutional forms, legal arrangements, and ways of talking about politics. By transforming political imagination about society, authority, and power in their time, they initiated liberal beginnings. This originality thus impelled us to revisit their writings. Refusing a simple binary choice, we decided to focus rather on the intersecting trajectories of republicanism and liberalism, all the while remaining attentive to variations in how each thinker navigated this shifting ground.

Our reading has implications. The book focuses primarily on the origins and development of liberalism as a quest to make a republic for modern times. In so doing, we do not proceed as if liberalism is a hermetically sealed, freestanding body of thought with distinct institutional applications that contends with rival doctrines and practices. This historical interpretation undercuts an artificial opposition demanding a stark alternative: opt for liberalism, or for one or another of its competitors. After a review of current historiographical trends that exhibit this excessively severe portrait, we will see how studying the beginnings of political liberalism not only can overcome this choice but also can advance a distinctive argument about the relevance of our reading to urgent problems today, warranting a reconceptualization and renewal of political liberalism.

II

Distinguished scholars of republicanism as diverse as Hannah Arendt, Gordon Wood, J. G. A. Pocock, Quentin Skinner, and Philip Pettit have portrayed a blunt conceptual opposition between two distinct intellectual and political projects that competed with each other.[10] Further, their depiction claims that liberalism decisively defeated and

[10] Hannah Arendt, "What Is Freedom?" in *Between Past and Present*, New York: Penguin Books, 1961, pp. 143–172; Pocock, *The Machiavellian Moment*, pp. 424, 545–546, 550–551; J. G. A. Pocock, *Politics, Language, and Time: Essays on Political Thought and History*, New York: Atheneum, 1971, p. 144; J. G. A. Pocock, "Virtue and Commerce in the Eighteenth Century," *Journal of Interdisciplinary History*, 3 (1972), pp. 120, 124–129; Pocock, "Virtues, Rights, and Manners: A Model for Historians of Political Thought," pp. 48–50; J. G. A. Pocock, "Cambridge School and Scottish Enlightenment," in *Wealth and Virtue: The Shaping of Political Economy in the Scottish Enlightenment*, ed. Istvan Hont and Michael Ignatieff, Cambridge: Cambridge University Press, 1983, pp. 244–250; Skinner, *Liberty before Liberalism*, pp. ix–x, 10, 12, 84–99; Pettit, *Republicanism*, pp. 297–303. Also, see Rowland

replaced republicanism.[11] Viewing this development elegiacally, these authors lament liberalism's victory and wistfully long for a republican renewal.[12]

The most ambitious recent elaboration of this approach is Quentin Skinner's vigorous *Liberty before Liberalism*. Conceptually, it insists that a radical difference distinguishes liberalism from an earlier republicanism. Methodologically, it offers an account of a historical disjunction. Building on his 1997 inaugural lecture as Regius Professor of Modern History at Cambridge University, this tightly argued text chronicles "the ideological triumph of liberalism" and the concurrent "fall within Anglophone political theory of what I have labeled a neo-roman understanding of civil liberty."[13] Informing this treatment is a particular version of the history of ideas based on an assertion that each to the other presents "a rival view of liberty," "a conflict within our inherited traditions."[14] Normatively, Skinner insists that the ultimate "liberal hegemony" has been very costly.[15] A better politics and practice of liberty understood as the absence of dependence has been sacrificed to a thinner, less robust version of human freedom as the absence of interference.[16]

Skinner's retrospective excavation, an effort to "re-enter the intellectual world we have lost," thus imagines a fateful historical "choice"

Betthoff, "Independence and Attachment, Virtue and Interest: From Republican Citizen to Free Enterpriser," in *Uprooted Americans: Essays to Honor Oscar Handlin*, ed. Richard L. Bushman, Boston: Little, Brown, 1979, pp. 97–124; Michael Zuckerman, "A Different Thermidor: The Revolution beyond the American Revolution," in *Transformation of Early American History: Society, Authority and Ideology*, ed. James A. Henretta, New York: Knopf, 1991, pp. 170–193.

11 Hannah Arendt, *On Revolution*, New York: Penguin Books, 1963, pp. 215–281; Wood, *The Creation of the American Republic, 1776–1787*, pp. 606–615; Pocock, "Virtue and Commerce in the Eighteenth Century," pp. 130–131, 134; Pocock, "Cambridge School and Scottish Enlightenment," pp. 240–243; John M. Murrin, "Self-Interest Conquers Patriotism: Republicans, Liberals, and Indians Reshape the Nation," in *The American Revolution: Its Character and Limits*, ed. Jack P. Greene, New York: New York University Press, 1987, pp. 224–229; Skinner, *Liberty before Liberalism*, pp. 96–99; Pettit, *Republicanism*, pp. 12, 21, 41–50.

12 For a critical discussion of the normative claims of republicanism in relation to liberalism, see Alan Patten, "The Republican Critique of Liberalism," *British Journal of Political Science*, 26:1 (1996), pp. 25–44.

13 Skinner, *Liberty before Liberalism*, pp. x, ix.

14 Skinner, *Liberty before Liberalism*, pp. x, 119.

15 Skinner, *Liberty before Liberalism*, p. x.

16 Skinner, *Liberty before Liberalism*, pp. 84, 92–93, 119.

in which "we in the modern West have embraced" the liberal tradition at the expense of the republican.[17] He asks, "Did we choose rightly?" He coyly responds, "I leave it to you to ruminate."[18] This is the basis of his desire to choose, once again, but more wisely, as if the game of selection simply continues.

We challenge this account. The two do not constitute entirely separate realms. Skinner has underplayed how both in fact are complex, as are their ties to each other. When Adam Smith and Adam Ferguson recognized the centrality of commercial society and how it affected republican institutions, values, and practices, they did not turn to a preexisting, fully formed liberal paradigm. Rather, they articulated a new theory of politics while remaining loyal to the spirit of republicanism. In so doing, they became liberal pioneers. When, as men of affairs, Madison and Paine confronted the immediate and pressing responsibility of instituting the globe's first modern republic – a task they expressed in republican terms – they actually established the world's first liberal regime. When Staël and Constant became disillusioned with the revolutionary excesses of classical republicanism, which they previously had endorsed and extolled, their constitutional proposals emplaced at the center of civic discourse in continental Europe a strong concern for individual rights and freedoms. Despite temporal, geographic, and intellectual differences, in each of these instances key features and aspects of republicanism were transmuted into what soon became a distinct liberal doctrine of government. This liberalism, emerging out of republicanism, came to occupy the space that the latter had not been able to fill after the collapse of monarchy.

There was, in short, no simple or radical break in which the one replaced the other. By averring that there was such a clear-cut substitution, Skinner stripped from liberalism key aspects of its republican lineage. To the contrary, modern liberalism was deeply influenced by republicanism. As republican philosophers sought to renovate the ancient republic for contemporary conditions, and as they struggled to modernize it, they invented ideas and institutions that transformed classical republicanism into what we know as liberalism. This effort was not primarily a planned change or, as Skinner argues, a malevolent

[17] Skinner, *Liberty before Liberalism*, pp. x, 119.
[18] Skinner, *Liberty before Liberalism*, p. 120.

exercise, but was the product of a direct grappling with pressing predicaments.

Associating the critical moment "with the rise of classical utilitarianism in the eighteenth century, and with the use of utilitarian principles to underpin much of the liberal state in the century following," Skinner proposed two explanations for the republican defeat.[19] First, republicanism came to be perceived as both anachronistic and inconsistent. "The social assumptions underlying" republican "theory began to appear outdated and even absurd . . . irrelevant to a polite and commercial age."[20] Second, this alteration to the perception of republicanism was neither accidental nor unintended. It was predicated on how its opponents maliciously caricatured republicanism as a confused approach to liberty. The enemies of republicanism successfully seized opportunities to discredit a still robust set of ideas. Republicanism was routed by making it seem "ludicrous."[21]

On this reading, the fall of republicanism was the result of manipulated misperception rather than inherent failings, institutional defects, or historical limitations in the doctrine itself. Liberalism's triumph was undeserved. It was not the best but the worst that emerged victorious in the clash of doctrines. We differ. Major political doctrines on the order of republican thought cannot simply be shunted aside by cunning or deception. Why, we must ask, was republicanism unable to respond either to the era's circumstances or to the ideological assault mounted against it?[22] Seen in this light, the notion that we are compelled to choose one or the other tradition is unpersuasive. Any renewal of republicanism would require a better understanding of its fall and its seeming conquest by the liberal other.

III

Each of the two bodies of political thought was deeply engaged with the other. We are not the first to notice this. Leading advocates of republicanism already have addressed this kinship.

[19] Skinner, *Liberty before Liberalism*, p. 96.
[20] Skinner, *Liberty before Liberalism*, pp. 96–97.
[21] Skinner, *Liberty before Liberalism*, p. 97.
[22] For one of the most compelling efforts to answer these questions, see Ventura, *Utopia and Reform in the Enlightenment*, pp. 18–46, 70–94.

In a prominent instance, the historian Gordon Wood revised his own earlier radical claims about an abrupt end of classical politics during the American Founding.[23] "I probably contributed my mite," he reflected, "to this distortion of past reality and to the mistaken notion that one set of ideas *simply replaced* another en bloc."[24] Wood now cautioned that it is an error to suggest that "the entire republican tradition came to an end in 1787–88 and was abruptly replaced by something called liberalism."[25] Rather, he insisted, "cultural changes of that magnitude do not take place in such a neat and sudden manner."[26] This insight has been reiterated by Maurizio Viroli, who likewise has challenged the idea "that republicanism is an alternative to liberalism."[27] "From a historical point of view, the relationship of liberalism to republicanism is one of derivation and innovation," he writes.[28] His claim that liberalism is a "transformation of classical republicanism" echoes Wood's suggestive proposition that "republicanism was indeed gradually transformed into something we call liberalism, but in subtle and complicated ways that kept many republican sentiments alive."[29] Viroli concurred with Wood that "liberalism is a doctrine derived from republicanism."[30]

These moves distinguish both Wood and Viroli from the strong alternative view advocated not only by Skinner but by Philip Pettit's influential *Republicanism: A Theory of Freedom and Government*, to which Skinner pays explicit homage as a primary influence.[31] It was Pettit, after all, who declared that "not only did the conception of freedom as non-interference displace the republican idea in the new

[23] Wood, *The Creation of the American Republic, 1776–1787*, pp. 606–615.

[24] Wood, *The Creation of the American Republic, 1776–1787*, p. xi (italics added).

[25] Wood, *The Creation of the American Republic, 1776–1787*, p. xi.

[26] Wood, *The Creation of the American Republic, 1776–1787*, p. xi. Wood may have been responding to critics such as Gary Schmitt and Robert Webking, who have questioned his earlier claim about a clean break between the two political traditions. See Gary J. Schmitt and Robert K. Webking, "Revolutionaries, Antifederalists, and Federalists: Comments on Gordon Wood's Understanding of the American Revolution," *Political Science Reviewer*, 9 (1979), pp. 195–229.

[27] Viroli, *Republicanism*, p. 6.

[28] Viroli, *Republicanism*, p. 58.

[29] Viroli, *Republicanism*, p. 8; Wood, *The Creation of the American Republic, 1776–1787*, p. xii.

[30] Viroli, *Republicanism*, p. 58.

[31] Skinner, *Liberty before Liberalism*, p. xi.

liberal tradition. It apparently succeeded in staging this *coup d'état* without anyone's noticing the usurpation," and who insisted, writing about liberalism, that "the new idea of freedom that emerged in the nineteenth century, and that eventually took over on all fronts, was socially as well as politically weaker than the older republican ideal."[32]

Despite their differences with Skinner and Pettit, however, the revisionist republican thinkers also have voiced regret – Wood, for example, deplored "how America moved into this liberal world of business, moneymaking, and the open promotion of interests," and Viroli, more intensely, lamented the "intellectual loss" entailed by the triumph of liberalism, which "can be considered an impoverished or incoherent republicanism."[33] Perhaps Wood and certainly Viroli, like Skinner, still pine for the return of a truer and more authentic republicanism, rather than the more limited and veiled kind found within liberalism. For better or worse, such a road no longer exists. There is little point in either republican nostalgia or utopianism. Rather, we should seek to grasp how and why the loss of republicanism happened and probe the character of the liberalism that emerged.

Notwithstanding this disagreement, the intellectual histories of Wood and Viroli do suggest an appealing thesis about the historical and conceptual ties linking republicanism to liberalism. Rather than endorse Pettit's and Skinner's claims of a paradigmatic break, they invite attention to the moment when liberal doctrine emerged in a complex relation to republican ideas.[34]

Unfortunately, neither Wood nor Viroli have followed up on these insights. Their suggestive formulations have remained underdeveloped. Viroli has kept silent about the mechanisms, means, and reasons republicanism was transformed into a new body of thought he considers demonstrably worse. Wood, by contrast, has provided a primarily cultural and socioeconomic explanation of American ideological history, a history mainly external to the trajectory of republicanism itself. He has emphasized that, as radical change was introduced by various means into social life, republicans had to adapt. The rise of mass

32 Pettit, *Republicanism*, pp. 50, 300, 21, 41.

33 Gordon Wood, "Ideology and the Origins of Liberal America," *William and Mary Quarterly*, 44:3 (1987), p. 635; Wood, *The Creation of the American Republic, 1776–1787*, pp. 610–613; Viroli, *Republicanism*, pp. 8, 61.

34 Wood, "Ideology and the Origins of Liberal America," p. 634.

evangelical Christianity from within a rapidly changing society produced irresistible popular energy that provoked a more liberal and egalitarian polity, economy, and society. Republican elites could not successfully resist.[35] Instead, he stressed, such elites were compelled to transmute their republicanism:

> People confronted particular problems, argued about them, and often presented new ways of dealing with them; in the process they inadvertently transformed important strains in the classical republican tradition. It was not that there were simply new kinds of people and new social groups emerging that required new values and new justifications for their behavior; though this was certainly true enough; it was also that circumstances often compelled those who wished to remain loyal to republican values to challenge and to subvert those values.[36]

One of our main goals is to explore these 'circumstances' and help reveal the mechanisms that accompanied and shaped this 'transformation.' We are particularly interested in observing and discerning the key features and underlying motivations that triggered this political and conceptual change. In so doing, we observe how liberalism developed not in a linear or teleological fashion that takes us from John Locke to Immanuel Kant to John Stuart Mill to John Rawls, as in many standard histories, and not from fully formed, transparent choices, but at critical junctures when other existing intellectual tools were insufficient to satisfactorily address pressing political and institutional matters. This way of thinking about the development of liberalism is more historical, more unpredictable, more heterogeneous and relational, and more oriented to practical affairs.

We dive into this history by closely examining key theoretical works that were written in the midst of demanding circumstances and arduous pressures and by tracing how republican themes and ideas turned in a liberal direction. The writings of Smith, Ferguson, Madison, Paine, Staël, and Constant allow us to witness this intellectual transformation. Concerned to attain a republic for the moderns, they never opted as such for liberalism rather than republicanism. Instead, their various quests to realize free government culminated in liberal formulations.

[35] Wood, "Ideology and the Origins of Liberal America," pp. 635, 636–640.
[36] Wood, *The Creation of the American Republic, 1776–1787*, p. xii.

IV

This history of ideas is not innocent. Recent debates about liberalism have been stylized by a series of oppositions that identify it exclusively with the primacy of the right over the good; neutral legal procedures rather than substantive values; interests, not virtues; negative instead of positive liberty; and individual persons as distinct from collectivities and the public good. With liberalism identified by both its advocates and skeptical critics with the first of each of these pairs, and as indifferent to the second, this tradition is doubly stressed. It denies to liberalism resources drawn from its own past. And it fashions a liberalism too thin for effective engagement with current conundrums.

This is a portrayal of forgetting.[37] In the eighteenth and nineteenth centuries, the key progenitors of modern liberalism refused to make just these distinctions. They did not abandon the good or disregard civic life. They did not glorify personal interests. They were not actors above the fray or outside history. But neither did they remain traditional republicans. They were both within and moved beyond, and sometimes against, republicanism. That singular association with this long-standing body of thought brought into being a rich, thick, historically grounded, sociologically sensitive, and institutionally oriented understanding to guide politics. Each thinker, albeit distinctively, recognized that the world's novel features demanded new ways to navigate the tensions and charged relations produced by the growth of modern states, the rise of commercial capitalism, the formation of pluralistic civil societies, and the development of global relationships. Because they approached these changes with never fully repudiated

[37] We are not alone in attempting to overcome this limited understanding of liberalism. See, among other efforts, Peter Berkowitz, *Virtue and the Making of Modern Liberalism*, Princeton, N.J.: Princeton University Press, 2000; Sharon R. Krause, *Liberalism with Honor*, Cambridge, Mass.: Harvard University Press, 2002; Thomas A. Spragens, *Civic Liberalism: Reflections on Our Democratic Ideals*, New York: Rowman and Littlefield, 1999; Richard Dagger, *Civic Virtues: Rights, Citizenship, and Republican Liberalism*, New York: Oxford University Press, 1997; Stephen L. Elkin, *Reconstructing the Commercial Republic: Constitutional Design after Madison*, Chicago: University of Chicago Press, 2006; and Istvan Hont, *Jealousy of Trade: International Competition and the Nation-State in Historical Perspective*, Cambridge, Mass.: Harvard University Press, 2005.

republican commitments, their political thought generated combinations of elements that joined what to many today appear as disjointed and competitive.

Much of our book explores these achievements. Adam Smith extracted his famous statement about human egoism from a deep conception of a good life as ethical recognition. Adam Ferguson sought to regulate and utilize formal law to tame human passions and the innate human propensity to conflict and to compete while appreciating the centrality of active citizenship. Thomas Paine and James Madison, in contributing to the creation of the first truly modern republic for a large and complex country, reinvented political virtue as political representation. Germaine de Staël's quest for a political center after monarchy's end led her to balance and at times combine polarized principles and values. Benjamin Constant distilled individual rights not from deductive abstraction but from a rich appreciation of historical development and cultural experience.

Of course, our world is not theirs. Yet present challenges are generated by not dissimilar sources. We continue to confront strains produced by economic inequality, the politics of global power, insecurity, and the scope of citizenship. Each source of pressure has characteristic features. The separation of sovereignty from property raises questions pertaining to how much inequality instigated by the operation of a market economy is consistent with the exercise of popular sovereignty, and which means might appropriately be deployed to reduce the tensions inherent in this division. The development of a global system of states, and of extra-state challenges to their authority, often pitches the pursuit of power by individual states against the pursuit of peace by international law and institutions. The persistence of violence and fear propels a pull for safety, intensifying the friction of liberty and security. And the establishment of liberalism as a coherent and independent body of concepts and practices inherently gives rise to the need to define criteria for inclusion in the polity, and thus to reconcile universal imperatives with particular cultural and historical divisions of humankind.

When we are asked by either dedicated republicans or committed liberals to select between their characteristic values, we are, perforce, being asked to sacrifice potential assets with which to address these quandaries. None has a singular or permanent resolution. Each defines a site of contestation in ideas and policies. Long ago, the six thinkers we discuss concluded that, on its own, the republicanism they had inherited simply was incapable of contributing effectively to debates about such crucial issues. The 'liberalism' they invented was the result of an active dialogue with one or more aspects of the modern world. Their liberalism was not sealed, but open; not uniform, but confidently heterogeneous. This situated and thick liberalism was born out of acts of sacrilege. Whenever they believed their own republican language excessively limited possibilities to envision and realize liberty, they transgressed its boundaries to search elsewhere. They brought back novel thoughts and arguments and initiated a reevaluation inside republicanism. In this way, they fundamentally altered both the perimeters and content of the civic tradition. Such were liberal beginnings.

2

The Rhetoric of the Market

Adam Smith on Recognition, Speech, and Exchange

Who can claim Adam Smith? For some strands of political thought, the stakes are high.[1] His writings have long been considered foundational texts for the economic dimensions of modern liberalism.[2] An alternative understanding, perforce, would compel a reevaluation of liberalism's canonical beginnings. Such a challenge, in fact, has been fashioned by thoughtful readers who associate Smith, alongside his colleagues in the Scottish Enlightenment, rather more with the republican tradition of civic humanism.[3] His rejection of the state of nature

[1] Donald Winch, "Adam Smith's 'enduring particular result': A Political and Cosmopolitan Perspective," in *Wealth and Virtue: The Shaping of Political Economy in the Scottish Enlightenment*, ed. Istvan Hont and Michael Ignatieff, Cambridge: Cambridge University Press, 1983, p. 253.

[2] F. A. Hayek has largely built on Smith in developing his liberal theory of the spontaneous order. See F. A. Hayek, *Law, Legislation and Liberty*, Vol. 1, Chicago: University of Chicago Press, 1973, pp. 20, 36–37, and *The Constitution of Liberty*, Chicago: University of Chicago Press, 1960, pp. 41, 161.

[3] For example, David Winch, *Adam Smith's Politics: An Essay in Historiographic Revision*, Cambridge: Cambridge University Press, 1978; Nicholas Phillipson, "Adam Smith as Civic Moralist," in Hont and Ignatieff, *Wealth and Virtue*, pp. 179–202; John Dwyer, "Virtue and Improvement: The Civic World of Adam Smith," in *Adam Smith Reviewed*, ed. Peter Jones and Andrew S. Skinner, Edinburgh: Edinburgh University Press, 1992, pp. 190–216. The debate over Smith's republicanism is much older, and its beginnings could be traced to John Rae's biography, *Life of Adam Smith*, London: Macmillan, 1895, p. 124, and to Joseph Cropsey's innovative study, *Polity and Economy: An Interpretation of the Principles of Adam Smith*, The Hague: M. Nijhoff, 1957, pp. 65–68, 94–95.

and his critique of social contract theory, as well as his denial that isolated individuals are the irreducible unit of social action, and his strong account of history and society as having moved through stages rather than having emerged out of a consensual founding, offer warrants for this effort to identify Smith as a "civic moralist."[4] Leaning heavily on Smith's *Moral Sentiments*, this ambitious reappraisal stresses the elements of sociality, sympathy, moral character, and passions to show the persistence and continued relevance of republican ideals for modern times.

Such readings are strained. Though rich with suggestive understanding, and often highlighting features that more-standard considerations of Smith either neglect or override, they nonetheless face overwhelming textual evidence that makes it impossible to simply appropriate him for a nonliberal tradition.[5] Accordingly, the leading practitioners of the 'republican' construal regularly acknowledge that Smith's writings are hybrids, combining elements from more than one legal and political discourse.[6] This assertion of syncretism is unmistakably correct, but it is incomplete in establishing how these strands in Smith's thought are entwined. This bracing literature thus leaves us with a historical challenge. How are Smith's 'republicanism' and 'liberalism' to be understood both within his own project and, more broadly, within the history of political ideas?

4 Phillipson, "Adam Smith as Civic Moralist," pp. 179–202.

5 Elie Halévy, *The Growth of Philosophic Radicalism*, trans. Mary Morris, London: Faber & Gwyer Limited, 1928, pp. 141–142; Duncan Forbes, "Sceptical Whiggism, Commerce, and Liberty," in *Essays on Adam Smith*, ed. Andrew S. Skinner and Thomas Wilson, Oxford: Clarendon Press, 1975, pp. 179–201; John Robertson, "Scottish Political Economy beyond the Civic Tradition: Government and Economic Development in the *Wealth of Nations*," *History of Political Thought*, 4:3 (Winter 1983), pp. 451–482; Michael Ignatieff, "Smith, Rousseau and the Republic of Needs," in *Scotland and Europe, 1200–1850*, ed. T. C. Smout, Edinburgh: John Donald, 1986, pp. 187–206; Shannon C. Stimson, "Republicanism and the Recovery of the Political in Adam Smith," in *Critical Issues in Social Thought*, ed. Murray Milgate and Cheryl B. Welch, London: Academic Press, 1989, pp. 91–112.

6 Joseph Cropsey, "Adam Smith and Political Philosophy," in Skinner and Wilson, *Essays on Adam Smith*, pp. 132–153; Winch, "Adam Smith's 'enduring particular result': A Political and Cosmopolitan Perspective," pp. 256, 262–269; David Winch, "Adam Smith and the Liberal Tradition," in *Traditions of Liberalism: Essays on John Locke, Adam Smith and John Stuart Mill*, ed. Knud Haakonssen, St. Leonards, NSW, Australia: Centre for Independent Studies, 1988, pp. 83–104.

If the liberal reading cannot be displaced, what is its standing? This more conventional and resilient account starts, of course, with the famous sentence in "Of the Principle which gives Occasion to the Division of Labour," the opening paragraph of the pivotal second chapter of *The Wealth of Nations*, that identifies the basis of political economy in the human "propensity to truck, barter, and exchange one thing for another."[7] This formulation plays both an analytical and a normative role. It offers an anthropological microfoundation for Smith's understanding of how commercial societies function as social organizations, which, in turn, provide settings for the expression and operation of these basic human proclivities. Together with the equally famous concept of the invisible hand, according to which "it is not from the benevolence of the butcher, the brewer, or the baker, that we expect our dinner, but from their regard to their own interest," this sentence defined the central axis of a new science designed to come to terms with economic production and exchange as a distinct, separate, independent sphere of human action that had begun to displace the once-ascendant positions of theology, morality, and political philosophy.[8]

Smith's formulation, moreover, transcends a purely descriptive account of the transformations that shook eighteenth-century Europe. A powerful normative theory about the emancipatory character of market systems lies at the heart of *Wealth*.[9] These markets constitute "the system of natural liberty" because they shatter traditional hierarchies, authorities, exclusions, and privileges.[10] Unlike mercantilism and other alternative mechanisms of economic coordination, markets

[7] Adam Smith, *An Inquiry into the Nature and Causes of the Wealth of Nations*, Indianapolis: Liberty Press, 1981 [1776], p. 25.

[8] Smith, *Wealth*, p. 27. For this interpretation, see Carl Schmitt, "The Age of Neutralizations and Depoliticizations" [1929], *Telos*, 96 (Summer 1993), p. 133; Hannah Arendt, *The Human Condition*. Chicago: University of Chicago Press, 1958, pp. 42, 48; Louis Dumont, *From Mandeville to Marx: The Genesis and Triumph of Economic Ideology*, Chicago: University of Chicago Press, 1977, pp. 104–107; Donald Winch, *Adam Smith's Politics: An Essay in Historiographic Revision*, Cambridge: Cambridge University Press, 1978, p. 187; and Philip Pettit, *Republicanism: A Theory of Freedom and Government*, Oxford: Oxford University Press, 1997, pp. 203–204, 224–227.

[9] Istvan Hont and Michael Ignatieff, "Needs and Justice in the *Wealth of Nations*: An Introductory Essay," in Hont and Ignatieff, *Wealth and Virtue*, p. 12.

[10] Smith, *Wealth*, pp. 687, 678, 670, 419–420.

are based on the spontaneous and free expression of individual preferences. Rather than change, even repress, human nature to accord with an abstract bundle of values, market economies accept the propensities of humankind and are attentive to their character. They recognize and value people's inclinations – not only human reason but the full panoply of individual aspirations and needs.[11] Thus, for Smith, markets advance economic liberty. This perspective has evident political implications. The liberal state should protect economic freedom, secure private property, and allow individuals to pursue their interests free from external interference under the protection of the rule of law. Smith's orientation thus offered an early formulation of what became a core feature of modern political liberalism – the value of negative liberty.

Also central to the liberal strand in Smith is the way he provided conceptual resources for an implicit theory of social integration based on strategic interaction among self-interested persons. Not just the economy but the larger social order is reproduced by free, unplanned behavior and processes, rather than by design. Smith considered a thick moral consensus and social homogeneity to have been eliminated by the large-scale social and symbolic transformations of his time. Thus, social order no longer could be secured by the features most prominent in republican thought. Additionally, with his emphasis on spontaneous coordination, Smith pointed to the possibility of a social order in which people could live in harmony with only a minimal coercive apparatus and limited political power. Notwithstanding its conflicts, capitalism produces stability and enjoys the advantage of a mechanism, the market, which maintains equilibria by continually adjusting competing interests, thus limiting the necessity of the state. Over time, these powerful theoretical propositions combined to produce a legitimating cornerstone for the robust defense of market capitalism, a particular ensemble of political institutions, and a specific line of justification for liberal ideas and values.

Itself, however, the liberal representation of Smith is not wholly compelling. Although the republican attempt to find a different Smith is even less persuasive, it nonetheless does capture elements within

[11] Joseph Cropsey has nicely discussed this double normative aspect in *An Interpretation of the Principles of Adam Smith*, Westport, Conn.: Greenwood Press, 1977.

his writings that cannot be contained within or reduced to a purely liberal account.[12] Smith, of course, is suitably if conventionally read as an exponent of material self-interest. Yet, as we show, his claim about propensities incorporates an older ethical understanding of the substantive content and intersubjective character of social relations mostly identified with the civic humanist tradition. This aspect of his thought sought to reconcile formal rights and the pursuit of interest with some ancient versions of ethical life. In so doing, he combined self-seeking propensities with a situational ethics grounded in history and local particularities.

Even as Smith announced the "propensity to truck, barter, and exchange," echoing Bernard de Mandeville's pioneering representation of human egoism, he immediately asked "whether this propensity be one of those original principles in human nature of which no further account can be given; or whether, as seems more probable, it be the necessary consequence of the faculties of reason and speech."[13] The pursuit of material self-interest, he thus suggested, may not be a primordial, constant or transhistorical, inclination. Stating that this inquiry "belongs not to our present subject to enquire," he left open the possibility that there exists an even deeper human desire – one, we will see, that is based on a craving for esteem and the avoidance of shame – which, under modern conditions, induces and sustains self-interested economic behavior.[14]

Smith did confront the vexing question he put aside in *Wealth*. He devoted considerable attention to it, not in a single, systematic study, but dispersed in three main texts: *The Theory of Moral Sentiments* (1759), *Letters on Rhetoric and Belles Lettres* (1762–1763), and

[12] For an acknowledgment of the civic qualities in Smith's work by the 'liberal' reading, see Duncan Forbes, "Sceptical Whiggism, Commerce and Liberty," in Skinner and Wilson, *Essays on Adam Smith*, pp. 179–201; Donald Winch, *Adam Smith's Politics: An Essay in Historiographic Revision*, Cambridge: Cambridge University Press, 1978; Winch, "Adam Smith's 'enduring particular result': A Political and Cosmopolitan Perspective," pp. 253–269; Donald Winch, "Commercial Realities, Republican Principles," in *Republicanism: A Shared European Heritage*, Vol. 2, ed. Martin van Gelderen and Quentin Skinner, Cambridge: Cambridge University Press, 2002, pp. 299–303, 308.

[13] Smith, *Wealth*, p. 24.

[14] Smith, *Wealth*, p. 24.

Lectures on Jurisprudence (1762–1763, 1766).[15] Despite their textual fragmentation, he developed a comprehensive and coherent answer. To better apprehend it, we invert the most common manner in which *Wealth* is located in the corpus of Smith, not as freestanding or as the place of departure for a larger grasp of his theoretical purpose, but as tightly linked to his prior writings. Doing so reveals his deeper philosophical objectives, and demonstrates how *Wealth* relies on a more inclusive social, aesthetic, legal, and moral theory.[16]

Smith valued speech and rhetoric as the main ligaments of social relations. Rather than consider markets to be sites solely for the economic exchange of commodities, he treated them more fundamentally as the modern analogue of previous institutional foundations for social order. Thus, in modern times, markets are not simply, or exclusively, arenas for the instrumental quest by competitive and strategic individuals to secure their material preferences. They are, additionally, a central mechanism for social integration derived from the inexorable struggle by human agents for moral approbation and social recognition. In modern times, the market became an institutional equivalent of ancient public spaces within which citizens of the classical *polis*, through speech and deed, struggled for recognition.[17] Smith understood, of course, that for the ancients the content of recognition as well as the location of the struggle differed from those of the moderns – greatness through public dedication to the common good rather

[15] Smith, *The Theory of Moral Sentiments*, Indianapolis: Liberty Press, 1976 [1759]; *Letters on Rhetoric and Belles Lettres*, Indianapolis: Liberty Press, 1985 [1762–1763]; and *Lectures on Jurisprudence*, Indianapolis: Liberty Press 1982 [first report: 1762–1763; second report: 1766].

[16] Glenn Morrow has noticed that "we know from the accounts given by his students that he followed in his lectures the usual fourfold division of Moral Philosophy into Natural Theology, Ethics, Jurisprudence, and Political Economy." Glenn R. Morrow, *The Ethical and Economic Theories of Adam Smith*, New York: Longmans, Green, 1923, p. 2. This claim has been affirmed by Richard F. Teichgraeber III in his *Free Trade and Moral Philosophy: Rethinking the Sources of Adam's Smith's "Wealth of Nations,"* Durham: Duke University Press, 1986, pp. xiii–xiv. For a more recent discussion, see Donald Winch, "Adam Smith: Scottish Moral Philosopher as Political Economist," *Historical Journal*, 35:1 (1992), pp. 94–97.

[17] On the centrality of recognition on classical republican discourses, see J. G. A. Pocock, *The Machiavellian Moment: Florentine Political Thought and the Atlantic Republican Tradition*, Princeton, N.J.: Princeton University Press, 1975, pp. 133, 253.

than greatness as material wealth, and the *ekklesia* rather than the *agora*. Undergirding both the ancients and the moderns, however, is the existence of an identical drive to acquire social approval, moral approbation, and civic praise. This, Smith believed, provides a universal motivation for human action, the main source in all societies of the various means by which they achieve cohesion and continuity.[18]

Smith, in short, drew upon the republican tradition, never wholly within, but never breaking with it. Rather, he relied on a concept we know as recognition to trace and explain the deepest motivations of actors within markets. He did so by transposing and redirecting the core ethical incentives that underlay republican thought into the new set of modern institutional arrangements. For the ancients, these motivations produced and sustained the republican quest for public excellence, active citizenship, patriotism, and martial glory. For the moderns, the very same traits induce the pursuit of liberty, rights, security, property, and wealth. Smith's liberalism thus might best be understood as a displaced republicanism.

The steps in our argument begin with a discussion of sympathy, the master concept of *Moral Sentiments*. This notion we retranslate, via approbation and esteem, into a theory of recognition.[19] We then demonstrate how Smith, in his *Rhetoric*, established the mutual constitution of recognition and speech. Finally, we carry this understanding to his *Jurisprudence*, where we discover Smith's first formulation of

[18] Like Benjamin Constant, who addressed how the liberty of the ancients could not be reproduced under conditions of modern social pluralism, Smith understood that the forms and institutional means they had designed to achieve social integration had become irrevocably extinct. Unlike Constant, however, who thought the liberty of the moderns had to be reinvented ex nihilo, Smith believed modern modalities for order would not differ radically from those of the ancients because both are based on the similar, and natural, quest for approbation and esteem. Of course, Smith, like so many in his age, acknowledged the break represented by modernity and capitalism; at the same time, he allowed room in his theoretical construction for continuity. Contrary to excessive celebrations of newness characteristic of many immoderate and presumptuous endorsements of modern times, Smith investigated the multiple configurations linking past and present. Benjamin Constant, "The Liberty of the Ancients Compared with That of the Moderns," in *Benjamin Constant: Political Writings*, ed. Biancamaria Fontana, Cambridge: Cambridge University Press, 1988 [1819], pp. 309–329.

[19] We rely in this regard primarily on Axel Honneth's theory of recognition, *The Struggle for Recognition: The Moral Grammar of Social Conflict*, Cambridge, Mass.: MIT Press, 1996.

his original theory of the market according to the terms derived from his earlier investigations in moral and social theory. Here, the market is revealed in its deepest sense.

I

Clearly influenced by David Hume, Smith further elaborated the seminal category of sympathy in an effort to explain the nature and the particular mechanisms of moral sentiments.[20] He inserted this concept as a mediating device between what he conceived to be two opposed poles that dominated secular moral philosophy: Frances Hutcheson's naturalistic theory of benevolence and Mandeville's ethics of self-love. For Smith, Hutcheson's assumptions about the kind, unselfish qualities of human nature made his moral system unrealistic, even utopian; it thus failed to take into account the complexity and ambivalence of the actual psychological motives of human action.[21] Mandeville, by contrast, Smith thought, successfully unmasked and demystified the type of idealization shared by such predominant moral theorists of his time as Lord Shaftesbury and Bishop Butler. But, in Smith's view, Mandeville also had adopted a reductionist model that leveled everything down to the universal, objective, and inexorable fact of self-interest.[22]

Smith refused both approaches, deeming them, despite their opposition, equally monistic and one-sided. To enrich our knowledge of moral psychology, he proposed instead a different moral theory, one based on sympathy.[23] On this view, moral judgments are derived from a person's ability to identify with someone else's situation and feelings through the faculty of imagination.[24] From this capacity to enter and experience the position of another, Smith extracted conceptual resources to elucidate the elementary processes by which people make valid moral evaluations, bridging the gap between the self and the other.

[20] David Hume, *Treatise of Human Nature*, book III, section i and section iii.

[21] Smith, *Moral Sentiments*, pp. 304–305.

[22] Smith, *Moral Sentiments*, pp. 312–313.

[23] Smith, *Moral Sentiments*, p. 43.

[24] Smith, *Moral Sentiments*, pp. 10–11, 71, 73, and, for the discussion of imagination, pp. 9, 13, 29.

The competence of individuals to undertake moral distinctions between the good and the bad, Smith argued, depends on their prior ability to sympathize. Through their passion, not reason, individuals communicate in depth with each other.[25] By such acts of imaginative identification, they reach moral conclusions. Thus, the measure of morality varies according to whether sympathy can be achieved.[26] Only when subjects can sympathize with the social and subjective situation of their interlocutors, and with their acts and passions, can they be judged as moral. The attributes of goodness and virtue are contingent, therefore, on whether they become objects of sympathy. By contrast, Smith discredited emotions with which the subject cannot sympathize as vicious and immoral.[27] Sympathy is the original basis on which notions of right and wrong, good and bad, are decided. According to this ethical system, humans adopt a moral stance toward the world, others, and themselves and judge the moral validity of facts and behavior by means of the faculty of sympathy. This affective capacity permits them to approve or disapprove of situations and events directly related to the feelings of pleasure and pain experienced by others. Hence, on the problem of how agents arrive at valid moral judgments, Smith identified psychological mechanisms involving the use of imagination and reflection. Sympathy, in short, is the chief criterion of moral judgment.[28] People do not empathize with virtuous intentions and situations as such, but some situations qualify as virtuous because individuals have sympathized with them.[29]

[25] Smith, *Moral Sentiments*, pp. 16, 27, 69.

[26] Smith, *Moral Sentiments*, p. 39.

[27] Smith, *Moral Sentiments*, pp. 49, 75–76, 109, 325–327. Here we disagree with Jeffrey Young, who argues that sympathy is exclusively an other-regarding principle in contrast to egoism, which is a self-regarding norm. Smith explicitly argued that sympathy is the main category with which we can judge and evaluate both the actions and passions of others as well as those of ourselves. Jeffrey T. Young, *Economics as a Moral Science: The Political Economy of Adam Smith*, Cheltenham: Edward Elgar, 1997, p. 31.

[28] Smith, *Moral Sentiments*, pp. 27, 49.

[29] Obviously, this approach is vulnerable to charges of subjectivism, emotivism, and individual arbitrariness. To avoid these criticisms, as the one expounded by Sir Gilbert Elliot, Smith introduced the idea of the "impartial spectator" gradually over the course of the six editions of *Moral Sentiments*, thus introducing a mechanism of objectivity and impartiality into his account. D. D. Raphael nicely has depicted and recounted this successive elaboration of the concept of the "impartial spectator." See D. D. Raphael, "The Impartial Spectator," in Skinner and Wilson, *Essays on*

For Smith, sympathy is neither an epiphenomenon of a deeper, more authentic, purely egoistic motive, a distant and disguised echo of self-love,[30] nor a mechanical and linear expression of a natural and unchangeable benevolent and altruistic disposition.[31] Furthermore, he did not attribute the origins of sympathy to an antecedent utilitarian principle.[32] To be sure, Smith alluded to this interpretation by noting that a person's ability to sympathize can be determined in part by the pleasure that can be derived from identifying with another's situation; reciprocally, one's aversion is informed by pain.[33] Notwithstanding, he insisted that "in all these cases, however, it is not the pain which interests us but some other circumstances."[34] Utility is not the driving force behind sympathy.[35] Indeed, for reasons of theoretical consistency, Smith rejected the utilitarian positions he already had criticized in the writing of Hume, Hutcheson, and Mandeville. Even more, he sought to transcend their arguments by developing a fresh moral stance, one that has "a synthetic character."[36]

But if utility does not provide the motivation that informs and shapes sympathy, why do humans empathize and identify with each other? Is sympathy the ultimate foundation of our moral abilities, a natural ground upon which we build our ethical evaluations? Is Smith's concept of sympathy his own particular version of the idea of a natural moral sense, the expression of a belief in "natural sentiments"?[37] Smith filled the vacuum left by his rejection of self-interest, benevolence, and utility as potential metatheoretical presuppositions with a theory of recognition. Despite the incompleteness and elusiveness of this account, he did, in fact, develop an extremely original and

Adam Smith, p. 91, and Andrew Steward Skinner, *A System of Social Science: Papers Related to Adam Smith*, Oxford: Clarendon Press, 1996, pp. 60–61.

30 Smith, *Moral Sentiments*, pp. 13, 317.

31 Smith, *Moral Sentiments*, p. 315.

32 Smith, *Moral Sentiments*, pp. 189, 306.

33 Smith, *Moral Sentiments*, pp. 45, 243.

34 Smith, *Moral Sentiments*, p. 30 and also p. 20.

35 Winch, "Adam Smith: Scottish Moral Philosopher as Political Economist," p. 102.

36 Skinner, *System*, pp. 52, 55. Similarly, Knud Haakonssen has claimed that Smith argued "against the idea that the useful tendency of characters and motives is the basis for moral evaluation." Knud Haakonssen, *The Science of a Legislator: The Natural Jurisprudence of David Hume and Adam Smith*, Cambridge: Cambridge University Press, 1977, p. 71.

37 Smith, *Moral Sentiments*, p. 159.

strikingly modern moral theory, by probing sympathy as the mechanism by which persons pursue the quest for esteem.

For Smith, a person's need for moral approbation, social approval, and intersubjective acceptance motivates the ability to sympathize with the other's emotions and passions.[38] We sympathize with fellow beings because we wish to be praised, admired, even loved. As Smith forcefully put the point, both the ability and inner drive for sympathy are based on the elemental compulsion "to be observed, to be attended to, to be taken notice of with sympathy, complacency, and approbation ... of our being the object of attention and approbation."[39] Thus, sympathy "is founded altogether in the desire of actual praise, and in the aversion of actual blame."[40] Embedded in the broader tissue of social relations, humans are attuned to sympathize with the emotional states and situations of others as a consequence of their more profound, substantive aspiration to be acknowledged as moral persons.

They pursue this goal indirectly. By sympathizing with other persons, we enter into their moral universe and thus can see ourselves through their perspectives and sentiments. By so doing, they become aware of the interpretative and axiological criteria with which they are judged and which, in turn, as interlocutors, they can satisfy to reciprocally gain praise and approval.[41] Neither nodal, isolated individuals nor products of reified societies and abstract norms, humans are instead continuously engaged in relations and networks within which they adopt perspectives of the other. As if through a "looking-glass," they see themselves from points of view rooted within the social relations in which they participate.[42] They become, in a metaphorical sense, "the impartial spectators of our own character."[43] Sympathy thus is an emotional, intersubjective form of seeing oneself through others and affirming one's personal worth through the approbation of fellow beings. Through empathy and imaginative identification, social

[38] A similar interpretation can be found in Eugene Heath, "The Commerce of Sympathy: Adam Smith on the Emergence of Morals," *Journal of the History of Philosophy*, 33 (July 1995), pp. 449–454. This essay, together with a significant selection of secondary literature on Adam Smith, also can be found in Knut Haakonssen, ed., *Adam Smith*, Brookfield, Vt.: Ashgate, 1998.

[39] Smith, *Moral Sentiments*, p. 50.

[40] Smith, *Moral Sentiments*, p. 131.

[41] Smith, *Moral Sentiments*, p. 112.

[42] Smith, *Moral Sentiments*, pp. 112, 110.

[43] Smith, *Moral Sentiments*, p. 114.

actors enlarge their mentalities, insert themselves within social and moral networks, and negotiate the qualities and content of mutual approval.[44] As Luigi Bagolini has observed, sympathy "is founded directly on the desire to receive the praise of others at once and, correspondingly, on the desire to avoid the immediate condemnation of others.... [It is also] based on the desire to possess these qualities and to achieve those actions that the judging subject himself admires in others."[45]

Smith's original understanding of these mechanisms crosscuts naturalistic theories positing the intrinsic sociability of individuals and those presenting an essentialist interpretation of social relations as effects of purely egoistic, self-regarding considerations. There is no self outside relations of intersubjective apperception. The ability to form a coherent personal, ethical identity is directly associated with the form and scope of the broader interpersonal structures of social interaction. With his focus on the complex, nuanced drive by individuals for moral and social approbation, Smith astutely struck a balance between self-love and benevolence; and, in contemporary terms, between the individual and the community, the good and the right, substantive ethics and formal morality.

This tension-ridden relation is characterized by a process of continuous adjustment and mutual reinforcement. It is true that with sympathy we come very close to satisfying an individual's need for praise and for advancing emotional, social, and symbolic well-being. What distinguishes sympathy from egoism and rational self-seeking, however, is that it is based on an explicitly intersubjective process that constitutes both identities and preferences via patterns of interaction. For Smith, the self is never disembedded or "unencumbered."[46] Rather, as he put

44 Smith, *Moral Sentiments*, pp. 58, 75. The relationship between sympathy, esteem, and praise is thoughtfully considered in Haakonssen, *Legislator*, pp. 49–50, 52–53, 57–58.

45 Luigi Bagolini, "The Topicality of Adam Smith's Notion of Sympathy and Judicial Evaluations," in Skinner and Wilson, *Essays on Adam Smith*, p. 106. For a similar point, see Hiroshi Mizuta, "Moral Philosophy and Civil Society," in Skinner and Wilson, *Essays on Adam Smith*, p. 121.

46 Michael Sandel, "The Procedural Republic and the Unencumbered Self," *Political Theory*, 12 (1984), pp. 81–96, and "The Political Theory of the Procedural Republic," *Revue de Métaphysique et de Morale*, 93 (1988), pp. 57–68. Haakonssen observes that "in Smith's view men ... are always living in a society and thus in the context of aims, values, and ideals. Moral evaluation is therefore only relevant in such a context." Haakonssen, *Legislator*, p. 62.

it, the other individuals' "approbation necessarily confirms our own self-approbation. Their praise necessarily strengthens our own sense of our own praise-worthiness. In this case, so far is the love of praise-worthiness from being derived altogether from that of praise; that the love of praise seems, at least in a great measure, to be derived from that of praise-worthiness."[47] This dialectic between the self and the other finds expression in sympathy, which provides, by linking self-esteem to social praise, the psychological and social mechanisms that can bind society together. "Nature," Smith argued, "when she formed man for society, endowed him with an original desire to please, and an original aversion to offend his brethren. She taught him to feel pleasure in their favourable, and pain in their unfavourable regard. She rendered their approbation most flattering and most agreeable to him for its own sake; and their disapprobation most mortifying and most offensive."[48]

For Smith, such imaginative identification rests on the inexorable fact that "man naturally desires, not only to be loved, but to be lovely; or to be that thing which is the natural and proper object of love."[49] Therefore, it is not sympathy as such that provides the ultimate criterion for moral judgment. Rather, it is the more profound human desire to be esteemed and praised, admired and applauded, which accounts for the nature and workings of morality.[50] In his subsequent studies of rhetoric, Smith went so far as to claim that "Men generally are more desirous of being thought great than good, and are more afraid of being thought despicable than of being thought wicked."[51]

In this respect, we find Smith to be strikingly modern. He anticipated not only Hegel[52] but more recent theories of recognition,

47 Smith, *Moral Sentiments*, p. 114.

48 Smith, *Moral Sentiments*, p. 116.

49 Smith, *Moral Sentiments*, p. 114.

50 Smith, *Moral Sentiments*, pp. 20, 159; Winch, "Adam Smith: Scottish Moral Philosopher as Political Economist," p. 104.

51 Smith, *Rhetoric*, p. 131.

52 G. W. F. Hegel, "The Oldest Systematic Programme of German Idealism," in *Hegel's Development: Toward the Sunlight*, ed. Henry S. Harris, Oxford: Clarendon Press, 1972; *Natural Law: The Scientific Ways of Treating Natural Law, Its Place in Moral Philosophy, and Its Relation to the Positive Sciences of Law*, trans. and ed. T. M. Knox, Philadelphia: University of Pennsylvania Press, 1975; and *"System of Ethical Life" [1802–1803], and "First Philosophy of Spirit" [Part III of the System of Speculative Philosophy, 1803–1804]*, trans. and ed. H. S. Harris and T. M. Knox, Albany: State University of New York Press, 1979.

notably including Axel Honneth's.[53] This philosophical approach helps us understand Smith's concern for the substantive content and intersubjective character of social relations. It also helps situate Smith's critique of social contract theory within a broader motivational framework, reconciling formal morality with ethical life. In so doing, he combined the natural jurisprudential language of rights with shared situational ethics, which now were challenged by cultural and

[53] Honneth, *Struggle*. See also his "Integrity and Disrespect: Principles of a Conception of Morality Based on a Theory of Recognition," in *The Fragmented World of the Social: Essays in Social and Political Philosophy*, ed. Charles Wright, Albany: State University of New York Press, 1995, pp. 247–290. We turn to Honneth because, in so doing, we can discern how Smith sought to solve key dilemmas of social, moral, and political theory at the intersection of the elements of individual and society that had been rent by the advent of postfeudal modernity. In his theoretical scheme, Honneth identifies the moral and psychological preconditions for undistorted ego development. The possibility of a positive relation-to-oneself, he argues, requires three different modes of recognition: self-confidence, self-respect, and self-esteem (*Struggle*, chap. 5). Each refers to distinct levels of social organization, spheres of personality, experiences of social disrespect, and forms of recognition. Individuals are deprived of recognition when their expectations are violated and their needs, rights, and moral claims disregarded. Translated into the psychological experience of injustice, this want triggers antagonisms directed against the established social, legal, and political order (*Struggle*, chap 6). Struggles for the recognition of one's identity, according to Honneth, explain the progressive evolution toward more inclusive political and institutional forms of social recognition and account for the social integration of previously excluded or marginalized groups into a normative social order that satisfies the needs and expectations of social actors. Honneth's understanding of recognition is worth attending to because, in underscoring two elements, it points us toward a reinterpretation of Smith's social and moral theory. First, he reintroduces a paradigm of recognition to contest the hegemony of the paradigm pivoting on material interests. Creatively combining Hegel's early philosophical works with George Herbert Mead's research in psychology, Honneth advances an intersubjective model of struggle for recognition of one's identity as an alternative to instrumental formal rationality and self-preservation. The category of conflict, he claims, erroneously has been materialist and utilitarian theories, which reduce political confrontation to instrumental calculation conceptualized in a reductionist manner as overly individualistic and strategic. He thus enlarges the domain of the political to include struggles concentrating on the ethical dimension of social interaction. Relying on an evolutionary model of social development, Honneth also attempts to overcome the tension between formal rights and substantive values by deploying the concept of a "formal conception of ethical life," a synthesis of Kant's and Hegel's moral philosophies, pointing toward a higher stage of social organization where enabling conditions for the development of individual identity are rooted in the institutionalization of substantive relations of solidarity. These, Honneth argues, do not privilege any specific conception of the good but make possible the self-realization of many forms of life. With the accent now on the goals and needs of embedded forms of collective life, the formal and abstract content of rights becomes more textured, contextual, and attentive to the shared experiences of groups and individuals.

social transformations within modern commercial societies. As Ernst Tugendhat correctly points out, Smith's critical engagement with Aristotle resulted in a "unique and genial" contribution providing an alternative to what later became known as Kantianism and utilitarianism. It enriched the universal core of secular morality with a theory focused on reciprocal affective relationships and substantive intersubjective forms of communication that transcend mere abstract rationality, utilitarian considerations, and purely contractarian formal exchanges among self-interested economic actors.[54]

II

More than a century ago, the political economist Edwin Cannan, a Smith scholar, introduced a new edition of *Jurisprudence* by remarking that an understanding of Smith's political economy would not be aided by attention to his lectures on rhetoric.[55] This view crystallized into what certainly has become conventional wisdom. It is misplaced. In fact, Smith's economic writings are best understood by reestablishing the tight, indeed constitutive, links joining them to his investigation of different forms of discourse.[56] In this approach, *Rhetoric* can be

[54] Ernst Tugendhat, *Vorlensungen über Ethik*, Frankfurt-am-Main: Suhrkamp Verlag, 1993, pp. 295–296, 308, 309. Once we take seriously Smith's elements of a theory of recognition, even the distance between him and Hegel contracts. Much like Hegel, Smith sought to blend the emergence of modern formal, legal rights with substantive ethics. Unlike Hegel, however, Smith believed, counterintuitively, that the market, rather than the state, could best achieve this goal. The clearest confirmation of the affinities between Smith and Hegel is found in their parallel criticisms of social contract theories. For both, a contract cannot be a legitimate foundation of the state for at least two reasons closely related to the very nature of contractual obligations as distinct from obligations that derive from law. In the first place, the bonds that unite the state to its citizens are permanent and irrevocable, whereas the parties can revoke their contractual bond. In the second place, the state can claim the legitimate right to punish its citizens independently of any written agreement. Smith, *Jurisprudence*, pp. 402–404.

[55] Edwin Cannan, "Introduction," in Adam Smith, *Lectures on Justice, Police, Revenue and Arms*, Oxford: Clarendon Press, 1896, p. xiv.

[56] Our discussion takes sustenance, even as our emphasis differs, from A. M. Endres, "Adam Smith's Rhetoric of Economics: An Illustration Using 'Smithian' Compositional Rules," *Scottish Journal of Political Economy*, 38 (February 1991), pp. 76–95. Endres demonstrates the relevance of *Rhetoric* for *Wealth* by arguing that the form of *Wealth* is better illuminated through the categories Smith developed in *Rhetoric*. For him, *Wealth* is a polemical book utilizing the rhetorical form of discourse in tandem

seen to connect the core themes of recognition and exchange through a theory of speech.[57]

Smith distinguished four forms of speech: poetic, narrative, didactic, and oratory or rhetoric (the last term he also deployed more generically to refer to each). We focus mainly on oratorical discourse, the primary function of which is to persuade an audience about a controversial issue through the communication of sentiments and emotions.[58] Unlike the other three genres, oratorical speech aims at neither the description of an object or experience in terms of aesthetic categories that produce pleasure and entertain listeners, nor an objective, precise narration of mere fact; nor even the transmission of abstract ideas by rational argumentation oriented toward truth. Rather, oration endeavors exclusively to persuade an audience and to gain its members' assent by influencing their emotions, enticing their sentiments, and shaping their feelings.[59] Oration is not directed to achieve truth but to change beliefs and opinions, to transform perceptions, and "to gain the assent of the readers."[60]

Even more interesting, the faculty of speech is grounded on a deeper and more essential human trait: the drive to be recognized by others. Smith deduced speech from the contest of moral approbation:

> The desire to be believed, the desire of persuading, of leading and directing other people, seems to be one of the strongest of all our natural desires. It is perhaps, the instinct upon which is founded the faculty of speech, the characteristic faculty of human nature.... Great ambition, the desire of real superiority, of leading and directing, seems to be altogether peculiar to man, and speech is the great instrument of ambition, of real superiority, of leading and directing the judgments and conduct of other people.[61]

with a scientific one in order to persuade its audience. This suggestive interpretation, we believe, understates the full significance of *Rhetoric* for reading *Wealth*. By contrast to Endres, we stress how *Rhetoric* is not only a form of argumentation but an integral part of Smith's economic theory. Thus, what Cannan severed, we seek to recombine.

57 Here we are in agreement with John C. Bryce, who correctly argued that one should approach "the *Rhetoric* and *Theory of Moral Sentiments* as two halves of one system, and not merely at occasional points of contact." See John C. Bryce, "Introduction," in Smith, *Rhetoric*, p. 19.

58 Smith, *Rhetoric*, pp. 36, 62, 164.

59 Smith, *Rhetoric*, p. 62.

60 Smith, *Rhetoric*, p. 36.

61 Smith, *Moral Sentiments*, p. 336.

Oration, moreover, is not practiced by means of reason but by touching human passions. The orator expresses a sentiment and communicates a feeling that, if successful, appeals to the emotions of the listeners and wins their approval. Smith thought the best historical settings for such speech had been classical agonistic politics in the ancient Greek democracies and the Roman Republic.

In ancient times, this entanglement between speech and recognition took place predominantly in the political realm. Citizens utilized rhetoric to strive for public excellence and eminence and compete for political greatness and admiration. Exercising civic virtue and demonstrating dedication to the common good of their cities, they tried to outdistance each other as virtuous and heroic. Ancient politics was informed by this underlying struggle for recognition, taking the form of persuading fellow citizens to support their proposed public policies. Recognition was reserved for the first citizens of the city who emerged triumphant as the leaders of the *demos*. Oration was the means by which the ancients gave political and institutional expression to a need for recognition and praise through acts of public greatness that concretely expressed one's love of the city. With such public discourses, citizens could come to enjoy the glory and honor that their fellow citizens bestowed on them.[62]

Of course, Smith knew that war was the main such instrument; oratory, the secondary one. When leaders avoided the solution of war, which glorified heroic acts of violence and physical sacrifice, they concentrated on the more prosaic, but still important, form of rhetorical speech as the main method to procure public eminence and popular distinction.[63] Thus, "among the candidates for excellence" the struggle for recognition took the form of an institutionalized fight, of an *agon*, to win the opinion and the veneration of the people by staging public contests of orations.[64] The ancient *ekklesia* emerges from Smith's writings as the institutional sphere within which individuals' drive for recognition was channeled and in which actions aimed at achieving moral approbation through glory unintentionally – a kind of invisible

62 Smith, *Rhetoric*, p. 139.

63 Smith, *Moral Sentiments*, p. 232. War, for the ancients, was an exceptional and extraordinary expression of public virtue. In normal times, speech and oration, were its equivalents.

64 Smith, *Moral Sentiments*, p. 123.

hand – procured social order, consolidated the integration of society, and fortified its collective identity.

Notwithstanding Smith's fascination, even admiration, for this manner to procure order, he deemed this type of social organization to have been extinguished irrevocably in modern times.[65] Though he lamented this loss, he acknowledged that commercial societies could not build social order by resurrecting the *ekklesia*. The scale of the postfeudal sovereign state made the quest to return to this republican model a misplaced nostalgia.[66] More important, the new forms of economic activity and the progress of the arts and sciences it facilitated had caused tremendous social, political, and cultural changes, which made going back to ancient forms out of the question.

Modernity, by its pacification of customs and refinement of habits, had discredited war as a struggle for recognition.[67] War itself had become, if anything, more prevalent during this moment, but it had been professionalized as an instrument of statecraft; "the rich would not take the field... and therefore it became necessary to employ mercenaries and the dregs of the people to serve in war."[68] The "savage patriotism" of ancient republics, according to Smith, had been replaced by a more tolerant and inclusive mentality of cooperation and compromise. The 'liberal mind' thus was more prone to negotiate and bargain with the enemy than engage in bloody conflicts of annihilation.[69]

In modern circumstances, moreover, human activities increasingly had been privatized and depoliticized. The modern individual now "would prefer the undisturbed enjoyment of secure tranquility, not only to the vain splendour of successful ambition, but to the real and solid glory of performing the greatest and most magnanimous actions."[70] Further, Smith understood democracy to be anachronistic,

[65] This element of appreciation of ancient rhetoric is totally missing from Wilbur Samuel Howell's otherwise instructive presentation of Smith's theory of rhetoric. In his account, the neglect of this element of historical continuity is accompanied by an underestimation of the underlying desire for recognition. See Wilbur Samuel Howell, "Adam Smith's Lectures on Rhetoric: An Historical Assessment," in Skinner and Wilson, *Essays on Adam Smith*, p. 21.

[66] Smith, *Jurisprudence*, p. 413.

[67] Smith, *Jurisprudence*, pp. 229, 235, 414–415; Smith, *Wealth*, p. 496.

[68] Smith, *Jurisprudence*, p. 412.

[69] Smith, *Moral Sentiments*, pp. 228–229.

[70] Smith, *Moral Sentiments*, p. 216.

suited to small, homogeneous societies characterized by a low level of economic and cultural development.[71] Under conditions of differentiation, heterogeneity, and division of labor, the public sphere of the *ekklesia* had become completely outmoded. Additionally, commercial societies, especially with the rise of modern cities,[72] had contributed to the erosion of traditional forms of social status, to the collapse of old hierarchies, and to the dissolution of patriarchal structures of dependency, thus undermining the aristocratic foundations of ancient political *agon*.[73] Writing in accord with the evolutionary philosophy of history expounded more broadly by the Scottish Enlightenment, Smith echoed Montesquieu, David Hume, and especially Adam Ferguson, to side with Western modernity, identified with the gradual and irresistible formation of civil society, with the market at its core.[74]

Smith elaborated the cultural repercussions of this massive transformation for the anthropological and psychological traits of modern individuals. Clearly, he did not treat strategic, self-interested individuals as natural or transhistorical. Rather, they were products of a particular time and process, most notably the constellation shaped by new kinds of markets. Modern *homo economicus* is a social-historical creation, not a universal fact. Smith's grounded philosophical anthropology connects modern subjectivity to novel economic structures and newly emergent capitalism, thus to both the material and symbolic "influence of commerce on the manners of a people."[75] Along with the division of labor, the historical advent and social extension of market relations were primary causes of a new kind of personhood characterized by "probity," "frugality," "punctuality," "industry," and "self-interest," all features that "lead[s] men to act in a certain manner from views of advantage," attributes that, not by chance, are "as deeply implanted in an Englishman as a Dutchman," the citizens of the two most economically marketized nations.[76] It is not a natural disposition for barter and exchange that gave rise to commercial

[71] Smith, *Rhetoric*, pp. 150–152; Smith, *Jurisprudence*, pp. 407, 413–414.

[72] Smith, *Wealth*, pp. 410–413.

[73] Smith, *Jurisprudence*, pp. 405, 486–487.

[74] Smith, *Jurisprudence*, p. 459.

[75] Smith, *Jurisprudence*, p. 538.

[76] Smith, *Jurisprudence*, pp. 538–539.

society, but "it is commerce that introduces probity and punctuality" into the human personality.[77]

If rhetoric has receded from modern politics, why focus on it? Has it not become obsolete? Notwithstanding the widening gap separating oration from politics, Smith believed there remained a close but unheeded connection between rhetoric and the drive for moral approbation and praise. The struggle for social recognition and the effort to be publicly esteemed continued to take place within rhetorical strategies of persuasion, though with a shift in venue: oration, over time, had moved from the sphere of politics to the realm of ethical theory, more particularly to the zone of sympathy. In an effort to attract the approbation of others and win the esteem necessary for one's own self-evaluation, the modern subject must captivate attention, invoke affection, and provoke a willingness to empathize. By carrying out this project, rhetorical discourse emerges as the natural language of recognition. Agents, struggling to win the sympathy of others, adopt strategies of speech and persuasion.

The entwining of recognition and rhetoric is manifested in two distinct, if interrelated, ways. A subject can induce others to sympathize with its emotional situation and thus secure approval. Or, the subject can try to enter into the emotional situation of others and, in so doing, transform itself into an object of admiration. In both, subjects make use of rhetorical means to present themselves as worthy of recognition. In the first instance, rhetoric serves as a medium for revealing feelings to others that will enable them to better identify with the actor. Here rhetoric plays a crucial role. It enables the actor to describe emotions in forms that can produce identification, incite sympathy, and procure moral approbation. For this reason, it is important that "the sentiment of the speaker is expressed in a neat, clear, plain and clever manner, and the passion or affection he is possessed of and intends, *by sympathy*, to communicate to his hearer, is plainly and clevery hit off, then and then only the expression has all the force and beauty that language can give it."[78]

In the second instance, the subject enters into the situation of the interlocutor, staging itself as an object whose qualities and attributes

[77] Smith, *Jurisprudence*, p. 528.
[78] Smith, *Rhetoric*, p. 25.

can be regarded as a target of admiration, respect, imitation, even honor. Rhetoric, in this particular circumstance, according to Smith, "shows [that] the Real design of the orator was to shew his own eloquence... [and that] to raise his own glory was plainly the motive of his undertaking."[79] This conclusion derived from Smith's strongly held belief that "Every thing that is created with Grandeur seems to be important. We watch the Sayings and catch the apothegms of the great ones with which we are infinitely pleased and are fond of every opportunity of using them."[80] We are inclined, in a sense, to approve and praise, thus to give recognition to what appears as eminent and illustrious. People, Smith observed, are prone to show approbation to someone who becomes "the object of their respect, their gratitude, their love, their admirations."[81]

In the first stratagem, recognition flows from a person deemed worthy of empathy; in the second, it flows from being worthy of exaltation. Despite this and other important differences, both depend on similar linguistic acts of self-revelation by actors in front of an audience. Rhetorical speech is a means to disclose oneself.[82] Through speech, persuasion, and use of emotions, the actor performs an act of self-exposure that brings into the light of a public its singular particularity and identity. Thus, different rhetorical styles reflect deeper differences in personality and character. Such speech acts rightly have been described as expressive, performative, and dramaturgical. They raise to the surface the subjective and emotional dimensions of speakers, in public, who attempt to reveal themselves in a manner geared to guarantee greater chances of having its needs and identity recognized.[83] This understanding informs Smith's critique of impersonal and rationalistic

[79] Smith, *Rhetoric*, p. 128.

[80] Smith, *Rhetoric*, p. 132.

[81] Smith, *Moral Sentiments*, p. 56.

[82] Andrew Skinner correctly has observed that one of the bonds linking Smith's moral theory to his writings on rhetoric is the relation between speech and sympathy. See Skinner, "Language, Rhetoric, and the Communication of Ideas," in *System*, p. 19.

[83] Jürgen Habermas, *Theory of Communicative Action*, Vol. 1, *Reason and the Rationalization of Society*, Boston: Beacon Press, 1984, pp. 90–94. Note the similarities between Smith's concept of rhetorical self-disclosure and Hannah Arendt's famous definition of political action as an act of appearance in public through speech and deeds. See Hannah Arendt, *The Human Condition*, Chicago: University of Chicago Press, 1958, pp. 50–52, 175–207.

forms of speech, which tend to conceal the character, qualities, and emotional state of the speaker who remains hidden behind abstract, formal argumentation.[84]

III

The question Smith left unanswered at the beginning of the second chapter of *Wealth* concerning the nature of the human person as disposed to truck, barter, and exchange now can be seen in a different light. Smith, you will recall, did not provide an account of the historical scope of this claim, thus facilitating the conventional understanding that he endorsed a universal and economically reductionist interpretation of human nature. He did, however, hint at an alternative grounded in the faculty of speech, though he did not directly address the potential links connecting this allusion to the microfoundations of his economic theory. When we take into consideration his posthumously published *Jurisprudence*, we discover that Smith, in fact, did provide such a formulation. This solution was unequivocal, powerful, and compelling. In a surprisingly revealing and crystalline passage, Smith declared:

> If we should enquire into the principle in the human mind on which this disposition of trucking is founded, it is clearly the natural inclination every one has to persuade. The offering of a shilling, which to us appears to have so plain and simple a meaning, is in reality offering an argument to persuade one to do so and so as it is for his interest. Men always endeavour to persuade others to be of their opinion even when the matter is of no consequence to them.... And in this manner everyone is practicing oratory on others thro the whole of his life. – You are uneasy whenever one differs from you, and you endeavour to persuade (?him) to be of your mind.[85]

[84] Smith, *Rhetoric*, pp. 56–58.

[85] Smith, *Jurisprudence*, pp. 352, 493–493. There is a striking similarity between Smith and Marx on this point. Despite their contrasting evaluations of the market, both commented on the unique language that characterizes modern economic transactions. In Marx's case, this language points to the alienation between the producers and their products, which had become independent entities controlling the lives of their producers – a process of alienation that he famously coined the fetishism of the commodity. Marx, insightfully, described the practices of commodity exchange in terms of a "social hieroglyphic." According to this view, which, from a descriptive perspective, does not differ from Smith's, "men try to decipher the hieroglyphic to get behind the secret of their own social product; for the characteristic which objects of utility have of being values is as much men's social product as is their language." See

Markets and persuasion do not inhabit separate realms. In classical times, persuasion had provided agents with the capacity to display themselves, convey their sentiments, and appeal to the emotions of others to be recognized as moral persons and as integrated members of a broader ethical civic community. In modern times, persuasion, an expression of the natural desire to be admired and praised, is utilized by market actors who, through their economic activity, struggle to win the approval and esteem of their own distinctively configured historical communities. For Smith, therefore, oration did not disappear from Western commercial societies after the erosion of the last remnants of republicanism in the Italian peninsula. Rather, this type of speech abandoned the ancient *ekklesia* to enter the modern *agora*, leaving behind, Smith thought, the now archaic language of politics and public virtues in favor of a freshly instantiated language of transactions, profit, and wealth. Crucially, the underlying motivation remained constant: the quest to seek moral approbation. Thus, speech, this "great instrument of ambition" and excellence, had found a new shelter.[86]

In his writings on the different types of discourse, Smith appears really fascinated by the gradual emergence and final triumph of market rhetoric, "the Language of Business,"[87] which, he believed, had become the predominant form of striving for recognition. If public deliberation and demonstrative speeches had been the main variants of ancient oration, prose now became dominant. As Charles Griswold observes, "Life in a market society," for Smith, "is an ongoing exercise in rhetoric."[88] Inserted into market relations, individuals strive to persuade their competitors and achieve social worth by using this new rhetoric, a style Smith considered to be more suitable for the cultural and social exigencies of commercial activity. He devoted many pages to understand this new kind of oration and its relationship not only to new economic structures but to modern social relations more broadly and, most important, to the human need for sympathy and recognition. "Prose," he observed, "is the Stile in which all the common affairs

Karl Marx, *Capital: A Critique of Political Economy*, Vol. 1, introd. Ernst Mandel and trans. Ben Fowkes, London: Penguin Books, 1990, p. 167.

86 Smith, *Moral Sentiments*, p. 336.

87 Smith, *Rhetoric*, p. 137.

88 Griswold, *Adam Smith and the Virtues of the Enlightenment*, Cambridge: Cambridge University Press, 1999, p. 297.

of Life, all Business and Agreements are made. No one ever made a Bargain in verse."[89]

Despite this important change, the content, role, and goal of rhetoric as such remained essentially consistent. It continued to provide, even within a new institutional context, linguistic means to express and channel the contest for recognition. Smith perceptively realized that, although modern individuals do not strive for public excellence within the political arena or seek such approbation openly in front of their fellow citizens, they still aspire to gain recognition from their peers, but now by economic means. Within the market, recognition can be achieved by increasing one's wealth under conditions of formal equality. Smith's comparison of the ancients to the moderns underscores how wealth had displaced public devotion to the city as the currency of greatness and recognition. But the underlying moral grammar of social conflict remained unaltered. "Wealth and greatness," he claimed, constitute the two sides of one and the same drive "to deserve, to acquire, and to enjoy the respect and admiration of mankind."[90]

Rather than fight with weapons of political speech, public achievements, civic deeds, or military valor, modern individuals make use of money.[91] Monetary exchange gradually had transformed itself from being a mere tool of convenient give-and-take into a complex symbolic system embodying forms of mutual recognition. Merchants and traders deploy currency and the effort to increase their capital to gain sympathy and obtain respect by persuading both rivals and peers that they are worthy. In ancient times, it was "Grandeur" that received "a tincture from them and is looked on in that light by the generality of People."[92] Now, it is wealth.

The descriptive and normative foundation for Smith's political economy is not the natural impulse to exchange. Rather, it is the persistent struggle for recognition and the search for social approval that explains the modern drive of individuals to accelerate accumulation. Smith was remarkably direct about the ethical and intersubjective motivation behind this process.

[89] Smith, *Rhetoric*, p. 136.

[90] Smith, *Moral Sentiments*, p. 62.

[91] In this way, the market transforms potentially disruptive forms of conflict for recognition into regularized, ordered competition.

[92] Smith, *Rhetoric*, p. 133.

It is because mankind are disposed to sympathize more entirely with our joy than with our sorrow that we make parade of our riches, and conceal our poverty. Nothing is so mortifying as to be obliged to expose our distress to the view of the public, and to feel, that though our situation is open to the eyes of all mankind, no mortal conceives for us the half of what we suffer. Nay, it is chiefly from this regard to the sentiments of mankind, that we pursue riches and avoid poverty.... From whence, then, arises the emulation which runs through all the different ranks of men, and what are the advantages we propose by that great purpose of human life which we call bettering our condition? To be observed, to be attended to, to be taken notice of with sympathy, complacency, and approbation, are all the advantages which we can propose to derive from. It is the vanity, not the ease, or the pleasure, which interests us. But vanity is always founded upon the belief of our being the object of attention.[93]

The ethos of the modern Western trader is homologous to that of the ancient citizen. Both desire to be esteemed by peers and their community.[94] The frugal bourgeois is the modern equivalent of the warrior-citizen.[95] Of course, the axes of ancient and modern values are inverted. The successful acquisition and enlargement of wealth in market exchange relations confers on the individual similar authority and recognition as in the *polis*. But unlike the ancients, who praised their demagogues, warriors, founders, and leaders, the moderns are more inclined to honor and admire the wealthy. The drive toward boundless accumulation, therefore, was derived for Smith from the natural need to win praise and secure respect, not from any universal propensity to barter and exchange. The agonistic politics of the ancients thus had been transmuted into the competitive, economic agonism of the moderns. For Smith,

93 Smith, *Moral Sentiments*, p. 50.

94 John Dwyer has argued that Smith should be read as an integral part of the civic humanist tradition and the neo-Harringtonian perspective because, "*Wealth of Nations*, continued to reflect a recognisably civic programme... [and] the moral vocabulary of the civic tradition." See Dwyer, "Virtue and Improvement: The Civic World of Adam Smith," pp. 191, 195.

95 Needless to say, like the *ekklesia*, the market, for Smith, was the realm of a privileged minority, in this instance, the bourgeoisie. The large mass of the population was excluded from participating in the struggle for recognition, as slaves, women, and visitors were from the political arena of the ancients. Thus even in this respect, the distance separating the ancients from the moderns was not as huge as we might have thought.

> superior wealth still more than any of these qualities (i.e. superior strength, age, etc.) contributes to confer authority. This proceeds not from any dependance that the poor have upon the rich, for in general the poor are independent, and support themselves by their labour, yet tho' they expect no benefit from them they have a strong propensity to pay them respect. This principle is fully explained in the Theory of Moral Sentiments, where it is shewn that it arises from our sympathy with our superiors being greater, than with our equals or inferiors: we admire their happy situation, enter into it with pleasure, and endeavour to promote it.[96]

In like manner, fortune and accumulation endow the merchant and manufacturer with social recognition. "The rich man glories in his riches, because he feels that they naturally draw upon him the attention of the world, and that mankind are disposed to go along with him in all those agreeable emotions."[97] The market elevates him to a "man of rank and distinction," whereby he "is observed by all the world. Every body is eager to look at him, and to conceive at least, by sympathy, that joy and exaltation with which his circumstances naturally inspire him. His actions are the objects of the public care. Scarce a word, scarce a gesture, can fall from him that is altogether neglected."[98] By contrast, but from the opposite perspective, financial failure represents an injury and a harm, the shame that comes from misrecognition and disrespect. "Bankruptcy," Smith admonished "is perhaps the greatest and most humiliating calamity which can befall an innocent man,"[99] an "everlasting infamy,"[100] a damage to one's reputation and public esteem. Thus, behind the fear of financial failure lies the deeper and more essential fear, "an anxiety about the public opinion,"[101] "to have its misery exposed to insult and derision, to be led in triumph, to be set up for the hand of scorn to point at.... Compared with the contempt of mankind, all other external evils are easily supported."[102] For Smith, insolvency was qualitatively similar to the symbolic and

[96] Smith, *Jurisprudence*, p. 401.
[97] Smith, *Moral Sentiments*, pp. 50–51.
[98] Smith, *Moral Sentiments*, p. 51.
[99] Smith, *Wealth*, p. 342.
[100] Smith, *Moral Sentiments*, p. 120.
[101] Smith, *Moral Sentiments*, p. 123.
[102] Smith, *Moral Sentiments*, p. 61.

psychological effects of a military defeat or a public ostracism on a person's self-esteem.[103]

Smith's theory of the market also is embedded in a theory of historical change. His moral philosophy grappled with vexing problems of continuity and discontinuity in Western history. In this respect, his critical engagement with republicanism is quite different from those of Montesquieu and Hume, notwithstanding some similarities. While Smith criticized the ancient republics, he sought neither to replace them with a completely novel system of political and social organization nor to distinguish as radically different the constitutive elements of these republics from those of modern sovereign states. Consequently, he sought to dig out such elements from the republican tradition. Essential for moral development and the security of the social order, they were transposed by Smith to institutional structures and norms consistent with modern realities.[104] In so doing, he accepted the underlying anthropological and philosophical presuppositions of republicanism, according to which the intentions and actions of the person – indeed, the entire individual personality – are constituted within intersubjective, public networks and moral relationships.

IV

Once we recover Smith's persistent emphasis on recognition, two crucial but relatively neglected dimensions of his social and political theory come into view. These are based on his distinctive understanding of modernity. Although he did not use the term, it seems clear that Smith believed the Enlightenment was not the product of an apocalyptic break or a world-historical rupture. Rather, it is best comprehended as the product of a gradual process of inversion and retraction, a rearrangement of premodern norms and patterns of meaning. Modernity thus signified traditional values turned upside down. Key features in

[103] The central role that disrespect plays in Smith's works also can be gleaned from his steady concern to penalize insult and intentional forms of humiliation and degradation. A person's injured reputation is as grave as physical injury and the violation of property. Smith even would go as far as to allude to a natural right to reputation. See Smith, *Jurisprudence*, pp. 399, 480–481.

[104] Phillipson, "Adam Smith as Civic Moralist," pp. 200–201.

Smith's work clarify this perspective. First is his historical understanding of the market. In spite of its newness, he thought it to be a modern institutional equivalent of previous mechanisms, which achieved social integration. Consider his discussion of how the merchant replaced the warrior as the most "honorable and esteemed" profession. In noncapitalist premodernity, "a merchant was reckoned odious and despicable. But a pirate or robber, as he was a man of military bravery, was treated with honour... When the trade of a merchant or mechanic was thus depreciated in the beginnings of society, no wonder that it was confined to the lowest rank of the people."[105] Over time, traditional heroic values lost their appeal and failed to create order.[106] As surrogates, the acquisition of material wealth became the distinguishing mark of status, prestige, and praise. Social integration came to be organized by material competition and economic struggle. What in the past was esteemed had come to be disdained; what then was scorned, today is admired. Modernity thus signifies an evaluative reversal, not an absolute beginning.[107]

The second feature is implied by Smith's historical explanation for the origins of commercial societies, an embryonic theory of modern capitalist development. It was the inexorable ethical quest to secure greatness, honor, and recognition, he argued, that conditioned the emergence of a new economic system. An unprecedented social

[105] Smith, *Jurisprudence*, p. 527.

[106] Of course, Smith was fully aware of the limits of his model of social integration based exclusively on the market. He recognized the unintended effects of growing poverty, increasing class polarization, the proletarization of the working class, the appearance of new forms of authority and domination, and some monopolistic tendencies. For this reason, he introduced the state as an important coercive mechanism with which to protect private property, secure the undisrupted functioning of the market, and repress potential forms of resistance and uprising by the excluded. That is, he understood the state to be, in the last instance, responsible for implementing order when the market fails peacefully to achieve integration. His concept of justice was deployed to contain the social pathologies created by modern commercial societies. See Smith, *Wealth*, pp. 265–267, 493–495, 708–710, 781–786.

[107] We do not mean by this claim to overlook Smith's well-known evolutionary and progressive model of history, according to which human societies have followed the four stages of "hunting, pasturage, farming, and commerce." We do think, however, that next to this typical Enlightenment image of history, Smith alluded to a more nuanced and rich philosophy of history. For the first claim, see *Jurisprudence*, p. 459.

transformation ensued from this search by the new middle classes to obtain social recognition. Now, they concentrated on what was fast becoming the predominant new institutional sphere, the market, within which transactions expressed the persistent human struggle for approbation and respect. This configuration of deep continuity and institutional innovation provided Smith with the means to develop an entirely novel theory of the intersubjective motivations for capitalist development. For Smith, the pursuit of moral approbation created the modern ethic of rational acquisition – that is, the spirit of capitalism.[108]

Following this line of reasoning in Smith, we can better see the status of republicanism in his 'liberal' theory of economics and politics. For Smith's texts, read together, reveal the republican origins of commercial society. Once displaced from the political forum to the economic sphere, the social contest for recognition authored a new bourgeois mentality devoted to accumulation, thrift, enterprise, and rational calculation.[109] To the question, "What is the reward most proper for encouraging industry, prudence, and circumspection?" Smith gave

[108] In fact, this theoretical proposition powerfully competes with Max Weber's famous thesis about the Protestant origins of capitalism. Max Weber, *The Protestant Ethic and the Spirit of Capitalism*, trans. Talcott Parsons and introd. Anthony Giddens, London: Routledge, 1995; "The Protestant Sects and the Spirit of Capitalism," in *From Max Weber: Essays in Sociology*, trans., ed., and introd. Hans H. Gerth and C. Wright Mills with a new preface by Bryan S. Turner, London: Routledge, 1991; and "Confucianism and Puritanism," in *The Religion of China: Confucianism and Taoism*, trans. and ed. Hans H. Gerth, Glencoe, Ill.: Free Press, 1951.

[109] Smith, *Moral Sentiments*, pp. 172–173. Similarly, Smith's allusions to the republican origins of modern markets challenge Albert Hirschman's claim that self-interest was perceived as a solution to the problem of violent passions. Whereas traditional political thought struggled to channel, repress, or displace the dangerous drive for honor and greatness, liberalism discovered a more peaceful and controllable human attribute, self-interest, that, according to Hirschman, easily could be controlled by new institutional devices, such as the market. In this view, the perilous passion of glory, on the one hand, and calm self-interest deployed for accumulation and wealth, on the other, represent two different principles that define the core of two distinct, even opposite, historical epochs. The transition to modernity thus signifies a shift from glory to interests. It is difficult to agree with Hirschman's reading of Smith as an exemplar of this cultural shift, in light of Smith's grounding of self-interest in the deeper, more essential, human drive for mutual recognition and social admiration. See Albert O. Hirschman, *The Passions and the Interests: Political Arguments for Capitalism before Its Triumph*, Princeton, N.J.: Princeton University Press, 1977.

an unambiguous answer: "Wealth and external honours are their proper recompense, and the recompense which they can seldom fail of acquiring."[110]

A republican nostalgia remained. It is implicit in all his texts, which regret a lost, unrecoverable past. Even if the underlying principle is similar to that which once characterized the ancient republics, the passing of important and crucial aspects of ancient life cannot be compensated fully by exchange and monetary relations confined to the acquisition of wealth. Lamentably, they had disappeared along with the *ekklesia*.[111]

Smith's attitude toward commercialization and pacification thus appears to have been multifaceted. Rather than unconditionally accept these aspects of modernity, Smith acknowledged important losses. Sounding more like a traditional republican than a liberal, he asserted, "Another bad effect of commerce is that it sinks the courage of mankind, and tends to extinguish martial spirit."[112] Commercial societies had become weak and privatized. War, for example, having been transformed into a new commodity, a specialization, and "a trade"[113] marked by the division of labor, had lost its civic character. "The defence of the country is therefore," Smith deplored, "committed to a certain sett of men who have nothing else to do. By having their

110 Smith, *Moral Sentiments*, p. 166.

111 For example, although he applauded the pacification of Western societies, for example, he never hid his attraction to the moral dimension of war. Despite all his positive references to the civilizing effects of commerce, Smith persisted in believing that "War is the greatest school both for acquiring and exercising this species of magnanimity.... In war, men become familiar with death, and are thereby necessarily cured of that superstitious horror.... The skilful and successful exercise of this profession, in the service of their country," he continued, "seems to have constituted the most distinguished feature in the character of the favourite heroes of all ages." Most important, more than a mere glorification of war, Smith perceived its political significance to have been its forging of a public spirit; however, he criticized the idea of a national army or a militia, an argument constitutive of the republican tradition, and scorned those "men of republican principles" because they feared a professional, mercenary army. Smith also acknowledged that "Foreign war and civil faction are the two situations which afford the most splendid opportunities for the display of public spirit." Smith, *Moral Sentiments*, p. 239; Smith, *Wealth*, pp. 706–707; Smith, *Moral Sentiments*, p. 232.

112 Smith, *Jurisprudence*, p. 540.

113 Smith, *Jurisprudence*, p. 540.

minds constantly employed on the arts of luxury, they grow effeminate and dastardly."[114] The market did not adequately substitute for this loss, with the consequence that the "heroic spirit is almost utterly extinguished."[115] Contrary to the moderns, he wistfully observed, the ancients "were not enervated by cultivating arts and commerce, and they were already with spirit and vigor to resist the most formidable foe."[116]

Smith not only was preoccupied with the moral and social effects of the demilitarization of modern societies. He also was concerned with the growing depoliticization and civic abstinence characteristic of the new middle classes. Rather than participate visibly and actively in public life, they devoted more of their energies to economic issues. Commenting on Demosthenes' effort to revive public virtue in a commercialized Athens on the verge of decay, Smith unexpectedly came to the defense of the Athenian orator, reproaching the people of Athens, who favored private economic activities instead of political participation, for having become "altogether idle and unnactive... Military Glory had then no weight.... The Athenians from being the most enterprising people in Greece were now become the most idle and innactive."[117] Here, Smith ascribed Athens' political decadence and democratic crisis to the expansion of commercial relations. These had led to a generalized civic atrophy, which had made Athens an economic power to the detriment of its political supremacy.[118]

We offer two principal conclusions. The first concerns one of the longest-standing, but deeply frustrating, theoretical debates about Smith, the so-called Smith Problem, the apparent contradiction between the early moral Smith who considers humans to be connected as if in a tuning fork producing sympathy and the late instrumental Smith focusing on interest-seeking, competitive individuals.[119] Broadly speaking, scholars have pursued two clusters of solutions. One might

[114] Smith, *Jurisprudence*, p. 540.
[115] Smith, *Jurisprudence*, p. 541.
[116] Smith, *Jurisprudence*, p. 541.
[117] Smith, *Rhetoric*, p. 151.
[118] Smith, *Rhetoric*, p. 152.
[119] For an early discussion of the "Adam Smith Problem," see Morrow, *Adam Smith*, pp. 1–12. For a more recent critical presentation of this literature, see Richard F. Teichgraeber III, "Rethinking *Das Adam Smith Problem*," *Journal of British Studies*, 20 (1981), pp. 106–110.

be called the thesis of compartmentalization. Modernity is marked, above all, by differentiation. Each sphere is motored by its own distinct set of principles and causal mechanisms. On this reading, each of Smith's books corresponds to a specific object of analysis. Intimate relations are pervaded by sympathy; economic exchange, by self-interest.[120] This approach reproduces rather than solves the 'problem.'[121]

A more compelling alternative treats Smith's range of writings as contributing to the development of a single, comprehensive, and realistic moral theory, instantiating the full complexity of the human person and of emerging capitalism.[122] Instrumental egoism and intersubjective sympathy are interwoven. This manner of reading tends to stop before specifying the mechanisms that link and underpin each. Situating ourselves within this orientation, we have sought to elucidate the missing ethical and social mediating processes by translating sympathy into a struggle for mutual recognition carried out by speech.[123]

120 Allan Silver, "'Two Different Sorts of Commerce' – Friendship and Strangership in Civil Society," in *Public and Private in Thought and Practice*, ed. Jeff Weintraub and Krishan Kumar, Chicago: University of Chicago Press, 1997, pp. 43–74; Vernon L. Smith, "The Two Faces of Adam Smith," *Southern Economic Journal*, 65:1 (1998), pp. 1–19.

121 Another attempt is made by Henry C. Clark. Writing in a historicist vein, he claims that Smith transcended this alleged tension by considering how commercial societies enhance possibilities for communication and conversation, making each individual increasingly connected to, and interested in, others, thus both softening and humanizing egoistic self-interest. This 'solution' pays insufficient regard to the link between the market and the struggle for recognition, thus eliding the impact of rhetoric within the market. In setting the market aside the zone of social intersubjectivity, he implicitly reproduces the conventional understanding of the divide in Smith's writings. Henry C. Clark, "Conversation and Moderate Virtue in Adam Smith's *Theory of Moral Sentiments*," *Review of Politics*, 54 (Spring 1992), pp. 194–195, 209.

122 Teichgraeber, *Free Trade and Moral Philosophy*, pp. 168–169, 176–178; Young, *Economics as a Moral Science*, pp. 20–28, 203–207.

123 This interpretation is close to Robert D. Cumming's claim that *Moral Sentiments* is a book concerned with the moral dimension of modern economic activities. He correctly defined this activity as "rhetorical" in the sense that the drive to accumulation is based on an anterior human need to persuade the other of our merit and worth. However, Cumming bifurcates Smith's work, arguing that in *Wealth* Smith abandoned this line of interpretation, looking instead at a totally different issue: unintended social consequences and not human motives. We have tried to show that the principles informing *Moral Sentiments* inform as well *Wealth*. See Robert D. Cumming, *Human Nature and History*, Vol. 2, Chicago: University of Chicago Press, 1969.

Our second conclusion informs how we might understand the relationship between the republican and liberal traditions in Smith's writings. In probing the microfoundations of both ancient and modern societies, he found and deployed attractive elements from within the republican tradition but never wholly identified with it. In a plaintive mood, Smith regretted the impossibility of holding tight to traditional republicanism. He realized that only by transposing the core moral insights and concerns from that tradition into a new set of institutional arrangements could they be safeguarded, if, alas, also diminished. In this way, he secured republicanism's ethical foundation in recognition by adapting and accommodating modernity's radical transformations.

3

Agonistic Liberalism

Adam Ferguson on Modern Commercial Society and the Limits of Classical Republicanism

A thinker associated with the republican tradition in the eighteenth century, Adam Ferguson, sometimes labeled a "Machiavellian moralist" or "the last 'neo-Roman,'" stands out for systematically grappling with the challenge of preserving republican government despite the emergence of modern commercial society.[1] This engagement, understood as an attempt to make republicanism fit for new conditions, has been at the center of important scholarship on Ferguson initiated by J. G. A. Pocock and carried forward by the Cambridge School.[2] It

[1] Duncan Forbes, "Introduction," in Adam Ferguson, *An Essay on the History of Civil Society*, Edinburgh: Edinburgh University Press, 1966, p. xxviii; Fania Oz-Salzberger, "The Political Theory of the Scottish Enlightenment," in *The Cambridge Companion to the Scottish Enlightenment*, ed. Alexander Broadie, Cambridge: Cambridge University Press, 2003, p. 168.

[2] J. G. A. Pocock, *The Machiavellian Moment: Florentine Political Thought and the Atlantic Republican Tradition*, Princeton, N.J.: Princeton University Press, 1975, pp. 499–505; J. G. A. Pocock, "Civic Humanism and Its Role in Anglo-American Thought," and "Cambridge Paradigms and Scottish Philosophers: A Study of the Relations between the Civic Humanist and the Civil Jurisprudential Interpretation of Eighteenth-Century Social Thought," in *Wealth and Virtue: The Shaping of Political Economy in the Scottish Enlightenment*, ed. Istvan Hont and Michael Ignatieff, Cambridge: Cambridge University Press, 1986, pp. 101–103, 235–252; Fania Oz-Salzberger, "Introduction," in *Ferguson: An Essay on the History of Civil Society*, ed. Fania Oz-Salzberger, Cambridge: Cambridge University Press, 1995, pp. vii–xxv; Marco Geuna, "Republicanism and Commercial Society in the Scottish Enlightenment: The Case of Adam Ferguson," in *Republicanism: A Shared European Heritage*, Vol. 2, ed. Martin van Gelderen and Quentin Skinner, Cambridge: Cambridge University Press, 2002, pp. 177–195; Fania Oz-Salzberger, "Scots, Germans, Republic

powerfully portrays him as having "modernised republicanism."[3] This orientation has displaced an older interpretation, famously identified with Friedrich Hayek, which had characterized Ferguson, like Adam Smith, as an early liberal, devoted to free markets, spontaneous orders, and limited governments.[4]

We offer an angular reading. Ferguson, in fact, did struggle to renovate and update republican ideas and values. In so doing, he sought to fashion a politics suitable for what he characterized as a new age of separations. He did not succeed. We will see how each of the three principal solutions he offered, ranging from primarily republican to increasingly liberal, failed to persuasively reconcile virtue and commerce. Yet, in emplacing pluralism, conflict, and sentiments, as well as the role of institutions and laws, at the center of his thinking, Ferguson did more than recast classical republicanism. In highlighting and deploying these features of politics, he pioneered what we can recognize as a distinctive kind of liberalism – not exclusively the economic liberalism sometimes attributed to him, but primarily a political liberalism best understood as agonistic.[5]

Further, in attending to this feature of Ferguson's political thought, we also can reconsider the immanent place of the republican tradition

and Commerce," in van Gelderen and Skinner, *Republicanism: A Shared European Heritage*, Vol. 2, pp. 197–226.

3 Oz-Sulzberger's work stresses Ferguson's "cautious restatement of classical republicanism." Oz-Salzberger, "Introduction," pp. xix, xxiv; Oz-Sulzberger, "Scots, Germans, Republic and Commerce," p. 204; Gary L. McDowell, "Commerce, Virtue, and Politics: Adam Ferguson's Constitutionalism," *Review of Politics*, 45 (October 1983), pp. 536, 542, 547.

4 Friedrich A. Hayek, *The Constitution of Liberty*, Chicago: University of Chicago Press, 1960, pp. 54–70; Friedrich A. Hayek, *Law, Legislation, and Liberty: A New Statement of the Liberal Principles of Justice and Political Economy*, London: Routledge, 1998, pp. 8–34; Ronald Hamowy, *The Political Sociology of Freedom: Adam Ferguson and F. A. Hayek*, Cheltenham: Edward Elgar Publishing, 2005. For a different, more nuanced and political, liberal reading of Ferguson, see Claude Gautier, *L'invention de la société civile. Lectures anglo-écossaises, Mandeville, Smith, Ferguson*, Paris: PUF, 1993.

5 Likewise, for Lisa Hill, Ferguson's work "represents a sustained attempt to nudge a space between classical civic humanism, on the one hand, and emergent liberalism on the other, in order to create a tradition all its own; a kind of 'liberal Stoicism.'" Lisa Hill, "Anticipations of Nineteenth and Twentieth Century Social Thought in the Work of Adam Ferguson," *Archives Européennes de Sociologie*, 37:1 (1996), pp. 203, 227–228.

within the development of modern liberalism. He is a particularly challenging but apt guide. Ferguson's work helps us rethink the origins and development of liberal theory by showing how the two doctrines were more than rivals. An engagement with his project thus can assist in understanding how a particular current of liberalism was cultivated within republican language, content, and values.

I

As he sought a republic for the moderns, Ferguson examined the socioeconomic origins, historical character, and political consequences of commercial society.[6] The central hallmark of modernity, he understood, is that the unity of society has been broken into a plurality of professions, skills, economic tasks, and social niches.[7] The emergence of this civil society, a large zone of human existence autonomous from political life, directly challenged the conditions that had made classical republicanism possible.[8] The division of labor, individual self-interest, private accumulation of wealth, luxury, and a taste for refinement produced a crisis that had destabilized the republican ideal of active citizenship that fosters the common good.[9] Ferguson's problem was

[6] In a rich but focused article, John Brewer underscores Ferguson's distinctive qualities: the "constant tension" in his work between civic discourse and modern sociological realism. Among Ferguson scholars, Brewer stands out as the most appreciative of the modern dimensions of his thought. John D. Brewer, "Adam Ferguson and the Theme of Exploitation," *British Journal of Sociology*, 37 (December 1986), pp. 472–473.

[7] Adam Ferguson, *An Essay on the History of Civil Society*, edited with a new introduction by Louis Schneider, New Brunswick, N.J.: Transaction Books, 1980, pp. 180–184; Adam Ferguson, "Of the Separation of Departments, Professions and Tasks Resulting from the Progress of Arts in Society," in *Collection of Essays*, ed. Yasuo Amoh, Kyoto: Rinsen Book, 1996, pp. 141–151. For a different reading of Ferguson's theory of civil society, which emphasizes the historical emergence of liberal rationality and the new strategies of governmentality, see Michel Foucault, *Naissance de la biopolitique. Cours au Collège de France, 1978–1979*, Paris: Gallimard Seuil, 2004, pp. 295–320.

[8] Ferguson, *Essay*, pp. 186–188.

[9] For a broader discussion of the ideological republican crisis caused by commerce and wealth, see Franco Venturi's still unsurpassed study, *Utopia and Reform in the Enlightenment*, Cambridge: Cambridge University Press, 1971, pp. 18–46, 55–94. For a more recent discussion of this crisis, see Donald Winch, "Commercial Realities, Republican Principles," in van Gelderen and Skinner, *Republicanism: A Shared European Heritage*, Vol. 2, pp. 293–310.

whether and how this crisis could be surmounted.[10] Once civil society had triggered the growth of manufacture and trade, could it sustain the value and practice of civic virtue? Had republicanism become an anachronism, as Montesquieu had assumed?

These questions, posed in more than one form, already are pivotal in his earliest text. In the first pages of *Reflections Previous to the Establishment of a Militia* (1756), he addressed the pressing need to find means "to mix the military Spirit with a civil and commercial

[10] Some four decades ago, David Kettler's still matchless consideration highlighted this challenging project at the heart of Ferguson's writings. Kettler's reading drew attention to Ferguson's persistent quest to reconcile republicanism with modern conditions. Kettler thus succeeds in organizing the frequently unsystematic qualities of Ferguson by placing this rapprochement at the center of his reading. Kettler couples this achievement with two additional insights. He recognizes the original qualities of Ferguson's political thought, rejecting the more common evaluation that has treated Ferguson as a minor thinker, at best. Further, Kettler's appreciation is not hagiographic. He understands Ferguson's significant limitations and hazards a plausible account of their cause. David Kettler, *Adam Ferguson: His Social and Political Thought*, New Brunswick, N.J.: Transaction Publishers, 2005, pp. xiv, 8, 124, 135. In a subsequent article, Kettler restated this tension and elaborated its significance. David Kettler, "History and Theory in Ferguson's Essay on the History of Civil Society: A Reconsideration," *Political Theory*, 5 (November 1977), pp. 442, 454–455. Richard Sher argues that this tension lies at the heart, more generally, of the Scottish Enlightenment. With this assertion, he illuminates the broader historical framework within which Ferguson developed his distinct thought. Richard Sher, "Adam Ferguson, Adam Smith, and the Problem of National Defense," *Journal of Modern History*, 61 (June 1989), pp. 242, 268. Hill's erudite study sheds light on the origins of Ferguson's conceptual innovations as she locates the significance of Ferguson in his innovative and idiosyncratic deployment of classical themes, especially drawn from Christian Stoic theology, to make sense of the dilemmas and challenges of commercial society. Hill, "Anticipations of Nineteenth and Twentieth Century Social Thought in the Work of Adam Ferguson," pp. 203–228. On the other hand, although Ernest Gellner recognizes Ferguson's recurring anxieties, he treats him partially, by representing Ferguson exclusively as believing the market to be a force for the corruption and decay of civic virtue. This reading fails to acknowledge Ferguson's more complex engagement with commercial society, seeing commerce not just as a problem but also as a hallmark of civilized progress. Gellner's insufficient reading, to be sure, is well intentioned. He was concerned to rejoin critics of the market and to secure a place for an affirmation of the price system as the only viable basis of liberty. Ernest Gellner, "Adam Ferguson and the Surprising Robustness of Civil Society," in *Liberalism in Modern Times: Essays in Honour of Hosé G. Merquior*, ed. Ernest Gellner and César Cansino, Budapest: Central European University Press, 1996, pp. 119–131. On Ferguson's attempt to reconcile civic virtue with commerce, also see Claude Gautier, "Introduction: Ferguson ou la modernité problématique," in Adam Ferguson, *Essai sur l'histoire de la société civile*, ed. Claude Gautier, Paris: PUF, 1992, pp. 15, 30, 37, 64, 70.

Policy."[11] Scotland, as the example at hand, had been transformed "into a Nation of Manufacturers, [in] which each is confined to a particular branch and sunk into the Habits and Peculiarities of his Trade. In this we consult the success of good Work; but slight the Honours of human Nature: We furnish good Work; but educate men, gross, sordid, void of sentiments and Manners."[12] Facing this combination of material change and human impoverishment, Ferguson sought to harmonize the "Degree of Civil Liberty" attained by modern societies with the "Cultivation of Moral Characters" and the realization of "National Greatness."[13]

Over the course of his life, Ferguson's objectives remained constant even as his terminology became more conceptual. His most renowned text, *An Essay on the History of Civil Society* (1767), observes that "democracy," by which he also means ancient republicanism, "is preserved with difficulty, under the disparities of condition, and the unequal cultivation of the mind, which attend the variety of pursuits, and applications, that separate mankind in the advanced state of commercial arts."[14] Nonetheless, he suggested that private wealth and public virtue, the individual and the community, can be reconciled and "mixed," as they "are opposed to one another but only by mistake."[15] The two, he argued, with a degree of optimism, could be joined. "If the public good be the principal object with individuals, it is likewise true, that the happiness of individuals is the great end of civil society: for in what sense can a public enjoy any good, if its members, considered apart, be unhappy?"[16] Hence, it is important to identify those institutional mechanisms, political arrangements, and social practices that might prevent such a mistake.

[11] Adam Ferguson, *Reflections Previous to the Establishment of a Militia*, London, 1756, p. 3. This insight about the early Ferguson can be found in John Robertson, *The Scottish Enlightenment and the Militia Issue*, Edinburgh: John Donald Publishers, 1985, p. 89. Robertson traces this reconciliatory project to a subsequent pamphlet by Ferguson, *The History of the Proceedings in the Case of Margaret, commonly called Peg, only lawful sister to John Bull, Esq.*, London, 1761, p. 179; cited in Robertson, *Scottish Enlightenment*, p. 114.

[12] Ferguson, *Militia*, p. 12.

[13] Ferguson, *Militia*, pp. 33, 12, 33.

[14] Ferguson, *Essay*, p. 187. A similar point is made by Robertson, *Scottish Enlightenment*, pp. 203, 205.

[15] Ferguson, *Essay*, p. 146.

[16] Ferguson, *Essay*, p. 58.

Later, in *Principles of Moral and Political Science* (1792), a volume of much-revised lectures, Ferguson's agonistic liberalism was most fully elaborated, but not without selectively holding to republican aspirations.[17] He advanced a vision of the modern state as a juridical instrument to protect the liberties of persons rather than to buttress a specific moral code. "It is a primary object of government on this and many other accounts," he claimed, "to secure the property of his subjects, to protect the industrious in reaping the fruits of his labour, in recovering the debts of which are fully due to him, and in providing for the fair decision of questions that may arise in the intercourse of trade."[18] Nonetheless, he concurrently insisted that the magistrate still must shut "the door to disorder and vice, to endeavour to stifle the ill dispositions of men; . . . to facilitate and encourage the choice of virtue, and to give scope to the best dispositions which nature has furnished."[19] Thus, he insisted, modern nations must "unite the public virtue with commerce."[20]

Ferguson translated these challenges concerning republicanism and commercial modernity into two distinct sets of tensions demanding resolution. The first is the conflict between political and individual autonomy and rights.[21] The second is the friction between public spirit and material self-interest. These distinctions connote different qualities. The former refers to competing concepts of liberty, anticipating Benjamin Constant's and Isaiah Berlin's well-known typologies.

[17] A first version of the *Principles* was published in 1769 as a comparatively small volume entitled *Institutes of Moral Philosophy* by Ferguson for the use of his students. Subsequently, it was substantially modified, amended, and expanded, appearing ultimately as a two-volume publication. Writing about his own efforts in the third person, Ferguson distinguished in his introductory "Occasion and Progress of the Following Work" to the 1792 edition of *Principles* that "he has treated the history of the species in a different manner; not without hopes that this his last method, in the order of progression may have gained some advantage over the former." Adam Ferguson, *Principles of Moral and Political Science*, 2 vols., Edinburgh, 1792, p. vii.

[18] Ferguson, *Principles*, *II*, p. 426.

[19] Ferguson, *Principles*, *II*, p. 318. Yet Ferguson remained uneasy. Even in this most liberal text, he never renounced his fear that the formal rule of law, by failing to apprehend the ethical and normative tissue of society, would leave unprotected the very sentiments and virtues necessary for a free political community. This underlying preoccupation is apparent in Ferguson's discussion of modern law.

[20] Ferguson, *Principles*, *I*, p. 254.

[21] For Ferguson's concept of rights, see *Principles*, *II*, pp. 184–202.

The latter refers to contrasting philosophical anthropologies and concepts of the good, signifying alternative motivations for human action.

Political autonomy includes the principles of democratic legitimation and popular sovereignty. 'Democracy' is often used as Ferguson's synonym for 'republic.'[22] An individual who has political rights must possess "a certain share in the government of his country."[23] He understood political autonomy to be a principle of legitimation for political authority, a criterion of validity for distinguishing between just and unjust governments. Treating political authority as the power of the state to monopolize the use of violence, he regarded the democratic kernel of republicanism to be a method that can transform force into a legitimate practice based on consent, a right "so long as the bulk of the people agree in opinion with their rulers, and think that the force of the state is properly applied"[24] – hence the distinction in his writings between "a government *de facto*" and "a government *de jure*."[25]

Individual autonomy, by contrast, denotes economic freedom and the individual right to private property in commercial market society. "Liberty," in such circumstances, consists "in every particular instance . . . in securing the fairly acquired conditions of men, however unequal."[26] Likewise, he observed, in advocating a limited state that "we must be contented to . . . expect justice from the limits which are set to the powers of the magistrate, and to rely for protection of the laws which are made to secure the estate, and the person of the subject."[27] Fashioned under the conditions of civil society, individual autonomy is grounded in circumstances marked by how "the materials of commerce may continue to be accumulated without any determinate limit," against external interference.[28]

[22] Ferguson, *Essay*, p. 126.

[23] Ferguson, *Essay*, p. 156; Geuna, "Commercial Society in the Scottish Enlightenment: The Case of Adam Ferguson," p. 188.

[24] Ferguson, *Principles, I*, pp. 215, 274, 284, 240–241.

[25] Ferguson, *Principles, II*, p. 245.

[26] Ferguson, *Principles, II*, p. 464.

[27] Ferguson, *Essay*, p. 161.

[28] Ferguson, *Essay*, p. 216.

Ferguson cautioned that the exclusive or even predominant realization of one form of autonomy or right can threaten the other. Neither should be sustained alone. Regarding circumstances in which private autonomy gains the upper hand, he wrote:

> If to any people it be the avowed object of policy, in all its internal refinements, to secure the person and the property of the subject, without any regard to his political character, the constitution indeed may be free, but its members may likewise become unworthy of the freedom they possess, and unfit to preserve it. The effects of such a constitution may be to immerse all orders of men in their separate pursuits of pleasure, which they may now enjoy with little disturbance; or of gain which they may preserve without any attention to the commonwealth. If this be the end of political struggles, the design, when executed, in securing to the individual his estate, and the means of subsistence, may put an end to the exercise of those very virtues that were required in conducting its execution.[29]

Notwithstanding its indispensability, in short, private autonomy generates huge inequalities and shapes new patterns of subordination and domination that undermine the moral and institutional conditions of a free political community.[30] As John Brewer established in his treatment of exploitation in Ferguson's work, "Ferguson perceives exploitation in modern terms, as inequality of power and control in the labour process, and involving situations where skills are not the determinant of economic reward and where workers are denuded, diminished, and impoverished."[31] Renewing a classical republican trope, Ferguson argued that capitalism corrodes public virtue and neutralizes the substantive content of popular government by transforming it into an ensemble of empty laws, making of it a sheer formality.[32]

[29] Ferguson, *Essay*, p. 222.
[30] Kettler makes a comparable argument in "History and Theory," p. 447.
[31] Brewer, "Exploitation," p. 473.
[32] "It is not in mere laws, after all, that we are to look for the securities to justice.... Statutes serve to record the rights of a people, and speak the intention of parties to defend what the letter of the law has expressed: but without the vigour to maintain what is acknowledged as a right, the mere record, or the feeble intention, is of little avail." *Essay*, p. 166. Also, see Gautier, "Introduction: Ferguson ou la modernité problématique," pp. 85–86; Geuna, "Commercial Society in the Scottish Enlightenment: The Case of Adam Ferguson," pp. 193–195.

Economic freedom and the "admiration of riches" promote social inequalities so huge that popular self-determination becomes impossible.[33] Manifesting an admirable degree of sociological realism and anticipating what, a century later, would become conventional wisdom, Ferguson underscored the socioeconomic structural preconditions for democracy. Built on extreme economic disparity, political equality becomes empty and ceremonial. "In every commercial state, notwithstanding any pretension to equal rights, the exaltation of the few must depress the many."[34] Even as a commercially oriented state may guard property rights, increase the wealth of a nation, promote cultural development, secure the private sphere of individuals, and protect the plurality of values, "the disparities of rank and fortune which are necessary to the pursuit or enjoyment of luxury, introduce false grounds of precedency and estimation." Democracy, in consequence, becomes impossible "if, on the mere consideration of being rich or poor, one order of men are, in their own apprehension, elevated, another debased."[35] Thus, commercial capitalism turns "the foundation [on] which freedom was built . . . to serve a tyranny."[36]

Yet, a full pendulum swing in the direction of political autonomy would also have dire consequences. On its own, this form of autonomy also is conducive to tyranny, that of the majority, encroaching private freedom mainly by threatening property through the equalization of the distribution of wealth.[37] For Ferguson, this amounts to the "despotism of many," which "is the more oppressive and the less restrained" than other forms of despotic power, as "there is indeed no species of tyranny under which individuals are less safe than under that

[33] Brewer shows how Ferguson considered the labor process itself to be antidemocratic. Despite this insight, Brewer fails to discuss the relation between quasi democracy and protocapitalism in Ferguson's writings. Brewer, "Exploitation," p. 468.

[34] Ferguson, *Essay*, p. 186.

[35] Ferguson, *Essay*, p. 250. "Luxury," he further observed, "may serve to corrupt democratical states, by introducing a species of monarchical subordination." Ferguson, *Essay*, p. 255.

[36] Ferguson, *Essay*, pp. 186, 262. Here, our argument resembles that of John Keane, who writes, "The dialectic between civil society and political despotism is basic to Ferguson's argument." John Keane, "Despotism and Democracy," in *Civil Society and the State: New European Perspectives*, ed. John Keane, London: Verso Books, 1988, p. 42.

[37] Ferguson, *Essay*, p. 157.

of a majority or prevailing faction."[38] In addition, political autonomy threatens to eradicate the plurality of perspectives, characters, and interests by destroying their sources in civil society.[39] Alone, public liberty ultimately is inimical to the liberalization of political structures, the benefits of diversity, and the gains of toleration. Further, a commercially prosperous state is more likely to enjoy tranquillity, as individuals are motivated by the quest for economic gain rather than honor, sacrifice, and conquest.[40] Even demographic growth, for Ferguson, is the fruit of peace and generates a steady source of revenue for common purposes.[41] Without such material and cultural gains, the modern state would remain predatory, even barbarous.

Likewise, an excessive role for political autonomy counteracts the material and cultural progress generated by new forms of economic relations. For it would threaten the startling advancements in wealth and the quality of commodities, the enrichment of society through the development of human plurality, the refinement of manners and higher and more complex experiences and pleasures, a broadened access to cultural goods, and thus the conditions of civilization brought about by commercial progress. The division of labor – "the separation of callings, and the subdivision of each into a convenient number of different branches" – that underlay the very crisis of republicanism is, nonetheless, the driving force for "the progress of commercial arts" and "their advancement."[42] Indeed, it is by "the separation of arts and professions" that "the sources of wealth are laid open" and "every species of material is wrought to the greatest perfection, and every commodity is produced in the greatest abundance." Without such a division of labor and the attendant gains to wealth, "a people can make no great progress in cultivating the arts of life."[43]

Fundamental to the division of labor that produces prosperity and drives progress is the pursuit of self-interest. "The commercial arts," Ferguson observed, "are properly the distinctive pursuit or concern of

38 Ferguson, *Principles, II*, pp. 436, 464.
39 Ferguson, *Essay*, pp. 187–188.
40 Ferguson, *Essay*, pp. 146–154, 180.
41 Ferguson, *Essay*, pp. 140, 144, 181, 233; Ferguson, *Principles, II*, pp. 418, 420–446.
42 Ferguson, *Principles, II*, p. 424.
43 Ferguson, *Essay*, pp. 180–181; Ronald Hamowy, "Adam Smith, Adam Ferguson and the Division of Labor," *Economica*, 35 (1968), pp. 244–259.

individuals, and are best conducted on motives of separate interests and private advancement."[44] Civil society is driven by "the principle of private interest, and with a view to private gain."[45] But this egoistic motivation, however, inherently has a strained relationship with the public good, and thus directly challenges the republican values of patriotism and civic commitment. Although echoing Mandeville in noting that the state benefits by having the production of collective goods made possible by private acts and aspirations, Ferguson insisted that "where the principle of trade is private interest," it is "farthest removed from public spirit, or any concern for a common cause."[46] Unlike Mandeville, he refused to project faith in the spontaneous and unintended creation of order to the political realm. In so doing, he repudiated the idea that the polity follows the same logic as the market.[47]

Self-interest not only reduces the moral and intellectual dimensions of individual character but also seriously undermines human freedom. Ferguson's vision of historical progress consists of a compelling critique of commercial modernity informed by the republican concept of corruption.[48] The 'spirit' of civil society is detrimental to social cohesion as it promotes fragmentation and atomization, placing individuals against each other in a competitive quest for material profit without limit.[49] Within this powerful dynamic of self-interest, "the individual is every thing, and the public nothing."[50] As a consequence, "the bands of society are broken" and the modern state risks decline and dissolution.[51]

In the political realm, this trend takes the form of depoliticization, that is, a retreat into one's private sphere and a corresponding "growing indifference to objects of a public nature."[52] Political participation falters, and politics becomes an activity for the few, who, moreover, tend to rule according to the narrow dictates of self-interest,

44 Ferguson, *Principles, I*, p. 244.
45 Ferguson, *Principles, II*, p. 421.
46 Ferguson, *Principles, II*, pp. 381, 425.
47 Oz-Salzberger, "Scots, Germans, Republic and Commerce," p. 200.
48 Forbes, "Introduction," pp. xxxi–xxxviii.
49 Ferguson, *Essay*, p. 19. Gellner, "Adam Ferguson and the Surprising Robustness of Civil Society," pp. 121–122, 126.
50 Ferguson, *Essay*, p. 56.
51 Ferguson, *Essay*, p. 19.
52 Ferguson, *Essay*, p. 256.

"without any attention to the commonwealth."[53] Commercial society thus directly threatens to cancel the benefits brought about by the republican government, because, as Ferguson noted, "the history of mankind... has abundantly shewn, in the instance of republican governments, that the attainments of knowledge, ability, and public virtues are proportioned to the concern which numbers are permitted to take in the affairs of their community; and to the exertion of ingenuity and public spirit, which they have occasion to make in national counsels, in offices of state, or public services of any sort."[54]

Ferguson's account of commercial states, in short, identifies an ominous dialectic between wealth, prosperity, and culture, on the one hand, and corruption, apathy, and decline, on the other.[55] Progress is accompanied by a neglect of common affairs that corrodes civic virtue and the public spirit, and undermines the foundations of political liberty.[56] Institutional arrangements, procedural rules, and legal norms require the active support and dedication of citizens. Without such a living and steady defense, a free constitution becomes corrupted, unable to sustain its freedoms, and becomes an easy prey to "despotical tyranny" and the personal ambitions of the few, the strong, and the powerful.[57] The principle of self-interest, for Ferguson, entails an implicit abdication of political rights. It is an act of servility.[58] "After all," he cautioned, "it is not in mere laws... that we are to look for the securities of justice, but in the powers by which those laws have been obtained, and without whose constant support they must fall to disuse. Statutes serve to record the rights of a people, and speak the intention of parties to defend what the letter of the law has expressed: but without the vigour to maintain what is acknowledged as a right, the mere

[53] Ferguson, *Essay*, p. 222.

[54] Ferguson, *Principles, I*, pp. 266–267.

[55] Ferguson, "Of the Separation of Departments, Professions and Tasks Resulting from the Progress of Arts in Society," p. 142. For the most systematic and comprehensive treatment of Ferguson's theory of progress and decline, see Lisa Hill, "Adam Ferguson and the Paradox of Progress and Decline," *History of Political Thought*, 18:4 (1997), pp. 677–706.

[56] Ferguson, *Essay*, p. 56; Christopher J. Finlay, "Rhetoric and Citizenship in Adam Ferguson's *Essay on the History of Civil Society*," *History of Political Thought*, 27:1 (2006), pp. 33–36.

[57] Ferguson, *Essay*, p. 222; Ferguson, *Principles, II*, p. 289; Keane, "Despotism and Democracy," pp. 42; McDowell, "Commerce, Virtue, and Politics: Adam Ferguson's Constitutionalism," p. 545.

[58] Ferguson, *Essay*, p. 262.

record, or the feeble intention, is of little avail."[59] The result can be dramatic – national decline, where the citizens of a free state become, "in this manner, like the inhabitants of a conquered province."[60]

This powerful indictment of self-interest, however, is not associated with romantic nostalgia for the republics of the ancients. After all, Rome itself succumbed to the forces of corruption and decline.[61] Ferguson remains resolutely modern. The "perfect virtue" required in a republic cannot be fully resuscitated.[62] Nor should it. Such a republican cure would be worse than the commercial malady. An attempt to institutionalize civic virtue would undermine the multiple advances of commerce and could endanger the security, diversity, and freedom of individuals.[63] The solution, he warned, is not to be found by regressing "to the misplaced ardours of a republican spirit," for that approach would undercut the profound and valuable modern distinction separating "the political from the moral character."[64]

II

Over the course of his intellectual life, Ferguson struggled to discover a solution to these tensions between commerce and virtue.[65] In *Militia*, the youthful Ferguson privileged a quite traditional cultural solution, the establishment of a national militia.[66] That institution, he believed, could counterbalance the spirit and pathologies of commerce by cultivating the necessary moral and patriotic sentiments to succor public virtue and strengthen devotion to the common good while protecting liberty.[67]

59 Ferguson, *Essay*, p. 166.
60 Ferguson, *Essay*, pp. 219, 256, 223–232.
61 Adam Ferguson, *The History of the Progress and Termination of the Roman Republic* (1783), Michigan Historical Reprint Series, Ann Arbor: University of Michigan, 2005.
62 Ferguson, *Essay*, p. 72.
63 Ferguson, *Principles, II*, p. 181.
64 Ferguson, *Essay*, p. 71; Ferguson, *Principles*, *II*, p. 413.
65 Kettler, *Adam Ferguson: His Social and Political Thought*, pp. 201, 211–213, 218–225, 264–296; Brewer, "Exploitation," pp. 472–473.
66 See Robertson, *Scottish Enlightenment*, pp. 90–91.
67 Sher, "Ferguson, Smith, and the Problem of National Defense," pp. 242–243, 245, 255–258. Even in this early, more republican, text, however, Ferguson never renounced the positive features of commercial society; he remained in all his writings within the horizons of modernity. He appreciated the "happy form of our

This simplified program, he later came to realize, was insufficient for modern conditions, as it flew in the face of the division of labor by envisioning the reunification of the soldier and the citizen. Ferguson then advanced a second solution in *Civil Society* at the midpoint of his theoretical development.[68] Influenced by Montesquieu, he supported a constitutional monarchy as the means to reconcile private wealth with political liberty, and self-interest with civic virtue through the organizational principle of honor.[69] "Birth and titles, the reputation of courage, courtly manners, and a certain elevation of the mind," he wrote, will check the democratic drive to total equality, the homogenization of society, and the eradication of social differences and hierarchies.[70] Simultaneously, it also will counterbalance the effects of "effemination" and pacification cultivated by the embourgeoisement of a commercial middle class that lost its military spirit, renounced the common good, and had come to lack concern for national greatness.

This plan also proved problematic. Its recourse to this form of rule was neither republican nor liberal, and it could not reconcile Ferguson's own diagnosis of modern economic relations as the hallmark of progress with his insightful understanding of its antirepublican effects.

government; the sacred Authority with which our laws execute themselves; the Perfection to which Arts are arrived; the Extent of our commerce, and Increase of our People; the Degrees of Taste and Literature which we possess; the Probity and Humanity which prevail in our manners; are circumstances of which a Nation may be allowed to boast of." His lament is not that modernity and its market relations are inherently defective and dangerous; rather, they "have already gone too far, in the opinion that trade and Manufacture are the only requisites in our country." Against this unbalanced and uncritical affirmation of economic liberalism, Ferguson proposed moral education through the creation of a system of national defense. However, Ferguson did not press this classical republican solution to the problems of excessive self-interest and moral corruption to the opposite extreme of abandoning modern liberties. The remedy must respect individual autonomy: "The entire force of the military Law cannot be applied here, because we do not propose to give up our liberties." Ferguson, *Militia*, pp. 11, 12.

68 Robertson wrongly argues that Ferguson lacked an institutional solution. Confusing Ferguson's theory of the origins of institutions with his account of their actual functioning, Robertson cites Ferguson's claim that "No constitution is formed by concert, no government is copied from a plan" to misleadingly conclude that "Ferguson saw little point in deliberate initiative in relation to institutions." Robertson, *Scottish Enlightenment*, p. 208. By contrast to Robertson, Gary McDowell places constitutionalism and the place of institutions at the center of Ferguson's thought. McDowell, "Commerce, Virtue, and Politics: Adam Ferguson's Constitutionalism."

69 Kettler, *Adam Ferguson: His Social and Political Thought*, pp. 6, 165, 254–258, 277–278.

70 Ferguson, *Essay*, p. 251; Keane, "Despotism and Democracy," pp. 42–43.

Neither a modern nor a viable solution, constitutional monarchy signaled a conservative inclination by a thinker who had yet to crisply choose his political and theoretical loyalties.[71] Rather than confront the republican-commercial antinomy directly, the commitment to constitutional monarchy was an act of avoidance.

In his maturity, Ferguson forced a resolution. He faced the dilemmas and oscillations of his previous writings by transforming his classical republican aspirations into a more decidedly modern liberal political form. He stressed, though not without reservation, the lexical priority of a predominantly neutral, liberal state that protects private property and secures existing economic and social inequalities. He thus tilted the balance between public and private autonomy to favor the latter.[72] In *Principles*, he placed the market as an analytical and normative category inside his political thought,[73] and he marginalized republicanism as antiquarian and potentially dangerous. Like Hume, Ferguson now described political autonomy as archaic, appropriate for small, rude, homogeneous, and militaristic societies "where the people may be defined to govern and to defend themselves, the habits of the statesman and the warrior are required as ordinary accomplishments of the citizen."[74] In this inverted formulation, Ferguson identified the primary source of tyranny not in private interest, the pursuit of profit, or the deepening of economic inequality, but in the "prevalence of democratic power," which features the "violence of popular assemblies and their tumults."[75] Faced with the prospect of a despotism by the majority, Ferguson produced a solution that limited political participation, asserted the priority of economic development, and reconsidered the purposes of the modern state.[76]

71 Here, we disagree with Keane, who finds the solution of constitutional monarchy to be "thoroughly modern." Keane, "Despotism and Democracy," p. 43. By contrast, Forbes, Kettler, and Robertson more perceptively grasp Ferguson's failure. Forbes, "Introduction," p. xli; Kettler, *Adam Ferguson: His Social and Political Thought*, pp. 277–296; Robertson, *Scottish Enlightenment*, pp. 208–209.

72 Kettler, *Adam Ferguson: His Social and Political Thought*, pp. 264–296.

73 Ferguson, *Principles, I*, pp. 252–265.

74 Ferguson, *Principles, II*, p. 414.

75 Ferguson, *Principles, II*, p. 464.

76 He declared its "primary object" is "to secure the property of its subjects, to protect the industrious in reaping the fruits of his labour, in recovering the debts which are justly due to him, and in providing for the fair decision of questions that may arise in the intercourse of trade." Ferguson, *Principles, II*, p. 426. This formulation, though syntactically parallel to a passage in the *Essay* where the object of the state

In the face of pluralism, Ferguson stressed, the state must not take stands on moral issues.[77] Virtue cannot be coercively enforced by law.[78] "We are not to expect," he argued, "that the laws of any country are to be framed as so many lessons of morality, to instruct the citizen how he may act the part of a virtuous man."[79] Rather than counterbalance the social fragmentation and moral corruption imposed by modernity, he reformulated the task of the state as that of being attentive to the security of the individual, the protection of property, and the stabilization of a market economy. Even inequality, which he mostly had treated in pejorative terms, now appears far more positively: "In these inequalities we find the first germe of subordination and government so necessary to the safety of individuals and the peace of mankind; and in these also we find the continued incentive to labour and the practice of lucrative arts."[80]

The tension between republicanism and commercial society, while it did not disappear, by now had become rather slack. Here, in a predominantly liberal formulation, Ferguson came close to abandoning the anxieties that had animated his prior work, and he relegated to secondary status his earlier powerful concern for the dislocative, community-destroying impulses of modern commercial societies. Republican impulses are still present, to be sure, but now appear without compelling coherence. As a telling example, the text advances strong Aristotelian assumptions about the political and social nature of human persons and the superiority of society over the individual, but terminates with an apologetic glorification of private autonomy as its axial political principle.[81]

We come, in this way, to a pivotal problem in Ferguson's political thought. He powerfully understood that commercial development,

is discussed, is subtly but substantively different. There, Ferguson wrote, "The great object of policy ... is to secure to the family its means of subsistence and settlement; to protect the industriousness in the pursuit of his occupation; to reconcile the restrictions of police, and the social affections of mankind, with their separate and interested pursuit." Ferguson, *Essay*, p. 144.

77 Ferguson, *Principles, II*, pp. 145–146, 181, 316–318.

78 Ferguson, *Principles, II*, pp. 181–182, 316–319, 413–414.

79 Ferguson, *Principles, II*, p. 145.

80 Ferguson, *Principles, II*, p. 463; Brewer, "Exploitation," p. 474.

81 Ferguson, *Principles, I*, pp. 21, 24; *II*, pp. 59, 85, 223–224; Pocock, *The Machiavellian Moment*, p. 500.

civil society, and pluralism posed new and profound challenges for republican government. Here lay his originality. Others, of course, also recognized this issue, but Ferguson – especially in the *Essay on the History of Civil Society* – resisted the two most common, yet opposite moves by thinkers of his time. Some, like James Harrington, Jean-Jacques Rousseau, and the Scot Andrew Fletcher, sought to mimic the ancients in order to save republicanism. Others, including most notably Montesquieu, thought such a return to be impossible. Modernity, which they understood to be deeply antithetical to republicanism, had triumphed.

By contrast, even as he came close at times to each of these poles, Ferguson probed to see how it might be feasible to achieve what these other thinkers thought to be unattainable – the reconciliation of virtue with commerce. Rather than simply identify virtue with conditions present in the distant past, he identified this moral impulse as a transhistorical possibility, rooted in a particular view of the nature of the human person as active and creative. Even in *Principles*, where he often came close to translating the oppositions between political and individual autonomy and self-interest and virtue into abstract and historically grounded antagonisms between tradition and modernity, he continued to stress how "the general disposition to excel, next to interest, is the most ordinary, even more than interest, a powerful motive to action, and an occasion of the greatest exertions incident to human nature."[82] This transhistorical anthropology serves as the basis for his faith in the continuing possibility of reconciliation, despite the great pressures exerted by modern conditions.

Yet this persistent theme is at odds with the character of exposition and the solutions with which he experimented in each of his three main works. In *Militia*, he restored to life the martial virtues of the heroic citizen-soldier; in *Civil Society*, he rescued an expiring monarchical form; in *Principles*, he downplayed both earlier resolutions, affirming commerce and wealth as he drew nearer to stylizing republicanism as premodern.[83]

[82] Ferguson, *Principles*, *I*, p. 125.

[83] On Ferguson's silence over the militia issue in his post-*Essay* publications, see John Robertson, *The Scottish Enlightenment and the Militia Issue*, Edinburgh: John Donald, 1985, p. 209; Sher, "Ferguson, Smith, and the Problem of National Defense," pp. 258–259. The causes of Ferguson's misapprehension of democracy are different

III

Ferguson's thought beckons us still. Notwithstanding their unresolved project of reconciliation, his writings contain a compelling compound of intuitions, ideas, and intentions. These elements include a persistent appreciation for the fact of plurality, a distinction between friend and enemy, the constitutive character of conflict, and an engaged, less neutral understanding of the legal order and the role of political institutions as conducive to bargaining and the adjudication of competing values and interests. If separated, each of these features can be identified as belonging to either the republican or the liberal tradition. But Ferguson should not be read this way. Each appears at every stage of his writing, albeit with varying emphases and configurations as they inform his trajectory from a predominantly republican to a primarily liberal orientation.

Rather, the persistence of these four dimensions of politics, to which we now turn, and the challenge that comes with this persistence, is of greater interest.[84] They bear on two vital issues. The first is historical. It concerns the beginnings of modern liberalism. The second is conceptual. It relates to the character of liberal possibilities and the continuing relevance of Ferguson's innovations.

Plurality

Modernity, Ferguson argued, marked by a new "proficiency in the liberal and mechanical arts, in literature, and in commerce," is distinct from the "rude ages."[85] Its social order is differentiated and fragmented as a result of the structural imperatives of commercial society, especially its revolutionary division of labor, which not only accelerates the

in each of his main works. In *Militia*, his understanding was mediated by his republican commitments. In the *Essay*, he sacrificed an immanent democratic solution to his conservative quest for order. In *Principles*, his suspicious liberalism with regard to democracy cannot be explained by the text alone. Ferguson's theory is permissive; that is, there is nothing inherently antidemocratic in his thought in the book. Rather, he adopted a common and prejudiced reading of democracy.

84 The reading that follows is selective in two senses. First, it hardly constitutes a comprehensive or even representative overview of Ferguson's thought in full. That is not our aim. Second, it appropriates some of his key concepts and claims and examines them in their own terms for our purposes independently of Ferguson's own specific theoretical ends.

85 Ferguson, *Essay*, pp. 205, 138.

rhythm of economic development but alters the character of relations in the productive process.[86] Contrary to simple and uniform traditional social structures, modern societies manifest an unusual degree of complexity and "diversity of ranks and professions," so much so that even the "rude or the simple observer would remark the variety he saw in the dwellings and in the occupations of different men," and "would find, in the streets of the same city as great a diversity, as in the territory of a separate people."[87] "Mankind," he maintained, "when in their rude state, have a great uniformity of manners; but when civilized, they are engaged in a variety of pursuits; they tread on a larger field, and separate to a greater distance."[88]

This novelty is responsible for the dissolution of the symbolic universe of traditional societies, conducing the collapse of their substantive and shared uniform ethical codes. By contrast, "polished nations"[89] are characterized by an inevitable plurality of values, beliefs, and interests that cannot be arrayed or compared on a single scale. In his appreciation and discussion of pluralism, Ferguson boldly advanced three sets of claims.

The first concerns pluralism's scope and content. Ferguson shared John Locke's sociological assumptions about differentiation and his political conclusions favoring toleration.[90] But Ferguson considered the range of diversity to extend beyond differences in religion to encompass a broader array of modes of living, which consists of a "motley assemblage of different characters, and contains ... some examples of that variety, which the humours, tempers, and apprehensions of men, so differently employed, are likely to furnish."[91]

The second insists that pluralism's sources and location are not restricted solely to an independent symbolic sphere of ideas and perceptions, operating above or outside economic and social relations.

86 Ferguson, *Essay*, pp. 180–181; Ferguson, *Principles, II*, pp. 424–425.

87 Ferguson, *Essay*, pp. 188, 189. For a reconstruction of the social, economic, and historical environment within which Ferguson came to an understanding of commercial society, see Brewer, "Exploitation," pp. 464–465.

88 Ferguson, *Essay*, p. 188.

89 Ferguson, *Essay*, p. 200.

90 John Locke, *A Letter Concerning Toleration* (1689), New York: Prometheus Books, 1990.

91 Ferguson, *Essay*, p. 189.

Integral to society, the new diversity is intrinsically linked to modernity's dynamic patterns of material and political organization and class structure. Displaying a fresh sociological imagination, Ferguson claimed that pluralism appears in societies in which "the citizens of any free community are of different orders" and "each order has a peculiar set of claims and pretensions."[92] In making this assertion, however, Ferguson refused to fully endorse the more materialistic and reductionist theory of pluralism of Adam Smith, who compressed the values of a "civilized society" to "two different schemes or systems of morality current at the same time; of which the one may be called the strict or austere; the other the liberal, or if you will, the loose system."[93] Contrary to this distinction by Smith strictly based on class differences, Ferguson elaborated a richer theory of plurality recognizing a diversity of groups, beliefs, values, and dispositions.[94] He did not constrain difference to socioeconomic categories; nor did he think of human variety simply in idealist terms as disembedded and autonomous. The roots of human difference, he believed, had become multiple. They now included those of class, profession, social geography, gender (understood patriarchally), belief, and nationality.[95]

The third, concerning pluralism's effects, advanced the conflictual properties of plurality. Like Smith, who argued that friction in modern society is due to a collision of objective interests between two structurally opposed social classes, Ferguson asserted the more a society is composed of different groups, the more "the admiration and the desire which they entertain for the same subjects; their opposite pretensions" create a "separation of interest" that takes the form of "an opposition of interest," transforming "variance and dissension" into "animosity."[96] Ferguson's analysis transcended simple rational and purposeful explanation.[97] He thought every value system and moral

[92] Ferguson, *Essay*, pp. 162, 131, 133, 135. For this point, see Lisa Hill, "Eighteenth-Century Anticipations of the Sociology of Conflict: The Case of Adam Ferguson," *Journal of the History of Ideas*, 62:2 (2001), pp. 289–290.

[93] Adam Smith, *An Inquiry into the Nature and Causes of the Wealth of Nations* (1776), Indianapolis: Liberty Classics, 1976, p. 794.

[94] Ferguson, *Principles, I*, p. 182.

[95] Ferguson, *Essay*, pp. 188–189.

[96] Smith, *Wealth*, p. 84; Ferguson, *Essay*, pp. 20, 22, 20.

[97] In two cases, Kettler, in rich and precise textual readings, has established that for Ferguson 'will' and 'power' are more determinative motives in political life than

ideal contain a nonrational, power-ridden component; hence disagreements about matters of evaluation and judgment inhere in pluralism, and these cannot be reconciled simply through the mediation of reason. Perhaps influenced by Hume and distancing himself from the more purely rationalist political theory of his contemporaries, Ferguson claimed that we observe in social collisions "the influence of angry passions that do not arise from an opposition of interest," and "which the regards to interests or safety cannot confine."[98] Rather, conflict emerges from different conceptions of the good that individual and collective actors hold, particularly from their disagreements about what is "*insult* and *wrong*."[99] Their different interpretations of these harms are not justified rationally but are infused with "prejudices," "jealously," "dislikes," "antipathies," and "honour," passions that are inescapably present when value systems cross paths.[100]

Friend/Enemy

Despite such nonrational and arbitrary origins, differences are not simply open, contingent, or arbitrary. Even though individuals and groups are divided by belief and opinion and are driven by their contingent passions and emotions, pluralism is ordered.[101] Anticipating Carl Schmitt by one and a half centuries, Ferguson discovered a key structural form undergirding differences, that of the 'friend' and the 'enemy.'[102] For collective entities with dissimilar value systems and antagonistic interests, he wrote, "Friendship and enmity are to

material interest and property. For this meticulous underpinning of Ferguson's distancing from Smith, see Kettler, "History and Theory," p. 453; Hill, "Anticipations of Nineteenth and Twentieth Century Social Thought in the Work of Adam Ferguson," p. 217.

98 Ferguson, *Essay*, pp. 213, 23, 33.

99 Ferguson, *Essay*, p. 33.

100 Ferguson, *Essay*, pp. 23, 24; Ferguson, *Principles, I*, pp. 32–33, 182.

101 Ferguson, *Principles, I*, p. 182. Here, we find Hill's discussion to be deficient. In arguing that Ferguson anticipated the concept of 'spontaneous order,' she considers conflicts as random, irrational, and private actions lacking purposive and deliberative qualities. Hill fails to take into account Ferguson's group-centered analysis of conflicts. Hill, "Anticipations of Nineteenth and Twentieth Century Social Thought in the Work of Adam Ferguson," p. 209.

102 In so doing, he refuted Schmitt's boastful claim that liberals cannot distinguish between friends and enemies. Carl Schmitt, *The Concept of the Political*, New Brunswick, N.J.: Rutgers University Press, 1976, pp. 61, 69–73.

them terms of the greatest importance; they mingle not their functions together; they have singled out their enemy, and they have chosen their friend."[103]

By deploying this insight, Ferguson avoided portraying hostility as purposeless, an accidental collision of randomly distributed worldviews, condemned to a "life and death" confrontation. Rather, this distinction constitutes the central mechanism of identity formation through which a group's sense of 'us' – thus its cohesion – is constructed by transforming the cacophony of conflicts into a coherent, meaningful opposition between a friend and an enemy. Each term of the relation simultaneously consolidates and threatens the identity of the other.[104] The "separation" between friend and enemy "has an effect in straitening the bands of society; for the members of each separate nation feel their connection the more, that the name of fellow-countryman stands in contradistinction to that of an alien."[105]

Ferguson's theory of friendship and enmity starkly contrasts both with abstract universalism and with essentialist explanations of group identity that fix once and for all the perimeters and content of group particularity according to an objective position within a system of structural determinations.[106] For instance, regarding the latter, his singular definition of the nation is free from any ethnic or racial attributes: "*any separate company of men acting under a common direction*, may be termed a *nation*: For any plurality of men so united, in the language of lawyers, is an artificial person, having power to act, and rights to defend."[107] Identities are not closed or self-referential essences. They are relational and interactively constructed. They depend on a 'constitutive outside,' designed as the 'enemy.'[108] Without the postulation

[103] Ferguson, *Essay*, pp. 101–102.

[104] Ferguson, *Essay*, p. 22. Not in his book, but in his subsequent essay, Kettler took up the question of the significance of conflict in Ferguson's thought. Kettler, "History and Theory," pp. 450, 453.

[105] Ferguson, *Principles, I*, pp. 33, 32.

[106] This point has been incisively noticed by Keith Tester, who understood the novelty of Ferguson's theory of identity formation. However, Tester restricts the development of this insight to issues of national identity situated in the context of international relations and its boundaries, thus losing the wider range of its potential application. Keith Tester, *Civil Society*, London: Routledge, 1992, pp. 46–48.

[107] Ferguson, *Principles, II*, p. 294.

[108] For the concept of the 'constitutive outside,' see Henry Stater, *Wittgenstein and Derrida*, Oxford: Basil Blackwell, 1985.

of a radical other, located in the threatening presence of an exterior space, it is not possible to define one's identity and particularity.

The plural character of modern societies generates differences, disagreements, and interactions; it does not create identities. Even if the fact of plurality helps specify the basis for social conflict, "it is vain to expect," Ferguson claimed, "that we can give to the multitude of a people a sense of union among themselves, without hostility to those who oppose them."[109] Thus, what accounts for the social construction of identity is not the sheer fact of pluralism or the postulation of class, religious, racial, or ethnic foundations, but an enemy whose existence configures "bands of affection" reinforced in the practice of hostility, opposition, and rivalry.[110] The force and clarity of Ferguson's argument are striking. Here we can see him as our contemporary, initiating a very modern consideration of the constitutive features of conflict.[111]

Political Conflict

Ferguson's distinctiveness is not limited to this relational theory of identity formation. He advanced a thorough analysis of conflict, focusing on its political nature.[112] Indeed, a centerpiece of his argument is the way he discriminated political antagonism from other forms of conflictual interaction. As a result, his thought is regarded today "as an anticipation of a pluralist theory of conflict."[113] Heralding what later became a central feature of Max Weber's analysis of politics, Ferguson treated the specificity of political conflict as consisting in the contestation of authority, the most intense and pervasive form in

[109] Ferguson, *Essay*, p. 25.

[110] Ferguson, *Essay*, p. 19.

[111] It is, he stressed, only the "frequent practice of war [that] tends to strengthen the bands of society, and the practice of depredation itself engages men in trials of mutual attachment and courage. What threatened to ruin and overset every good disposition in the human breast, what seemed to banish justice from the societies of men, tends to unite the species in clans and fraternities; formidable, indeed, and hostile to one another." *Essay*, p. 101. For a further elaboration, see Louis Coser, *The Functions of Social Conflict*, Glencoe, Ill.: Free Press, 1956; and Hill, "Eighteenth-Century Anticipations of the Sociology of Conflict: The Case of Adam Ferguson," pp. 281–299.

[112] Forbes, "Introduction," pp. xvii–xix, xxix.

[113] Hill, "Anticipations of Nineteenth and Twentieth Century Social Thought in the Work of Adam Ferguson," p. 215; Hill, "Eighteenth-Century Anticipations of the Sociology of Conflict: The Case of Adam Ferguson," pp. 289–293.

which the "party which has an advantage in the actual state of society endeavor to avail themselves of it; and the party that is aggrieved, strives to obtain relief."[114]

Ferguson sought to embrace the political significance and implications of pluralism. More than being a sheer fact to be tolerated pragmatically because it cannot be abolished, he affirmed and at times glorified political conflict, even war, as the hallmark of any "civilized, polished nation."[115] Laying the foundation for an 'agonistical' liberal theory, he highlighted two advantageous consequences. At the level of the political community, Ferguson stressed the constitutive role of conflict because, as he asserted, "Without the rivalship of nations, and the practice of war, civil society itself could scarcely have found an object, or a form."[116] Equally important, Ferguson approached political conflict as the central mechanism of political innovation and change as well as of incorporation and stabilization.[117] Opposition counteracts corruption engendered by commercial self-interest, thus preserving free constitutions.[118] Conflicts are an indispensable corrective to the negative effects of the private drive for wealth and the tendency to isolate and detach oneself from public activities.[119] They support and defend free governments.[120] As Lisa Hill correctly observes,

> One of the most compelling aspects of Ferguson's history is his reliance upon conflict in the explanation of historical processes.... Conflict brings with it many positive unintended consequences: it leads to the formation of large-scale communities, the state, and formal defence institutions and plays a pivotal role in the development of the moral personality. Conflict also contributes to the maintenance of social cohesion and the preservation of free constitutions. Ferguson seems to anticipate a dialectical view of history but

[114] Ferguson, *Principles*, *II*, p. 264.

[115] Ferguson, *Essay*, pp. 220–221, Geuna, "Commercial Society in the Scottish Enlightenment: The Case of Adam Ferguson," pp. 191–192. On Ferguson's views on war, see Hill, "Eighteenth-Century Anticipations of the Sociology of Conflict: The Case of Adam Ferguson," pp. 286–289.

[116] Ferguson, *Essay*, p. 24.

[117] Ferguson, *Essay*, p. 59.

[118] Ferguson, *Essay*, p. 256.

[119] Pocock, *The Machiavellian Moment*, pp. 499–501.

[120] Hill, "Eighteenth-Century Anticipations of the Sociology of Conflict: The Case of Adam Ferguson," pp. 289–291; Geuna, "Commercial Society in the Scottish Enlightenment: The Case of Adam Ferguson," pp. 187–188.

if anything it should be regarded as an anticipation of a pluralist theory of conflict.[121]

Relying on an idiosyncratic, predominantly republican, conception of human psychology, Ferguson advanced the substantive, controversial thesis that, at the level of the individual, "the virtues of men have shone most during their struggles, not after the attainment of their ends."[122] Here, he endowed the political realm with strong substantive content, transcending the classical liberal neutral state that is concerned exclusively with the protection of life, property, and liberty. Implying the good life is that of a public *agon*, something to be politically affirmed, Ferguson claimed that "the rivalship of separate communities, and the agitations of a free people, are the principles of political life, and the school of men."[123]

Hence, although Ferguson's agonistic notion of politics focuses primarily on identity formation and group consolidation, it nonetheless is premised on a novel theory of individualism and on what David Kettler has called an "activist conception of virtue."[124] Struggles and antagonisms improve the moral and intellectual qualities of persons by developing and perfecting their "highest powers."[125] It is here that Ferguson's agonism mediates between Machiavelli's republican appreciation of conflict as the underlying source of political freedom and a perfectionist and progressive understanding of the person that later achieved clear expression in John Stuart Mill's liberal individualism.[126] Political adversity is simultaneously the main driving force of historical and social progress, the living foundation of freedom, and the prod for individual development and improvement. An active political life enhances the faculties of power, free choice, and judgment to enable the attainment of superior forms of happiness and gratification. For Ferguson, "the most animating occasions of human life, are calls

121 Hill, "Anticipations of Nineteenth and Twentieth Century Social Thought in the Work of Adam Ferguson," p. 215.
122 Ferguson, *Essay*, p. 206.
123 Ferguson, *Essay*, p. 61.
124 Kettler, *Adam Ferguson: His Social and Political Thought*, pp. 150, 164, 176–183.
125 Ferguson, *Principles, II*, p. 17.
126 Forbes, "Introduction," p. xxxv. For an informed discussion of Ferguson's notion of the human person as a progressive being, see Kettler, *Adam Ferguson: His Social and Political Thought*, pp. 126–131.

to danger and hardship, not invitations of safety and ease.... In all which, his disposition to action only keeps pace with the variety of powers with which he is furnished; and the most respectable attributes of his nature, magnanimity, fortitude, and wisdom, carry a manifest reference to the difficulties with which he is destined to struggle."[127]

Law and Institutions

This model of conflict raises, Ferguson understood, vexing problems of justice and social peace. Given the pervasiveness of antagonism and struggle and the place of power, how can a just political order be developed, maintained, and reproduced?[128] True to his preference for spontaneous social orders, he not only rejected the naturalistic, Aristotelian tradition that deduces criteria of validity from the historical and social naturality of human societies and the voluntaristic classical republican myth of the heroic founding legislator, the architect of free constitutions. He also turned aside the individualistic logic of social contract theory that postulates the existence of a general rational – prudential or moral – consensus among asocial individuals as the normative basis of society.[129]

Ferguson set aside the social contract as a source of legitimacy and, indeed, the possibility that society can act as a single collective actor in the face of human pluralism. The acknowledgment of this plurality is not a mere rhetorical device, for it carries factual weight. Beginning from the premise of inescapable and incommensurable differences, one must accept that a "perfect agreement in matters of opinion is not to be obtained in the most select company; and if it were, what would become of society?"[130]

[127] Ferguson, *Essay*, pp. 45, 47.

[128] Kettler is distinguished from other Ferguson scholars by his recognition that Ferguson grappled with this question. Kettler, "History and Theory," p. 453.

[129] Ferguson, *Essay*, pp. 4, 17, 121–123; Ferguson, *Principles, I*, pp. 199, 262; Ferguson, *Principles, II*, pp. 192, 206, 218–225, 244. On Ferguson's rejection of theories of social contract and founding legislators, see Forbes, "Introduction," pp. xxiii–xxiv; Kettler, *Adam Ferguson: His Social and Political Thought*, pp. 188–193; Gautier, "Introduction: Ferguson ou la modernité problématique," pp. 53–54, 79–80; Lisa Hill, "The Invisible Hand of Adam Ferguson," *European Legacy*, 3:6 (1998), pp. 48–51; and Oz-Salzberger, "The Political Theory of the Scottish Enlightenment," pp. 164–165.

[130] Ferguson, *Essay*, p. 62.

Ferguson directly attacked the fiction of a general founding consensus, and he sought to undermine its normative function. An attempt to reach agreement among all members of society to justify particular policies and institutional arrangements "amounts to something that has never been realized in the history of mankind, still more, if its objects be such as cannot be realized, there is reason not only to doubt its validity, but actually to consider it as altogether nugatory and absurd."[131] The search for unanimous consensus, moreover, is not only impossible but dangerous. Only violent suppression can transcend pluralism to impose an artificial agreement on substantive issues. Sounding a theme to which he often returned, Ferguson strongly cautioned that "Nothing . . . but corruption or slavery can suppress the debates that subsist among men of integrity."[132]

His insistence that it is neither possible nor desirable to seek a general consensus is supported by a crucial epistemological assumption about the scope and content of reason. Ferguson attacked the optimistic view that humans can coordinate their wills to control and determine their environment.[133] Institutional arrangements, he insisted, do not derive from deliberation and universal agreement; they are, rather, the "result of human action, but not the execution of any human design."[134] As he put it succinctly, "No constitution is formed by concert, no government is copied from a plan."[135] They are the product of political struggle and strategic action. By undermining the autonomy of reason in this manner, Ferguson sought to subvert the normative foundations of consensual arguments and reveal their credulous fragility.

Ferguson thus laid the ground for an alternative understanding of legitimate political order. His central analytical devices in this regard are the concepts of law and institution. His novelty lies in the way he fused within this framework three elements that are usually

[131] Ferguson, *Principles, II*, pp. 470–471.

[132] Ferguson, *Essay*, pp. 62.

[133] "The deliberate actions of leading men," Kettler writes in his interpretation of Ferguson's political thought, "do in fact produce political consequences that none of them intends. That is because of the contests among them and because of the interplay with circumstances, and this is the stuff of the history of nations." Kettler, "History and Theory," p. 450.

[134] Ferguson, *Essay*, p. 122.

[135] Ferguson, *Essay*, p. 123.

kept apart: prudential agreement, a shared symbolic horizon, and compulsion.[136]

In terms reminiscent of Thomas Hobbes but with considerable modifications, Ferguson analyzed order as pragmatic compromise.[137] He defined law as a "treaty" achieved through a process of strategic interaction among rival political groups that possess asymmetrical power.[138] They struggle over the acquisition of the state apparatus, but none is strong enough to impose a permanent legal and institutional arrangement over the others. On the contrary, "while they pursue in society different objects, or separate views, [they] procure a wide distribution of power," forming a nexus of instrumental interaction based on the uneven diffusion of power that precludes the possibility of a one-sided victory.[139] Even the most powerful find themselves in a situation of mutual dependence, compelling them to enter into prudential compromises that transform situational balances of power into a temporally stabilized political order. In consequence, the legal system of modern society is the outcome of struggle, bargaining, and strategic compromise. For Ferguson, "laws are never, perhaps, dictated by the interests and spirit of any order of men: they are moved, they are opposed, or amended, by different hands; and come at last to express that medium and composition which contending parties have *forced* one another to adopt."[140] By way of this pragmatic, iterated process, social norms and political institutions that solidify complex, contingent, and relational structures of power are generated.

Although he highlighted the power, bargaining, and compromise contained in the legal and institutional fabric of society, Ferguson

[136] Although McDowell appreciates the centrality of constitutionalism, institutions, and law for Ferguson, he reduces their role to an educative one, thus producing an unwarrantedly strong republican interpretation of their significance. McDowell, "Commerce, Virtue, and Politics: Adam Ferguson's Constitutionalism" pp. 548–549.

[137] Ketter, "History and Theory," p. 453. Ferguson critiques Hobbes on the social contract by deploying insights from Pufendorf. From our perspective, however, he makes two especially important departures from Hobbes. Ferguson primarily focuses on political collectivities rather than on individuals, and he is concerned far less with the foundations of a political order than with behavior and activity inside its folds.

[138] Ferguson, *Essay*, pp. 155, 165.

[139] Ferguson, *Essay*, p. 237.

[140] Ferguson, *Essay*, p. 128 (emphasis added).

understood that a legitimate and stable political order cannot be constructed solely as a by-product of strategic conflict. He was a realist, but his realism never was separated from normative considerations. Ferguson proposed a critical political theory directed to generate principles that could prescriptively assess political arrangements.[141] By itself, a bargained compromise cannot produce criteria required to distinguish between just and unjust governments and policies. Though Ferguson ventured "to reject the idea of an *original compact*... either in the formation of society itself, or in the establishment of any actual government," he nonetheless strongly believed the legitimacy of a political order once fashioned in the crucible of conflict depends on normatively motivated consent by society's members.[142] Norms are valid, he argued, only when "the parties concerned, upon trial of the situation in which they find themselves placed, agree to the conditions which are required in the exercise of government."[143]

Ferguson's adoption of such a theory of consensual legitimacy was motivated by the two most basic substantive assumptions of his philosophical anthropology: the person is both autonomous and active.[144] Autonomous, because "every person... is the absolute master of his own will";[145] and active because "happiness is not that state of repose, or that imaginary freedom from care, which at a distance is so frequent an object of desire," but is the quest to grapple with "danger and hardship" deploying "dispositions to action" keeping pace "with the variety of powers with which he is furnished."[146] Autonomous and active, "Man is by nature an artist, endowed with ingenuity, discernment, and will."[147]

This concept of the person necessitates that a political order be legitimated not merely by strategic interests and bargains but requires something like a broadly axiological system that respects, represents, and promotes the core features of the person. The principle of autonomy

141 For a comparable discussion, see Kettler, *Adam Ferguson: His Social and Political Thought*, pp. 224, 268–269.

142 Ferguson, *Essay*, p. 244.

143 Ferguson, *Principles, II*, p. 245.

144 For a comment on Ferguson's progressive conception of the person, see Kettler, *Adam Ferguson: His Social and Political Thought*, pp. 176–177.

145 Ferguson, *Principles, I*, p. 202.

146 Ferguson, *Essay*, pp. 49, 45.

147 Ferguson, *Principles, I*, p. 200.

requires the citizen to be the author as well as the subject of the law. Political obligation not only is the prudential outcome of the pursuit of preference or the absence of reasons to defect. It must also be rooted in the normative endorsement of the institutional fairness of the legal system as the basis for this achievement and assume the form of a procedurally permissive agreement between political actors about social norms and political institutions. A "fair convention," he argued, "is consistent with the welfare of the whole" while honoring the core attributes of the person.[148]

Ferguson's explication of the normative content of political institutions, however, was conditioned by his realistic understanding of modern society.[149] The formation of plural groups, values, and interests challenges the possibility and validity of a universal consensus. Because political actors are divided by class, profession, belief, passion, and unequal social and economic power, they cannot simply agree to establish social norms. Rational agreement – prudential or moral – potentially involves exclusion by force of those who fundamentally dissent from the values and institutions of the political order.[150] Agreements can remain valid even in cases that omit certain parts of the political community as long as they are able to construct a broad basis of political support and incorporate representative numbers of dissimilar political forces.

Ferguson is very clear about the limits of any agreement. First, no consensus, as wide as it may be, can overcome the fact of enmity, which requires that the political community protect itself through exclusion. While Ferguson defended toleration as a prerequisite for pluralism and conflict, he never endorsed the fiction of universal inclusion, adopting instead the position that diversity and conflict need to be affirmed to the point that they do not self-destruct. He sought arrangements that could accommodate conflict and diversity and capture their dynamism but not at the price of the dissolution of the political and social order. He thus thought an appeal to the principle of toleration could not by itself constitute a normative criterion. If toleration is the only valid

148 Ferguson, *Principles, I*, p. 304; *II*, p. 245; *I*, p. 303.

149 Forbes, "Introduction," pp. xix, xli.

150 "The idea of men in any society, great or small having ever assembled upon a foot of absolute equality, and without exclusion of any individual, to dispose of their government is altogether visionary and unknown in nature." Ferguson, *Principles, I*, p. 262.

principle, groups holding values inimical to and irreconcilable with those of a free political community would have to be granted rights self-defeating to the very existence of that community. "Even the furious zealot who is pleased to inculcate his doctrines under the terror of the rack and fire," he wrote, and yet thinks "that he is active in the cause of truth or in propagating a faith which is necessary to the salvation of mankind" must be excluded from the polity.[151] Hence, any political community based on the plurality and representation of groups, values, and interests must confront two questions "still open for discussion: 1st, Who are to be admitted on the rolls of the people, and to have a deliberative or elective voice? 2nd, In the case of a people too numerous to meet in any one body, in what divisions are they to act?"[152]

Second, contrary to the optimistic belief that general agreement dispenses with force, Ferguson, ever the realist, reminded his contemporaries that violence is an inherent aspect of any political arrangement. He counterposed the tendency to neglect and conceal its persistence, stressing that "the object of reason never can be to abolish the relation of power and dependence."[153] Force is a permanent characteristic of politics because any political regime, including the most desirable, suppresses alternative choices and, in so doing, mobilizes bias in favor of some while endangering other ideas, identities, and interests. Legal and institutional arrangements create order, but not neutrally. They orient power and value around certain basic norms – group and value plurality, private property, and the autonomous and active person – that generate social standards for the distribution of political power, mechanisms for the exclusion of enemies, and, not least, rules for political competition.

Ferguson possessed a rich and strikingly modern institutional imagination. He had a prescient sense that under circumstances of modernity institutions – themselves the outcome of bargaining under conditions of plurality – are vital settings and resources for the expression, validation, and channeling of diversity via the adjudication of deeply held differences.[154] His institutional orientation was an outcome of his search

[151] Ferguson, *Principles, II*, p. 319.
[152] Ferguson, *Principles, II*, p. 471.
[153] Ferguson, *Principles, I*, p. 263.
[154] Kettler takes up this issue in *Adam Ferguson: His Social and Political Thought*, pp. 255–258, and in "History and Theory," p. 453.

to avoid two competing options: the estimations that social order must depend on universal norms and rational consent or, conversely, that all conflict is merely instrumentally strategic or tactical. By contrast, he offered the vision of a bounded politics that could combine organizational stability, active participation, and productive conflict inside actually lived history marked by deep differences in power, interests, ideas, and cultural practices.

Rather than shunt conflicts into the private realm, Ferguson sought to secure the possibility for persons and groups to pursue their competing conceptions of the good within a legitimate political and institutional framework. This choice was informed by his confidence that institutions, as constituted by both norms and organizational arrangements, "form a political establishment" that not only provides security, "the essence of freedom," but confers identities, selects issues and capabilities, and defines the scope of choice by establishing boundaries between legitimate and illegitimate agendas and projects.[155] Although institutions contain sets of procedures to adjudicate social and political disputes while not directly privileging any specific actor or conception, they also circumscribe boundaries and fix limits in accord with the four principles of plurality, difference, public contest, and autonomy, without erasing diversity or insisting on artificial or undesirable degrees of homogeneity.

As an anti-utopian, Ferguson wanted to avoid the identification of institutional arrangements with a single moral order. He clearly distinguished "the political from the moral," noting that "habits proper to the political" delineate a specific domain within which multiple values, leaving their isolated private homes, meet and contend within formal political institutions.[156] The task of creating such institutions faces a host of historical constraints. "We are not now inquiring what men ought to do," he tells us, "but what is the ordinary tract in which they proceed.... Mankind must be contented to act in the situations in which they find themselves placed."[157] The goal of an institutionalized political establishment cannot be the creation of an ideal order but of a polity that cultivates and protects diversity and the active

[155] Ferguson, *Principles, II*, p. 461.
[156] Ferguson, *Principles, II*, p. 412.
[157] Ferguson, *Principles, I*, p. 263.

character of persons in the face of an ineradicable "overbalance of power."[158]

Politics regularizes the competitive character of political antagonists through the use of frameworks for bargaining and provisional outcomes. Majorities are temporary, not fixed; each group and member of society can aspire to be in the majority with regard to particular matters. "It seldom happens," Ferguson observes, "the whole is unanimous.... The majority is no more than a government *de facto*, until the people at large, finding their account in the observance of some such rule, and every individual, in his turn, availing himself of his advantage in being of the majority, by his acquiescence, gives it a right of convention."[159] This situational majoritarianism made of Ferguson what we would call a liberal democrat.

Legitimate institutions, Ferguson underscored, must not aim to eliminate or even contain difference. They should convene forums for political struggle but not burst the bounds of a shared system for adjudication and decision. Institutions paradoxically affirm conflict through the exclusion of total conflict – that is, conflict that threatens plurality, difference, public contest, and the autonomous, active person. These four basic elements make also his theory substantive, rather than simply procedural. They constitute core values outside and prior to the realm of neutral procedures. If respected, they implicitly set rules for discriminating between various political ideas and practices.

A theory of agonistic liberalism, Ferguson's political thought implies, must possess traits that connect substantive values to formal procedures. The definition of 'friends' must be broad and inclusive. It must conform to the value of pluralism. Even "the promiscuous multitude should be admitted by themselves, or their representatives, to restrain any unfair advantages that might be taken of the distinctions or power established in favor of any part of the community."[160] For only "[w]hen parties of every description are thus fairly consulted, and accede to acts of legislation, the result is a fair convention and may be justly enforced by persons entrusted with power for this purpose."[161]

[158] Ferguson, *Principles, I*, p. 263.
[159] Ferguson, *Principles, II*, p. 470.
[160] Ferguson, *Principles, I*, p. 304.
[161] Ferguson, *Principles, I*, p. 304.

Public debate valorizing *agon* and esteeming difference must be premised on free speech and vigorous contestation. Ferguson observed that in "free states, even where men do not act from any culpable defect of understanding or criminal disposition, they are seldom of one mind, on any subject whatsoever. The conversation of good men very often takes the form of debate or controversy; and it is indeed in this form they are most likely to receive from one another mutual instruction and improvement of thought."[162]

Last, Ferguson hypothesized that institutional frameworks move in a series "of successive conjunctures."[163] Each instance of bargaining has a fresh and open quality, for a "[l]egislature in this form is a *continued negotiation*" located in a zone between deliberation, strategic positioning, and force.[164] Outcomes, consequently, are not conceived or planned, but are products of contestation and bargaining that, "by a species of chance, arrive at a posture for civil engagements, more favourable to human nature than what human wisdom could ever calmly devise."[165] In this, Ferguson anticipated themes of "balance, counterpoise, and mutual correction" that, in the twentieth century, became central concerns for modern American political science.[166]

IV

Ferguson's multiple efforts to reconcile virtue with wealth, political freedom with individual rights, and republicanism with commerce did not produce crisp, viable solutions. He did not craft a comprehensive, well-integrated political theory suitable for modern times – either exclusively republican or liberal. But his writings did generate the four elements we have discussed, which represent an important moment for each tradition. For republicanism, they are the instruments with which to confront and manage modern commercial reality. Faced with the prospect of anachronism, these were the means through which Ferguson believed this tradition could struggle for continued viability in a radically altered situation. For liberalism, the very same effort by

162 Ferguson, *Principles, II*, p. 510.
163 Ferguson, *Principles, I*, p. 304.
164 Ferguson, *Principles, I*, p. 304 (emphasis added).
165 Ferguson, *Essay*, p. 237.
166 Ferguson, *Principles, II*, p. 512.

Ferguson produced features that, in the hands of others, became key aspects of an originating endeavor. The liberal imagination enlarged and substantially altered with the effort of republicanism to remain germane.[167]

A great irony was at work. At just the moment when in both North America and Europe revolutionary actors sought to create modern republics for large, increasingly complex and commercial societies, Ferguson turned away. Placing a desire to protect the interests of constitutional monarchy and the British Empire first, he failed to engage sympathetically with the very unfolding in historical time of the project he sought to advance theoretically.

Replying to Richard Price, who had argued in 1776 that the justification for national independence of the American colonies stemmed from a prevailing right of political self-determination, Ferguson adopted the contrary position.[168] "Is Great Britain then to be sacrificed to America," he asked, "and a state which has attained high measures of national felicity, for one that is yet in expectation, and which, by attempting such extravagant plans of Continental Republic, is probably laying the seeds of anarchy, of civil wars, and at last of a military government?"[169] From a broader theoretical point of view, a democratic republic, which he had valued in his prior writings, albeit in a specific form, now was turned into an outdated and dangerous institution, feasible only for ancient cities.[170] Compared to monarchy, such a regime, he now argued, "is tolerable only in small states ... [and] is of all others the most unstable, capricious, and arbitrary; bound by

[167] Ferguson thus helps us see liberalism through a glass, darkly. His writings compel present-day liberalism to see parts of its republican lineage that are not commonly recognized.

[168] Richard Price, "Observations on the Nature of Civil Liberty, the Principles of Government, and the Justice and Policy of the War with America," in *Price: Political Writings*, ed. D. D. Thomas, Cambridge: Cambridge University Press, 1991, pp. 20–75.

[169] Ferguson, *Remarks on a Pamphlet Lately Published by Dr. Price, intitled, Observations on the nature of civil liberty, the principles of government, and the justice and policy of the war with America, &c., in a letter from a gentleman in the country to a member of Parliament*, London: T. Cadel, 1776, p. 59. Also see Kettler, *Adam Ferguson: His Social and Political Thought*, pp. 63–65, 85–89, and Yasuo Amoh, "Adam Ferguson and the American Revolution," *Kochi University Review*, 37 (1990), pp. 55–87.

[170] Ferguson, *Dr. Price*, p. 23.

no law, and subject to no appeal."[171] To delegitimate the claims of the American colonists to independence, therefore, Ferguson diminished the political novelty of their enterprise, claiming that the "Americans . . . seek no innovation; they are the parties that contend for the ancient establishment."[172] And, as it is evident "from the history of the world," he concluded, "plunging at once into military government" is "the fate that has ever attended Democracies attempted on too large a scale."[173]

In a similar vein, he critically observed that in France, with the Revolution, "the sovereignty was vested in the whole not in a part; and this mysterious sovereign who never could act precluded the right of every pretender to power."[174] It also is conducive to terror. After he assessed French republicanism in wholly negative terms, his silence about the efforts by the French revolutionaries to establish the first European republic for a large prosperous state was equally conspicuous. Rather than appreciatively engage with this development while holding it to appropriate standards, he accused the members of the constituent National Assembly of having proceeded "to execute a tyranny more bloody and terrible than any that is known in the history of mankind."[175]

Ferguson's too-simple acts of rejection thus missed a remarkable moment in the political history of modern republics. After all, despite

171 Ferguson, *Dr. Price*, pp. 10, 9.

172 Ferguson, *Dr. Price*, p. 24.

173 Ferguson, *Dr. Price*, p. 23. In a much later, unpublished text, Ferguson reiterated his objection to the American War of Independence and advised Britain what concrete military steps it needed to take in order to ensure the American colonies will remain within the empire. Adam Ferguson, "Memorial Respecting the Measures to be Pursued on the Present Immediate Prospect of a Final Separation of the American Colonies from Great Britain," in *Collection of Essays*, pp. 302–306. Also, see Oz-Salzberger, "Introduction," p. xxiii. For a detailed discussion of Ferguson's support of the British Empire and of the importance it played in his thought, see James Steven Sheets, "Adam Ferguson: The 'Good Preceptor' of Empire," Ph.D. dissertation, Department of Political Science, University of Rochester, 1993.

174 Adam Ferguson, "On the French Revolution with Its Actual and Still Impeding Consequences in Europe," in *Collection of Essays*, p. 134.

175 Ferguson, "On the French Revolution with Its Actual and Still Impeding Consequences in Europe," p. 134. For a detailed presentation of Ferguson's views on the French Revolution, see Kettler, *Adam Ferguson: His Social and Political Thought*, pp. 80–81, 90–96, and Yoshikazu Kubo, "Adam Ferguson and the French Revolution," *Kwansei Gakuin University Annual Studies*, 11 (1962), pp. 165–173.

their vexing problems, these revolutions self-consciously were fashioned as republics for the moderns. We turn, therefore, to understand this development and navigate its contours by concentrating on thinkers who addressed Ferguson's project not just in theory but as leading participants.

4

After the King

Thomas Paine's and James Madison's Institutional Liberalism

The relationship between republicanism and liberalism that was so central to the theoretical explorations of Adam Smith and Adam Ferguson was transformed into a demanding practical and historical political endeavor for the founders of the American republic. Rather than reflect on hypothetical possibilities, James Madison, Thomas Paine, and their colleagues moved the question of whether a republic could be built for modern times into a concrete political project. A luminous generation of revolutionaries grappled with how a persistent commitment to the classical republican tradition could guide their choices and actions. Pursuing this path, they confronted issues and challenges already identified by prior thinkers, as they turned to the design of institutions to secure a viable and enduring free government.

The creation of the American republic is a decisive site for understanding how republican themes and ideas turned in a liberal direction. Key theoretical works, written in the midst of this unprecedented situation, highlight the conceptual changes and institutional innovations that were advanced as the globe's first modern republic became the world's most archetypical liberal democracy. As it unfolded, this complex undertaking became the explicit and focused object of an almost obsessive analysis by the period's leading thinkers and political actors.

Among this group, we have selected the work of Paine and Madison for particular attention. They were, of course, figures of enormous influence. "I know not whether any man in the world," John Adams opined in October 1805, "has had more influence on its inhabitants or affairs for the last thirty years than Tom Paine."[1] Madison was his generation's most important thinker, often regarded as the Father of the Constitution.[2] But it is not for their uncommon impact on their contemporaries, or even the longevity of their writings, that we are focusing on their thought. They were central actors in a revolutionary program that inscribed a new and mutually constitutive relationship between an older republican tradition and a newer liberal impulse. Interestingly – perhaps even provocatively – these two thinkers cover an enormous political range, spanning a continuum from radical democracy to elitist commitments. Yet these familiar differences prod us to see how Paine and Madison in fact shared a common political project. As deep as their dissimilarity, even deeper is their respective and broadly aligned quest to discover the essential and necessary features of republican government under modern conditions. They sought to discern "the distinctive character of the republican form" and "what republicanism was, or is."[3]

Their primary objectives, of course, were the success of the War of Independence and the creation of lasting constitutional government. They were political actors, above all, and their thought was disciplined by these purposes. But their texts offer a good deal more than strategic and rhetorical interventions into the day-to-day struggles of their time. They also compose major reflections on – indeed, interventions into – the nature of republicanism, which, after all, was central to their political purposes, for it bore on the values, content, and aims of the American Revolution. Their commitments at the level of ideas ran deep

[1] John Adams in *Familiar Letters of John Adams and His Wife Abigail Adams*, ed. Charles Francis Adams, New York: Hurd and Houghton, 1876, p. 167.

[2] It was Charles Jared Ingersoll who in 1825 proposed this famous title for Madison. See Irving Brant, *James Madison: Commander in Chief, 1812–1836*, Indianapolis: Bobbs-Merrill, 1961, p. 471. For this characterization, also see Clinton Rossiter, *1787: The Grand Convention; The Year That Made a Nation*, New York: Macmillan, 1966, pp. 247–252; Harold S. Schultz, "James Madison: Father of the Constitution?" *Quarterly Journal of the Library of Congress*, 37 (1980), pp. 215–222; Robert A. Rutland, *James Madison: Father of the Constitution*, New York: Macmillan, 1986.

[3] James Madison, "The Federalist No. 39," in *Writings*, ed. Jack Rackove, New York: Library of America, 1999, p. 211; Thomas Paine, "Rights of Man," in *Collected Writings*, ed. Eric Foner, New York: Library of America, 1995, p. 565.

and exceeded the circumstances within which they wrote. By attending to their writings, and especially by observing and understanding transmutations and combinations in their thought, we can better grasp the complex relationship between republicanism and liberalism.

Paine and Madison invested new meanings, arguments, and justifications into existing republican ideas and political forms. We examine this transformation by first portraying how these two intellectual and political figures challenged the understandings of their contemporaries regarding how to judge whether a regime qualifies as a republic. From their historical and comparative perspective, ancient and modern republics were found to be equally deficient, lacking the fundamental attributes of an authentic republican form. Paine and Madison traced this republican deficit to the wider problem of political power and its institutionalization. For this reason, they explored the meaning of sovereignty, representation, and liberty and the right balance among them. Though not unknown to prior republicans, representation and popular sovereignty previously had occupied an ambivalent and subordinate place to such master commitments as the public good, civic virtue, rule of law, strong citizenship, mixed government, patriotism, and the contest for excellence and glory. Equally significant, they also imported theories of natural individual rights, religious freedom, and social contract that earlier had found no persisting expression or integrated place within republican doctrines of private property, civic religion, and political authority. In so doing, they placed these concepts at the very center of their visions of free government, drastically affecting the meaning and character of classical republicanism.

At chapter's end, we briefly engage with the large body of scholarship that has probed the doctrinal identity of Madison's and Paine's ideas as either primarily republican or liberal. This choice, we will have shown, forces a classification that is excessively stark. We argue, as noted, that both thinkers remained republican as they became liberal. By searching for a "republican remedy for the diseases most incident to republican government," each, in his own way, arrived at a liberal constitutional cure.[4] Of course, the liberal doctrine that ushered out of their republicanism was not uniform or fixed, but included, in a

[4] James Madison, "The Federalist No. 10," in *Writings*, p. 167.

wide spectrum, Paine's radical artisanal democratic liberalism as well as Madison's elitist liberalism.[5]

I

In redefining republican government, Paine and Madison critically considered the prevailing understandings, shared by both critics and advocates of classical republicanism alike. They defended the republican project against disparagements targeted at ancient republics, from which they also distanced themselves, and dismissed as ersatz republics modern regimes that wrongly claimed to be free governments. Only the young United States, they believed, qualified as a country that had developed nascent and authentic republican government, by making adjustments that we would recognize as demonstrably liberal.[6]

In the first instance, it was necessary to transcend how the "science of government," Madison observed, utilized the term republic "with extreme inaccuracy ... in political disquisitions."[7] Paine likewise complained about the tendency by the "political craft of courtiers and court-governments to abuse something which they called republicanism."[8] The "inaccuracy" and "abuse" against which both protested referred primarily to the cities of ancient Greece and Rome, as well as contemporary self-designated republics.

These misleading characterizations, Paine and Madison recognized, were not politically indifferent or theoretically inconsequential. Critics of classical republicanism, they noticed, underscored the most doleful

[5] See, for example, Norman Jacobson, "Political Science and Political Education," *American Political Science Review*, 57:3 (1963), pp. 561–569; Eric Foner, *Tom Paine and Revolutionary America*, Oxford: Oxford University Press, 1976, pp. 88–89.

[6] For an illuminating discussion of the conceptual dispute over the meaning of republic, see Terence Ball, "A Republic – If You Can Keep It," in *Conceptual Change and the Constitution*, ed. Terence Ball and J. G. A. Pocock, Lawrence: University Press of Kansas, 1988, pp. 237–164; Franco Venturi, *Utopia and Reform in the Enlightenment*, Cambridge: Cambridge University Press, 1971; Claude Nicolet has examined a parallel conceptual and intellectual debate in France in his *L'idée républicaine en France (1789–1924)*, Paris: Gallimard, 1982, pp. 23–28, 48–81, 479–484. For a different, less convincing, interpretation, see Garrett Ward Sheldon, *The Political Philosophy of James Madison*, Baltimore: Johns Hopkins University Press, 2001, p. 67.

[7] James Madison, "The Federalist No. 37," in *Writings*, p. 197; "The Federalist No. 39," p. 211.

[8] Paine, "Rights of Man," p. 565.

or no longer germane features of ancient free governments. They did so to dismiss republicanism as anachronistic, irretrievable, and dangerous. Arguing in this manner, they asserted that this antiquarian system could not be a viable option for modern, large commercial societies.

Paine and Madison rejected these criticisms. As Paine put it, "the opinion that the system of *Republicanism* is only adapted to a small Country" is but a fallacy propagated by "Monarchic Ignorance or knavery."[9] Such a dismissal wrongly confounded the essence of republicanism with ancient patterns of government.[10] Despite the common formulations of their contemporaries, Madison and Paine insisted that republicanism cannot be reduced to "pure democracy"; "ancient," "single," and "pure" republics; or "original simple democracy."[11] For Madison, there were two "great points of difference between a democracy" and "other antient republics" "and a [modern] republic." First is representation, "the delegation of the government . . . to a small number of citizens elected by the rest." Second is scale, "the greater number of citizens, and greater sphere of country."[12] From Paine's perspective,

9 Paine, "Rights of Man," p. 377.

10 Here, Madison and Paine differed in their emphases and vocabularies. What for Paine had been an ancient democracy was for Madison a small republic. Paine, "Rights of Man," p. 564; Madison, "Speech in the Federal Convention on Suffrage," in *Writings*, p. 133; James Madison, "Letter to Thomas Jefferson, October 24, 1787," in *Writings*, pp. 149–150. On Paine's and Madison's attitude toward the ancients, see A. Owen Aldridge, "Thomas Paine and the Classics," Eighteenth-Century Studies, 1:4 (1968), pp. 370–380; Carl J. Richard, *The Founders and the Classics: Greece, Rome, and the American Enlightenment*, Cambridge, Mass.: Harvard University Press, 1994, pp. 104–107, 109–118, 139–141, 154–158, 215–217, 235–237; Jennifer Tolbert Roberts, *Athens on Trial: The Antidemocratic Tradition in Western Thought*, Princeton, N.J.: Princeton University Press, 1994, pp. 179–193; and Caroline Winterer, *The Culture of Classicism: Ancient Greece and Rome in American Intellectual Life, 1780–1910*, Baltimore: Johns Hopkins University Press, 2002, pp. 10–76. For a broader approach, see Charles F. Mullett, "Classical Influences on the American Revolution," *Classical Journal*, 35 (1939–1940), pp. 92–104; Richard Gummere, "The Classical Ancestry of the United States Constitution," *American Quarterly*, 14 (1962), pp. 3–18; Edwin A. Miles, "The Young American Nation and the Classical Word," *Journal of the History of Ideas*, 35:2 (1974), pp. 259–274.

11 Madison, "The Federalist No. 10," p. 164; Madison, "Letter to Thomas Jefferson," p. 149; James Madison, "The Federalist No. 51," in *Writings*, p. 296; James Madison, "The Federalist No. 58," in *Writings*, p. 336; James Madison, "The Federalist No. 63," in *Writings*, pp. 348–350; Paine, "Rights of Man," p. 567.

12 Madison, "The Federalist No. 10," p. 164; Madison, "The Federalist No. 63," p. 348.

"Representation was a thing unknown in the ancient democracies."[13] This absence, he observed, made them obsolete "as these democracies increased in population, and the territory extended." Regarding size, he continued, "the simple democratical form became unwieldy and impracticable; and as the system of representation was not known, the consequence was, they either degenerated convulsively into monarchies, or became absorbed into such as then existed."[14] Madison and Paine, in short, deduced that the political regimes of the Greek city-states and ancient Rome were deficient as republics and thus should not be reproduced under modern conditions. Moreover, they believed that modern republicanism now had features lacking in the past but indispensable for more complex and pluralistic circumstances.

Both thinkers also rejected the claim several modern governments made to be genuinely republican. They resisted this self-description as deceptive because it tamed the doctrine's most attractive egalitarian and popular impulses. Thus, just as ancient republics often were portrayed as overweeningly participatory, factional, and unstable, their modern equivalents now did not qualify as republics because of their close and unhappy affinities with aristocracy and monarchy. Writing in *Federalist* 39, Madison observed:

> Holland, in which no particle of supreme authority is derived from the people, has passed almost universally under the denomination of a republic. The same title has been bestowed on Venice, where absolute power over the great body of the people, is exercised in the most absolute manner, by a small body of hereditary nobles. Poland, which is a mixture of aristocracy and of monarchy in their worst forms, has been dignified with the same appellation. The government of England, which has one republican branch only, combined a hereditary aristocracy and monarchy, has been with equal impropriety been frequently placed on the list of republics.[15]

Strikingly, in *Rights of Man*, Paine concurred:

> Various forms of government have affected to style themselves a republic. Poland calls itself a republic, which is an hereditary aristocracy, with what

[13] Paine, "Rights of Man," p. 564.
[14] Paine, "Rights of Man," pp. 564–565.
[15] Madison, "The Federalist No. 39," p. 211.

is called an elected monarchy. Holland calls itself a republic, which is chiefly aristocratical, with an hereditary stadtholdership.[16]

Earlier that year, he had already expressed similar thoughts:

> The states at present styled *Republican*, as HOLLAND, GENOA, VENICE, BERNE &c. are not only unworthy of the name, but are actually in opposition to every Principle of a *Republican* Government, and the Countries submitted to their Power are, truly speaking, subjected to an *Aristocratic* Slavery.[17]

By contrast, only the adoption of the new American Constitution fully abolished monarchy and hereditary aristocracy, two of republicanism's most distinct and central yearnings. Paine adamantly underscored the incompatibility of kingship and republicanism.[18] At its core, monarchy "signifies *the absolute Power of a single Individual*, who may prove a fool, an hypocrite, or a tyrant" – the very obverse of republican principles. As a model for others, including revolutionary France, the new North American federal union, he observed, "can now afford to Monarchy no more than a glance of disdain."[19] Likewise, for Madison "monarchy is even more unfit for a great state, than for a small one."[20] He also attended to the irreconcilability of aristocracy and republicanism. "Could any further proof be required," he asked, "of the republican complexion of this system, the most decisive one might be found in its absolute prohibition of titles of nobility, both under the federal and the state governments."[21] Paine, similarly, deplored aristocracy as "a law against every law of nature, and Nature herself calls for its destruction."[22]

From this common perspective, to live under monarchy is to live as a slave. Paine sought to explain why the possession of individual sovereignty by a single person must ineluctably produce tyranny. Citizens are rendered as slaves by a monarchical sovereign who commands limitless and absolute capacity to the exclusion of all other agents. Slavery, "being subject to the will of another," is best understood

[16] Paine, "Rights of Man," p. 566.
[17] Paine, "To the Authors of *The Republican*," in *Collected Writings*, p. 378.
[18] Jack P. Greene, "Paine, America, and the 'Modernization' of Political Consciousness," *Political Science Quarterly*, 93:1 (1978), pp. 80–83.
[19] Paine, "To the Authors of *The Republican*," p. 377.
[20] James Madison, "Government," in *Writings*, p. 501.
[21] Madison, "The Federalist No. 39," p. 213.
[22] Paine, "Rights of Man," p. 478.

from Paine's point of view as exclusion from sovereign power – that is, when the people are banned from "a power over which there is no control, and which controls all others."[23] In a monarchy, "this power is lodged in a single person, or sovereign," and the king's subjects are wholly dependent on the arbitrary and discretionary desires of an individual "whose will is law; which he declares, alters, or revokes as he pleases, without being accountable to any power for so doing."[24] Perhaps even more oppressive is the forfeiture of the right by future generations to choose the form of rule and the persons who will govern them. Monarchy offers the people "a perpetual exclusion" from sovereignty.[25] The key word here is perpetual. It is the hubris of monarchical government, grounded in a theory of hereditary rights, to extend a monopoly of sovereign power not only in space but in boundless time.

Madison shared this concern, though for slightly different reasons. Rather than highlight the absolute and arbitrary character of kingship, he drew attention to threats of partiality and militarism. Moving from the scope of power to its content and direction, he noted, "In absolute Monarchies, the prince is sufficiently, neutral toward his subjects, but frequently sacrifices their happiness to his ambition or avarice."[26] But although monarchy is a putative site of neutrality, the king "too often forms interests of his own repugnant to those of the whole."[27] Madison also described the monarchies that "oppress . . . in almost every country of Europe, the quarter of the globe which calls itself the pattern of civilization, and the pride of humanity," as governments "operating by a permanent military force, which at once maintains the government and is maintained by it."[28] By nature, executives are prone to war. Monarchies, as unlimited executives, thus are especially militaristic. On their watch, "the propagation and management of alarms has

[23] Thomas Paine, "On First Principles of Government," in *The Thomas Paine Reader*, ed. Isaac Kramnick, New York: Penguin Books, 1987, p. 461; Paine, "Dissertations on Government, the Affairs of the Bank, and Paper Money," in *The Thomas Paine Reader*, p. 167.

[24] Paine, "Dissertations on Government, the Affairs of the Bank, and Paper Money," p. 168.

[25] Thomas Paine, "Common Sense," in *Collected Writings*, p. 16.

[26] James Madison, "Vices of the Political System of the United States," in *Writings*, p. 79.

[27] Madison, "Vices of the Political System of the United States," p. 82.

[28] James Madison, "Spirit of Government," in *Writings*, p. 510.

grown into a kind of system," reinforcing the capacity of rulers to extract resources and control their populations.[29]

Having decisively rejected monarchy, Madison searched for a non-monarchical site of impartiality, placing this quest at the center of his republicanism. This pursuit informed much of his attention to constitutional innovation. But he could not turn to the model of the ancients, for they, too, did not, indeed could not, satisfactorily identify a site of neutrality. In such settings, "the sovereign will is sufficiently controuled from such a Sacrifice of the entire Society, [it] is not sufficiently neutral towards the parts composing it."[30]

Madison thus understood the main challenge confronting modern republicanism to be the invention of a compound institutional configuration that successfully could address the problem of neutrality without endangering popular sovereignty or eradicating the plurality of interests and passions always found among free people in complex civil societies. "The great desideratum which has not yet been found for Republican Governments," he powerfully asserted, thus charting a direction for fellow republicans, "seems to be some disinterested & dispassionate umpire in disputes between different passions & interests in the State."[31]

II

Focusing on problems of absolute power and partial authority, Paine and Madison thus converged on a sharp critique of monarchy and inauthentic republics. For solutions, they combined popular sovereignty with political representation.

Because they were motivated by a common fear of tyranny, their point of departure was popular sovereignty. In the new American republic, the place of the king unambiguously was taken by the people, "the fountain of power," as Paine put the point.[32] "The people, not the government, possess absolute sovereignty," Madison concurred.[33]

[29] James Madison, "Political Reflections," in *Writings*, p. 605.

[30] Madison, "Vices of the Political System of the United States," p. 79.

[31] Madison, "Vices of the Political System of the United States," p. 81.

[32] Paine, "Dissertations on Government, the Affairs of the Bank, and Paper Money," p. 168.

[33] James Madison, "On the Alien and Sedition Acts," in *Writings*, p. 645. Also, see Joshua Miller, "The Ghostly Body Politic: The Federalist Papers and Popular Sovereignty," *Political Theory*, 16:1 (1988), pp. 99–119; John Ferejohn, "Madisonian

He not only rejected vesting sovereignty in a monarch but insisted on placing it with the people. Consonant with Paine, he thus reserved the term republic exclusively for "a government which derives all its powers directly or indirectly from the great body of the people."[34] Reasoning along these lines, he exhorted, "It is *essential* to such a government, that it be derived from the great body of the society, not from an inconsiderable proportion, or a favored class of it; otherwise a handful of tyrannical nobles, exercising their oppressions by a delegation of their powers, might aspire to the rank of republicans, and claim for their government the honorable title of republic."[35]

We can see how Madison applied the principle of popular sovereignty in the recommendations he offered for the ratification of the new Federal Constitution. Discussing this issue at the Constitutional Convention, he distinguished the Articles of Confederation, approved by agreement among the states, from the new charter, which, he insisted, should require popular electoral assent in order to convey sovereignty from ordinary legislatures to the people themselves.[36] In Philadelphia, he is reported to have argued "the difference between a system founded on the Legislatures only, and one founded on the people, to be the true difference between a *league* or *treaty*, and a *Constitution*."[37] Precisely because such a federal union, as distinct from a confederation of states, would be created by the people, it could not be dissolved by the decision of any single party to exit without "the authority of the people themselves."[38]

In advancing popular sovereignty, Paine put even more emphasis on the problem of arbitrary power. Committed to the normative ideal that the object of politics is the public good, he reasoned that such a goal requires the incorporation of all members of the polity into the

Separation of Powers," in *James Madison: The Theory and Praxis of Republican Government*, ed. Samuel Kernell, Stanford, Calif.: Stanford University Press, 2003, p. 150.

34 Madison, "The Federalist No. 39," pp. 211–212; Madison, "Government," p. 502; Madison, "Spirit of Governments," p. 511.

35 Madison, "The Federalist No. 39," p. 212.

36 But he favored each state one at a time, creating a compound, federal nation, not a simple nation with a single people. Madison, "The Federalist No. 39," p. 214.

37 James Madison, "Speech in the Federal Convention on Ratification," in *Writings*, p. 129.

38 Madison, "The Federalist No. 39," p. 214; Edmund S. Morgan, *Inventing the People: The Rise of Popular Sovereignty in England and America*, New York: W. W. Norton, 1988, part III, pp. 239–306.

sphere of sovereignty. Such inclusion makes each person a free citizen, eliminates subjection by discretionary personal will, and hence accomplishes the critical initial step in effectuating "the interest of the public, as well individually as collectively."[39] With this accomplishment, "the sovereign power . . . remains where nature placed it – in the people."[40]

Though "essential," Madison and Paine thought it is not "sufficient" for republican government to be based on popular sovereignty.[41] The derivation of legitimate authority from the people qualifies a government as "popular" but not, on its own, as a republic. Both insisted that a republic, above all, must emplace political representation at its center, alongside popular sovereignty. Not just Madison, who famously argued that a republic is "a government in which the scheme of representation takes place," but Paine underscored the pivotal standing of representation.[42] Addressing Abbé Sieyès in 1791, he declared, "By Republicanism. . . . I understand simply a government by representation."[43]

Of course, their views concerning the objective of political representation starkly diverged. For Madison, it was, among other purposes, a check on pure majoritarianism and unbridled passion. For Paine, it was a means to better actualize democratic values. But what they shared must not be gainsaid. It constituted nothing less than positioning political representation at the core of republican doctrine. In this way, Madison and Paine definitively resolved in the same way a long-standing ambivalence among republicans. Some of its leading thinkers, notably James Harrington and Algernon Sidney, previously had favored this institutional device.[44] Yet, famously,

39 Paine, "Rights of Man," p. 565.

40 Paine, "Dissertations on Government, the Affairs of the Bank, and Paper Money," p. 168; Howard Penniman, "Thomas Paine – Democrat," *American Political Science Review*, 37:2 (1943), pp. 245–252.

41 Madison, "The Federalist No. 39," p. 212; Paine, "Rights of Man," p. 567.

42 Madison, "The Federalist No. 10," p. 164.

43 Thomas Paine, "Letter to the Abbé Sieyès," in *Collected Writings*, p. 380.

44 James Harrington, *The Commonwealth of Oceana* and *A System of Politics*, ed. J. G. A. Pocock, Cambridge: Cambridge University Press, 1992; Algernon Sidney, *Discourses Concerning Government*, ed. Thomas G. West, Indianapolis: Liberty Fund, 1996. Also, see J. R. Pole, *Political Representation in England and the Origins of American Revolution*, Berkeley: University of California Press, 1971, pp. 7–16, and Quinter Skinner, *Liberty before Liberalism*, Cambridge: Cambridge University Press, 1998, pp. 32–36.

Rousseau's distinctive version of republicanism had abjured representation.[45]

By contrast, Paine and Madison almost immediately turned to representation when they addressed the centrality of popular sovereignty for the republican program. For each, representation under modern conditions realizes, while superseding, the normative ambitions of the ancients. Madison understood that a republic standing primarily on the foundation of popular sovereignty loses the capacity to discern "its general interest" and thus becomes exposed to self-subversion by a "blow mediated by the people against themselves."[46] Independent of the ethical qualities and political virtues of its citizens, direct democracy produces turbulent and intemperate outcomes. "Had every Athenian citizen been a Socrates," Madison wrote, "every Athenian assembly would still have been a mob."[47] Without representation to secure "the benefits of free consultation and discussion," the citizenry becomes a mass, prone to passion, lacking means to transcend "temporary or partial considerations" or discern "the true interests of their country."[48]

Madison's celebrated anxiety about factions was allayed by this reliance on appropriate representation. By itself, the popular sovereign cannot be "sufficiently neutral" without this institutional mediation. Passionate, unfiltered, and mobilized, the populace – whether ruling directly or via large popular assemblies – inescapably divides into parts "united and actuated by some common impulse of passion, or of interest, adverse to the rights of other citizens, or to the permanent and aggregate interest of the community."[49] Where such factionalization is rampant, "the sovereign will... is not sufficiently neutral towards the parts composing it."[50] True and effective republics can redeem the promise of popular sovereignty by producing neutrality only through

[45] Jean-Jacques Rousseau, "Du contract social; ou, Principes du droit politique," *Œuvres complètes*, Vol. 3, Gallimard: Bibliothèque de la Pléiade, 1964, book III: xv, pp. 429–430.

[46] Madison, "Letter to Thomas Jefferson," p. 152; Madison, "The Federalist No. 63," p. 347.

[47] Madison, "The Federalist No. 55," in *Writings*, p. 316.

[48] Madison, "The Federalist No. 55," p. 316; Madison, "The Federalist No. 10," p. 165.

[49] Madison, "The Federalist No. 10," p. 161.

[50] Madison, "Letter to Thomas Jefferson, October 24, 1787," p. 152.

the institutionalization of representation. Unaided, the sovereign people cannot discover a common good. By contrast, inside a system of representation, "it may well happen that the public voice pronounced by the representatives of the people, will be more consonant to the public good, than if pronounced by the people themselves convened for the purpose."[51]

Guardianship of the public weal, an emblematic feature of Roman republicanism, found its highest expression, Madison thought, in the American national legislature and its elected representatives. They were, as he put it, "the guardians of the people, selected by the people themselves."[52] Here, too, we discern a suggestive resemblance with Paine, who likewise found in representation the means to realize the cherished republican pursuit of "RES-PUBLICA, the public affairs, or the public good; or, literally translated, the *public thing*."[53] Such a discovery, he strongly asserted, "most naturally associates with the representative form."[54]

Paine and Madison did not agree about the novelty of modern representation. Madison argued that the ancients knew the institution through their practice of delegation. Notwithstanding, they never integrated it into their dominant political forms. As a result, they could not effectively discern the public good in the face of an inherent tendency to faction.[55] For Paine, however, representation is an entirely modern invention, whose absence had wounded ancient democracy.[56]

51 Madison, "The Federalist No. 10," p. 165.

52 Madison, "The Federalist No. 55," p. 319. Also, see Madison, "The Federalist No. 10," p. 165; Madison, "The Federalist No. 56," p. 324. This republican element of Madison's approach to political representation is commonly underplayed or overlooked even in highly informed treatments, which instead emphasize the 'liberal' aspect of Madison's theory of representation that stresses the balance of interests and not the search for a common, public good. An important example is Hanna F. Pitkin, *The Concept of Representation*, Berkeley: University of California Press, 1972, pp. 191–198. For two notable exceptions, see Sunstein, "Beyond the Republican Revival," pp. 1559–1561; Garry Wills, *Explaining America: The Federalist*, New York: Penguin Books, 2001, pp. 180–264. For a detailed and informed presentation of the debate regarding Madison's theory of representation, see Alan Gibson, "Impartial Representation and the Extended Republic: Towards a Comprehensive and Balanced Treatment of the Tenth *Federalist* Paper," *History of Political Thought*, 12 (1991), pp. 263–304.

53 Paine, "Rights of Man," p. 565.

54 Paine, "Rights of Man," pp. 565–566.

55 Madison, "The Federalist No. 63," pp. 349–350.

56 Paine, "Rights of Man," p. 564.

When faced with an enlarged territory and a greater population, such government "degenerated convulsively into monarchies" as the result of a "want of some method to consolidate the parts of society, after it became too populous, and too extensive for the simple democratical form."[57] Here, and in many other discussions, Paine underscored representation as a solution to "unwieldy and impracticable" empirical problems caused by size.[58] This justification subtly differs from Madison's. Madison found inherent structural flaws within unrepresentative democracy. Paine, it would seem, thought such regimes could function well under conditions of modest scale but not in large polities.

Paine also hinted at a deeper normative argument in favor of representation, a redolent claim that trumps direct democracy under all conditions. A representative republic, he wrote, "is preferable to simple democracy even in small territories. Athens, by representation, would have outrivalled her own democracy."[59] This strong declaration calls to mind Madison's arguments. To be sure, Paine did not copiously explain his reasoning, but the hints he provided offered points of contact with Madison. Like Madison, he claimed that the representative system "concentrates the knowledge necessary to the interest of the parts, and of the whole. It places government in a state of constant maturity."[60] "The representative system is calculated to produce the wisest laws, by collecting wisdom from where it can be found," because it brings a range of knowledge and talents into politics, and "because the representative system admits of none but men properly qualified into the government," it remedies "at once the defects of the simple democracy."[61]

These observations were concerned with more than the changes associated with magnitude. Paine also alluded to the plurality of interests. Representation, he argued, is "capable of embracing and confederating all the various interests."[62] Regimes without representation lack this capacity. Regrettably, Paine did not explicitly discuss why direct popular assemblies are unable or less able to include and

[57] Paine, "Rights of Man," p. 565.
[58] Paine, "Rights of Man," p. 564.
[59] Paine, "Rights of Man," p. 568.
[60] Paine, "Rights of Man," p. 568.
[61] Paine, "Rights of Man," pp. 563, 567; Thomas Paine, "Letter Addressed to the Addressers on the Late Proclamation," in *The Thomas Paine Reader*, p. 376.
[62] Paine, "Rights of Man," p. 567.

affiliate "various interests," but we can make a reasonable inference. What representation does is draw the various interests into what he calls "a common center, in which all the parts of society unite."[63] He insisted, further, that "this cannot be accomplished by any method so conducive to the various interests of the community, as by the representative system."[64] The method of representation can achieve this goal by closely associating useful knowledge, plural interests, and political power. Any society, he believed, composed of "the various and numerous circumstances of a nation, its agriculture, manufacture, trade, commerce, &c. &c. requires a knowledge of a different kind, and which can be had only from the various parts of society. It is an assemblage," he continued, "of practical knowledge."[65] Without the institution of representation, simple democracies are too decentered, and thus, for Paine, unstable, and without harnessing sufficient knowledge to configure the public good. This simple or direct democracy leans naturally toward "ignorance and incapacity."[66]

Of course, the reasoning here is not the same as that of Madison. Paine thought representation to be the key means by which to enhance democracy. A modern representative republic is more, not less, democratic than the democracies of the ancients. Madison, by contrast, understood representation to be a limiting corrective to democracy. Representation confines democracy by turning the "pure democracies of Greece" into a new 'impure' type of regime that can, precisely because of this impurity, reach successfully for the public good. Madison's representative republic is less democratic and thereby superior to the governments of the ancients, both Greeks and Romans.[67] For Madison, representation elevates reason and checks passion. His ideal representative is distinguished by wisdom and the ability to transcend partial interests. In fact, it is the republican constitution, whose aim is "to obtain for rulers men who possess most wisdom to discern, and most virtue to pursue the common good of the society," that allows the selection of the most virtuous citizens.[68] For Paine, representation

[63] Paine, "Rights of Man," p. 568.
[64] Paine, "Rights of Man," p. 568.
[65] Paine, "Rights of Man," pp. 566–567.
[66] Paine, "Rights of Man," p. 567.
[67] Madison, "The Federalist No. 63," pp. 350–352.
[68] Madison, "The Federalist No. 57," in *Writings*, p. 326.

generates social knowledge that both integrates interests into national legislative considerations and improves the character of public statutes. Though his model legislator did not have the elevated qualities stressed by Madison, he nonetheless still possesses the expertise of particulars and the skill of combining and blending them "for the interest of the public, as well individually as collectively."[69]

Notwithstanding this discrepancy in tone, evaluation, and strategy, at the deepest level both thinkers strongly advocated representation as the best available means to achieve the republican ideal of a common interest. Moreover, in grappling with the problem of societal fragmentation, their views of the role of representation were compatible. They shared a deep disquiet about what Madison identified as faction and Paine described as decomposition – that is, the inability of nonrepublican governments to find a neutral center and hold it together while facing social complexity, various interests, and plural preferences.

These views concerning political representation display a deep republican lineage. As the institutionalized quest for the public good under conditions of heterogeneity, representation does not need to abandon the ideal of civic virtue. To the contrary, in Madison's thought, civic virtue finds a particular locus in the legislature. Members of Congress in both houses exhibit virtues reminiscent of classical republican citizens – wisdom, patriotism, vigilance, honor, manly spirit, and distinction. Such representatives, people of "wise and enlarged patriotism," are deeply dedicated to "the public welfare" and "popular rights."[70] These qualities promote the interest of the whole against the interests of the parts.

The republican strand in Madison, however, was not limited to the legislative arena. In a more traditional vein, and despite his view that human motivation is informed by interests, power, and egoism, he identified key parts of the wider society as inclined toward civic virtue and public-oriented action.[71] Speaking as a member of Congress in

[69] Paine, "Rights of Man," p. 565.

[70] James Madison, "Seventh Annual Address to Congress," in *Writings*, pp. 716, 718; James Madison, "Charters," in *Writings*, p. 502.

[71] Drew R. McCoy provides an illuminating discussion of the relationship between citizenship and virtue in Madison. See Drew R. McCoy, *The Last of the Fathers: James Madison and the Republican Legacy*, Cambridge: Cambridge University Press, 1989, pp. 175, 192–207.

1792, he identified the country's farming population as "the class of citizens" who are "the most truly independent and happy. They are more: they are the best basis of public liberty, and the strongest bulwark of public safety. It follows, that the greater the proportion of this class to the whole society, the more free, the more independent, and the more happy must be the society itself."[72] Such is their role because of the "reciprocity of dependence" that inspires "a dignified sense of social rights."[73] Relying on agrarian, and other, sources of such republican virtues, Madison could invoke "the people" as the "guardians" of "constitutional liberty" and "every good citizen" as "a centinel over the rights of the people."[74] Classical republicanism echoes in the summons to citizens, counseling them that "their eyes must be ever ready to mark, their voice to pronounce, and their arm to repel or repair aggressions on the authority of their constitutions; the highest authority next to their own, because the immediate work of their own, and the sacred part of their property, as recognizing and recording the title to every other."[75]

A corollary was Madison's apprehension about "corrupt influence."[76] Affirming a typical fear by republicans, he deplored the contamination of the public by the private, a feature he thought had become characteristic of the English political system. He thus cautioned against "a government... substituting the motive of private interest in place of public duty... accommodating its measures to the avidity of a part of the nation instead of the benefit of the whole."[77]

Writing in a republican idiom, Paine charged the English regime with a proclivity toward corruption, stressing the danger inherent in combining concentrated economic resources with political power – that is, combining "the man who is in the receipt of a million a year" with "the power of creating and disposing of places" and "the power of making laws."[78] Paine's emphasis on civic virtue, however,

[72] James Madison, "Republican Distribution of Citizens," in *Writings*, pp. 512–513.
[73] James Madison, "Fashion," in *Writings*, p. 514.
[74] Madison, "Government," p. 502.
[75] James Madison, "Government of the United States," in *Writings*, p. 509.
[76] Madison, "Spirit of Government," p. 510.
[77] Madison, "Spirit of Government," p. 510.
[78] Paine, "Rights of Man," pp. 590, 592, 510; Thomas Paine, "The American Crisis No. V," in *Collected Writings*, p. 170; Thomas Paine, "The American Crisis No. VII," in *Collected Writings*, p. 200.

was more prominent than Madison's. It drew more on the egalitarian impulses of the ancient republics than on the aristocratic strains and institutional commitments also present in the republican vision. Fully agreeing with Madison's characterization of the desirable qualities of elected representatives, Paine, more emphatically, underscored that the virtues of representatives, though necessary, are insufficient. In a modern republic, as in an ancient one, the "criterion of public spirit" also must be widely diffused, not confined in the legislature.[79] Representation should lean on the social and economic bases of citizenship, exemplified above all in the classical republican figure of the independent farmer, "citizens of the first necessity."[80] In this respect, Paine and Madison shared a surprisingly similar appreciation not only for the rural basis of civic virtue but for the complementary relationship between the design of institutions and the ethical support offered by key groups in a free society.

III

To meet their criteria for the existence of a genuinely modern republic, Paine and Madison looked to individual rights, especially religious freedom. They believed that ancient republics and simple democracies did not, indeed could not, address social complexity, value plurality, and individual autonomy, given their relatively small scale and homogeneous composition. Modern republics cannot avoid these challenges. Their size, diverse population, division of labor, extension and intensification of commerce, and fragmentation of Christendom had reconfigured the relationships linking diversity and order, freedom and authority, and the individual and the community. Turning decisively away from civic religion, value homogeneity, and an exclusive reliance on strong citizenship, they redefined republicanism to include the twin pillars of institutionalized religious freedom and natural individual rights. Both had been underestimated in the republican canon.[81]

79 Thomas Paine, "The Necessity of Taxation," in *Writings*, p. 313.

80 Thomas Paine, "Letter to Henry Laurens," in *Writings*, p. 211.

81 For the absence of theories of natural rights from classical republicanism, see Maurizio Viroli, *Republicanism*, trans. Antony Shugaar, New York: Hill and Wang, 2002, p. 7. For a contrary interpretation of the relationship between republicanism and

Instead, that tradition had privileged civic religion as a pathway to social harmony. In classical republican texts, the zone of the gods possessed an unmediated relationship to the zone of the political. Worshiping each particular god connoted a specific political meaning. This relationship had a spatial dimension. Loyalty to a god (or gods) equaled loyalty to a city.[82] These gods sustained urban political communities. A central feature of civic religion thus was its capacity to forge social unity and political solidarity by fashioning citizens with shared civic commitments to the common realm and to its republican institutions. These were citizens willing even to sacrifice their lives for the superior good of their city and country.[83] Religion, as Rousseau had argued in writing about the "religion of the citizen," "combines the divine cult and love of the laws and by making the homeland the object of the citizens' prayers, it teaches them that to serve the State is to serve its tutelary God."[84] To this positive contribution in molding and sustaining a collective patriotic ethos was attached the corresponding negative task of transcending the impulses of self-interest and self-love that could threaten the stability of the republic. Civic religion thus was perceived as a powerful and efficient tool, a means to contain and neutralize egoistic passions, if not to erase them.[85]

Paine adamantly rejected this constitutive aspect of classical republicanism. His principal concern was fear of persecution. "Persecution," he argued, "is always the strongly-marked feature of all law-religions, or religions established by law."[86] The solution to this threat was the

natural rights, see Philip Pettit, *Republicanism: A Theory of Freedom and Government*, Oxford: Oxford University Press, 1997, pp. 101, 303–304, and Skinner, *Liberty before Liberalism*, pp. 18–21. A more detached and historically informed approach can be found in Nicolet, *L'idée républicaine en France*, pp. 338–348, 356–357. For a serious attempt to address and solve the tension between republicanism and rights, see Frank Michelman, "Law's Republic," *Yale Law Journal*, 97:8 (1988), pp. 1493–1537.

82 Rousseau, "Du contract social," book IV: viii, p. 460.

83 Niccolò Machiavelli, *Discourses on Livy*, trans. Harvey C. Mansfield and Nathan Tarcov, Chicago: University of Chicago Press, 1996, book I: xi–xvi, pp. 34–47.

84 Rousseau, "Du contract social," book IV: viii, pp. 464–465.

85 For a recognition by Viroli of republicanism's dependence on civic religion and his attempt to address the threats posed by this relationship with its secularized version of patriotism, see *Republicanism*, p. 92. Also, see Nicolet, *L'idée républicaine en France*, pp. 473–507.

86 Paine, "Rights of Man," p. 484.

institutionalization of religious freedom. The justification he offered was based on a theory of universal and individual natural rights. With this turn, Paine inserted into his republican stance a decidedly external element. Those rights, he wrote, "which appertain to man in right of his existence," are outside and prior to the political organization of society.[87] Such inalienable and "pre-existing" individual rights,[88] as we know, were not present in classical republicanism, where the individual most often was understood not as freestanding, but as integrated within, indeed constituted by, the community.

For Paine, by contrast, political society is the product of the collective choice individuals make prior to any political structure. The introduction of this concept of rights into republican discourse altered thinking about the ends of government, whose prime goal is to protect each individual against the depredation of others while enhancing the capacity of all to achieve collective goals.[89] These are the primary purposes of Paine's theory of social contract. Moreover, such rights are integral to the delineation and circumscription of the legitimate scope of political power. "Rights of the mind" or "intellectual rights" – that is, the liberty of individual conscience and religion – are absolute, and set explicit, nonnegotiable limits on political authority.[90]

Unlike Roman republicanism, therefore, Paine's approach based the foundations of political society on a distinct version of social contract theory, according to which the creation of government must be predicated on securing religious and intellectual freedom. In a stateless condition, "this state of natural liberty," individuals lack power or capacity to protect their freedom from human vices and the "defect of moral virtue."[91] In an account of the passage from a state of nature, composed of twenty individuals, to an organized political community, Paine expressed the fear that without adequate government "the consequence would be that each might be exposed, not only to each

[87] Paine, "Rights of Man," p. 464.

[88] Paine, "Rights of Man," p. 465.

[89] Thomas Paine, "Letter to Thomas Jefferson, 1788," in *Collected Writings*, pp. 368–369.

[90] Paine, "Rights of Man," pp. 464–465; Thomas Paine, "The Age of Reason," in *Collected Writings*, p. 665.

[91] Paine, "Common Sense," pp. 7–8; Paine, "Letter to Thomas Jefferson, 1788," p. 368. For a discussion of the relationship between social contract theories and republicanism, see Nicolet, *L'idée républicaine en France*, pp. 362–374.

other, but to the other nineteen."[92] Collective safeguards replace fear. "It would then occur to them that their condition would be much improved, if a way could be devised to exchange that quantity of danger into so much protection, so that each individual should possess the strength of the whole number."[93] The creation of government also facilitates the achievement of collective ambitions. By entering into a mutual agreement to partially give up some liberty, mainly the right to property, members of society increase their overall capacity by aggregating the power of each and every individual.[94] That which is "defective in the individual in point of power, and answers not his purpose, . . . when collected to a focus, becomes common to the purpose of every one."[95]

Government, on this view, "is a badge of lost innocence."[96] It is a solution that is necessary because it protects. But government is also potentially dangerous because it can threaten natural rights. In articulating this anxiety – one not found in the republican tradition – Paine expressed distrust in public authority and doubt about the superior worth of political life. Observing that "government even in its best state is but a necessary evil," thus recognizing an inherent disjunction and tension between state and society, Paine's political thought took on a cast we now appreciate as unmistakably liberal.[97] Fundamental is the protection of "natural rights which are retained in the individual" and are both prior to and outside the scope of legitimate public intervention. At the core of these rights lies the "sacred" sphere of religious freedom, the cornerstone of Paine's constitutional doctrine.[98] Quite suggestively, this natural-rights justification for religious freedom was identified by Paine as the "liberal principle" positively welcoming the "diversity of religious opinion among us" as a social good.[99]

Reciprocally, Paine did not remain unaffected by the insertion of these liberal ideas into his republican imagination. His approach to

[92] Paine, "Letter to Thomas Jefferson, 1788," p. 368.
[93] Paine, "Letter to Thomas Jefferson, 1788," p. 368.
[94] Paine, "Common Sense," p. 7; Paine, "Letter to Thomas Jefferson, 1788," p. 368; Paine, "Rights of Man," p. 465.
[95] Paine, "Rights of Man," p. 465.
[96] Paine, "Common Sense," p. 7.
[97] Paine, "Common Sense," p. 6.
[98] Paine, "The American Crisis, No. III," in *Collected Writings*, p. 135.
[99] Paine, "Common Sense," p. 43.

social contract, as an example, continued to be shaped by this broader political perspective. What stands out from Paine's distinct theory of the social contract is his claim that its purpose is to increase the total sum of collective power. His founding covenant aims at augmenting rather than diminishing power "by a condensation of all the parts."[100] In this version, the contracting parties form an alliance that gathers together the isolated strength of all the allied partners and binds them into a new power structure in which all the coassociates partake, "so that each individual should possess the strength of the whole number."[101] This approach differs from theories in which the contracting members give up, in the form of a transfer, their personal powers to create a political state. The classical version of social contract tends to disempower and dispossess the covenanting parties, who, far from gaining a new power, and possibly more than they had before, resign their powers as such.

There is an additional difference. Paine's natural individual has a "propensity to society."[102] Egoism and the motivation of self-interest do not exhaust "man" because nature "has implemented in him a system of social affections."[103] In fact, although it originally placed him in "a state of natural liberty," "nature has created him for social life."[104] According to Paine's reasoning, the political state is the final realization of the state of nature. With this reformulation of human nature, Paine not only inserted a social teleology in his concept of the natural state; he also introduced a republican anthropology into his understanding of "man." This reformulation of the social contract transformed it from an instrumental act of self-interested selfishness to a collective founding political deed.[105]

Like Paine, Madison understood religious freedom to be a natural, unalienable right, marking the limits of politics.[106] Madison's

[100] Paine, "Letter to Thomas Jefferson, 1788," p. 368.

[101] Paine, "Letter to Thomas Jefferson, 1788," p. 368.

[102] Paine, "Rights of Man," p. 552.

[103] Paine, "Rights of Man," p. 552.

[104] Paine, "Common Sense," p. 7; Paine, "Rights of Man," p. 551.

[105] For Paine's unique theory of the constituent power and his proposal for a constituent convention, see Paine, "Rights of Man," pp. 572–581; Paine, "Common Sense," pp. 32–34.

[106] James Madison, "Memorial and Remonstrance against Religious Assessments," in *Writings*, p. 30.

approach, however, differed slightly from Paine's in that it incorporated a deeper awareness of the weakness of classical republicanism. In Madison, discourses of civic religion reveal a particular and truly unique vulnerability for republics. As this form of government depends on the internalization of common values, its existence is conditional on the subjective orientation of its members. Having renounced the coercive option of discretionary force and the tyrannical use of fear, both of which, by contrast, are available to monarchies, republics constantly are exposed to threats of violent discord, internal strife, even secession – hence, as an empirical matter, their short life-span.

With the exception of Montesquieu and David Hume, perhaps no one recognized this problem besetting ancient and modern republics better than Madison, who identified as their "mortal disease" their "factitious spirit."[107] Endemic to republics, factions can endanger the public good, subvert justice, threaten freedom, and undermine order. Searching for a cure, Madison dismissed the standard republican solution of giving "to every citizen the same opinions, the same passions, and the same interests."[108] Value pluralism and diversity of interests that in a free, popular government could lead to factional conflicts

[107] Montesquieu, *The Spirit of Laws*, ed. Anne Cohler, Basia Miller, and Harold Stone, Cambridge: Cambridge University Press, 1992, book IX, chap. i, vi–vii, pp. 131–132, book VIII, chap. i, pp. 112–114. David Hume, "Whether the British Government Inclines More to Absolute Monarchy, or to a Republic," "On Parties in General," "On Civil Liberty," "On Commerce," "Idea of a Perfect Commonwealth," in *Essays Moral, Political, and Literary*, ed. Eugene F. Miller, Indianapolis: Liberty Press, 1987, pp. 47–53, 54–63, 87–96, 253–267, 512–529; Madison, "The Federalist No. 10," pp. 160, 161. In addition, see Douglas Adair, "'That Politics May Be Reduced to a Science': David Hume, James Madison, and the Tenth *Federalist*," in *Fame and the Founding Fathers: Essays by Douglas Adair*, ed. Trevor Colbourn, New York: W. W. Norton, 1974, pp. 93–106; Theodore Draper, "Hume and Madison: The Secrets of Federalist Paper No. 10," *Encounter*, 58 (1982), pp. 34–47; Edmund S. Morgan, "Safety in Numbers: Madison, Hume, and the Tenth *Federalist*," *Huntington Library Quarterly*, 49 (1986), pp. 95–112; Marc M. Arkin, "The Intractable Principle: David Hume, James Madison, Religion, and the Tenth Federalist," *American Journal of Legal History*, 39:2 (1995), pp. 148–176; James Conniff, "The Enlightenment and American Political Thought: A Study of the Origins of Madison's *Federalist Number 10*," *Political Theory*, 8:3 (1980), pp. 381–402; Anne M. Cohler, *Montesquieu's Comparative Politics and the Spirit of American Constitutionalism*, Lawrence: University Press of Kansas, 1988; Judith N. Shklar, "Montesquieu and the New Republicanism," in *Political Thought and Political Thinkers*, ed. Stanley Hoffman, Chicago: University of Chicago Press, 1998, pp. 244–261.

[108] Madison, "The Federalist No. 10," p. 161.

are, for Madison, ineradicable facts. Consequently, "in all civilized Societies, distinctions are various and unavoidable."[109] "We know," he wrote," that no society ever did or can consist of so homogeneous a mass of citizens."[110] Therefore, attempts to eradicate diversity not only fail, but backfire. They abolish liberty, and ultimately can lead to the collapse of the republic.

If religion is used to homogenize beliefs, habits, mores, and interests, the result can only be tyranny, oppression, and persecution. Turning the logic of the civic religion doctrine on its head, Madison proclaimed that publicly sponsored religion degrades civil society by creating "a spiritual tyranny" and by upholding "the throes of political tyranny."[111] In this way, arguing from republican principles against republican practices, Madison showed how the public good, a conception to which he held fast, was undermined rather than advanced by politically inflected religion as a means to impose uniformity.

Extending the republican critique of political subjection to the symbolic sphere of religious belief, and deploying the central republican fear of tyranny, but this time in the zone of religion, Madison concluded that the independent citizen could flourish only when protected from a state-sponsored religious establishment. If such religion had prevailed, the young Madison wrote, "it is clear to me that slavery and Subjection might and would have been gradually insinuated among us."[112] Not just Paine, therefore, well known for his antipathy to religious authority, but Madison judged the fruits of official Christianity to be "pride and indolence in the Clergy, ignorance and servility in the laity, in both, superstition, bigotry, and persecution" – hardly proper bases for a free republic.[113]

In an extended 1787 letter to Thomas Jefferson, the fullest statement on this subject he produced, Madison explained why religion accompanied by civic status is extremely dangerous for a republic. Rather than create solidarity based on shared religious faith and practice, the joining of the state and religion produces two distinct sources

109 Madison, "Letter to Thomas Jefferson," p. 150.

110 Madison, "Letter to Thomas Jefferson," p. 150.

111 Madison, "Memorial and Remonstrance against Religious Assessments," p. 33.

112 Madison in Ralph Ketcham, *James Madison: A Biography*, Charlottesville: University of Virginia Press, 1995, p. 57.

113 Madison, "Memorial and Remonstrance against Religious Assessments," p. 32.

of passionate division, each a kind of factionalism. The first is wanton majoritarianism. When the religion of the majority is sanctioned by government, "even in its coolest state, it has been much oftener a motive to oppression than a restraint from it."[114] When religion unites a population in this manner, there is a high probability that the majority "cannot be restrained from repressing the minority."[115] The second is the response of "depressed sects."[116] In a variety of interventions, Madison signaled a concern that under conditions of majority oppression, "a religious sect, may degenerate into a political faction," and that "turbulence, violence, and abuse of power, by the majority, trampling on the rights of the minority," can result in the production "of factions and commotions."[117]

We infer from this assessment of the harms of state-sponsored religion that any quest for homogeneity based on civic religion, as for any other basis of uniformity, was, for Madison, horribly ill-conceived, even what he called "altogether fictitious."[118] If civic religion cannot solve a republic's endemic problem of social strife based on factionalism, what can? One solution, monarchical imposition, is ruled out by republican commitments. It is impermissible to solve the problem of factions by eliminating the liberties that facilitate their composition.[119] This remedy, he asserted, "is worse than the disease," and in the past "Torrents of blood have been spilt in the old world," Madison wrote, "by vain attempts of the secular arm to extinguish Religious discord, by proscribing all difference in Religious opinion."[120]

What is needed in light of the lack of guidance that can be obtained either from classical republicanism or from monarchical power is a new, modern impulse based on the proposition that "a just Government," as Madison wrote, "will be best supported by protecting every Citizen in the enjoyment of his Religion with the same equal hand which protects his person and his property; by neither invading the

114 Madison, "Letter to Thomas Jefferson," p. 151.

115 Madison, "Letter to Thomas Jefferson," p. 151.

116 Madison, "Letter to Thomas Jefferson," p. 151.

117 Madison, "The Federalist No. 10," p. 167; James Madison, "Speech in the Virginia Ratifying Convention in Defense of the Constitution," in *Writings*, p. 355.

118 Madison, "Letter to Thomas Jefferson," p. 149.

119 Madison, "The Federalist No. 51," p. 297.

120 Madison, "The Federalist No. 10," p. 161; Madison, "Memorial and Remonstrance against Religious Assessments," p. 34.

equal rights of any Sect, nor suffering any Sect to invade those of another."[121] Freedom of religion, in short, was his answer to this aspect of the problem of factionalism. The challenge was not to eliminate the sources of religious division, an impossible quest with pernicious consequences, but to discern "the means of controlling its *effects*."[122]

Madison's main answer was to enlarge the scope of freedom by conferring it on all manner of religious beliefs, by giving them equal rights, and by refusing public privilege to any. In such circumstances, no religious group can dominate or overwhelm others. Religious freedom solves the problem of religious factionalism by enhancing the likelihood of religious plurality and altering asymmetrical relations of power into horizontal structures of controlled and peaceful interaction. Whereas classical republicanism thought such diversity to be the deep source of factionalism, Madison's modern republicanism drew the opposite conclusion. Pluralism, supported by equal rights to faith and not buttressed by political power, itself was the cure.

Writing about religious as well as civil rights, Madison explained that by extending freedom and increasing pluralism "society becomes broken into a greater variety of interests, of pursuits, of passions, which check each other whilst those who may feel a common sentiment have less opportunity of communication and concert."[123] The American experience already had demonstrated the capacity of freedom "to assuage the disease."[124] Individual freedom and diversity have "exhibited proofs that equal and compleat liberty, if it does not wholly eradicate it, sufficiently destroys its malignant influence on the health and prosperity of the state."[125]

Religious freedom thus alters the context and logic of collective action.[126] In so doing, this tempering device weakens dispositions that are "adverse to the rights of other citizens, or to the permanent and aggregate interests of the community," while permitting depoliticized

[121] Madison, "Memorial and Remonstrance against Religious Assessments," p. 33.
[122] Madison, "The Federalist No. 10," p. 163.
[123] Madison, "Vices of the Political System of the United States," p. 79.
[124] Madison, "Memorial and Remonstrance against Religious Assessments," p. 34.
[125] Madison, "Memorial and Remonstrance against Religious Assessments," p. 34.
[126] For a detailed discussion of Madison's understanding of the problem of collective action that draws different conclusions regarding his constitutional proposals against factionalism, see Keith L. Dougherty, "Madison's Theory of Public Goods," Kernell, *James Madison: The Theory and Praxis of Republican Government*, pp. 55–56.

forms of metaphysical belief that are not inimical to either the public good or the principle of equal freedom.[127] To prevent the formation of religious factions from flooding the polity with their partial interests and private passions, Madison understood that more, not less freedom and diversity are required. With such freedom and diversity, religious groups that otherwise might harbor ambitions of domination "will find sufficient motives to restraint... from oppressing the minority."[128] It is religious freedom in the context of the perpetual threat of republican factionalism that can cool down harmful passions while respecting "the diversity in the faculties of men."[129] As Thomas Lindsay has correctly argued, in Madison's discussion of religious liberty his "concern all along was political liberty from tyrannical majorities."[130] Generalized free exercise of religion, therefore, is not only a protection of faith but also a protection of the public good from religious factionalism. As a tempering mechanism, it is Madison's pathway to reasonable pluralism.[131]

IV

A central concern of the vast literature on Madison and Paine is the political character of their writings, especially the tradition – republican, liberal, or both – to which these belong. This concern, of course, has resonated in the even larger body of work on the intellectual and ideological qualities of the American Revolution, which has wrestled with the respective influence of Niccolò Machiavelli and John Locke. Both sets of questions are nested within an even broader quest to understand the historical and conceptual relationships between

[127] Madison, "The Federalist No. 10," pp. 160, 163.

[128] Madison, "Letter to Thomas Jefferson," p. 150.

[129] Madison, "The Federalist No. 10," p. 161.

[130] Thomas Lindsay, "James Madison on Religion and Politics: Rhetoric and Reality," *American Political Science Review*, 85:4 (1991), p. 1333. Also, see Lance Banning, "The Practicable Sphere of a Republic. James Madison, the Constitutional Convention, and the Emergence of Revolutionary Federalism," in *Beyond the Confederation: Origins of the Constitution and American National Identity*, ed. Richard Beeman, Stephen Botein, and Edward C. Carter II, Chapel Hill: University of North Carolina Press, 1987, pp. 183–185.

[131] James Conniff, "The Obsolescence of the General Will: Rousseau, Madison, and the Evolution of Republican Thought," *Western Political Quarterly*, 28:1 (1975), pp. 47–58.

republicanism and liberalism during the turbulent eighteenth and nineteenth centuries.

As with Smith and Ferguson, much writing about these thinkers has sought to classify each as either republican or liberal.[132] The result has been an oversimplification. Fortunately, this kind of construction has been challenged and superseded by richer and considerably more nuanced bodies of work. Instead of searching for differences and oppositions, such scholarship also has probed ties and affinities. If we broadly summarize, two types of reading stand out. There is, first, the thesis of a new arrangement, arguing that both Madison and Paine created hybrids of republicanism and liberalism (with variation regarding

[132] For the 'liberal' Madison, see J. G. A. Pocock, *The Machiavellian Moment: Florentine Political Thought and the Atlantic Republican Tradition*, Princeton, N.J.: Princeton University Press, 1975, pp. 531, 535; Gordon Wood, *The Creation of the American Revolution, 1776–1787*, Chapel Hill: University of North Carolina Press, 1998, p. 608; John Patrick Diggins, *The Lost Soul of American Politics: Virtue, Self–Interest, and the Foundations of Republicanism*, New York: Basic Books, 1984, pp. 48–54; Isaac Kramnick, "The 'Great National Discussion': The Discourse of Politics in 1787," *William and Mary Quarterly*, 45:1 (1988), pp. 3–32; Thomas L. Pangle, *The Spirit of Modern Republicanism: The Moral Vision of the American Founders and the Philosophy of Locke*, Chicago: University of Chicago Press, 1988, pp. 46–47, 125–126; Jerome Huyler, *Locke in America: The Moral Philosophy of the Founding Era*, Lawrence: University Press of Kansas, 1995, pp. 261–264; Richard K. Matthews, *If Men Were Angels: James Madison and the Heartless Empire of Reason*, Lawrence: University Press Kansas, 1995, pp. 1–25; and Gary Rosen, *American Compact: James Madison and the Problem of Founding*, Lawrence: University Press of Kansas, 1999, pp. 1–9. For the 'republican' Madison, see Neal Riemer, "The Republicanism of James Madison," *Political Science Quarterly*, 69:1 (1954), pp. 45–64; David F. Epstein, *The Political Theory of the Federalist*, Chicago: University of Chicago Press, 1984, pp. 67–68, 109–110; Ralph Ketcham, "Publius: Sustaining the Republican Principle," *William and Mary Quarterly*, 44:3 (1987), pp. 576–582; M. N. S. Sellers, *American Republicanism: Roman Ideology in the United States*, New York: New York University Press, 1994, pp. 199–210; Iseult Honohan, *Civic Republicanism*, London: Routledge, 2002, pp. 102–110. For the 'republican' Paine, see Wood, *The Creation of the American Republic*, p. 92; Foner, *Tom Paine and Revolutionary America*; Michael Durey, "Thomas Paine's Apostles: Radical Emigres and the Triumph of Jeffersonian Republicanism," *William and Mary Quarterly*, 44:4 (1987), pp. 661–688; Bernard Vincent, ed., *Thomas Paine ou la Republique sans frontières*, Nancy: Presses Universitaires de Nancy, 1993; For the 'liberal' Paine, see Isaac Kramnick, "Republican Revisionism Revised," *American Historical Review*, 87:3 (1982), pp. 637, 644, 649, 651; Isaac Kramnick, "Editor's Introduction: The Life, Ideology, and Legacy of Thomas Paine," in *The Thomas Paine Reader*, pp. 22–29; Joyce Appleby, "Republicanism and Ideology," *American Quarterly*, 37:4 (1985), p. 470; Richard Ellis, "Radical Lockeanism in American Politics," *Western Political Quarterly*, 45:4 (1992), pp. 825–849.

which political tradition predominates).[133] There is, second, the theory of intellectual transitions, moving, depending on the particular scholar, either from republicanism to liberalism or even, counterintuitively, from liberalism to republicanism.[134]

Despite the advances made by these strands of scholarship, its authors continue to rely on just the dichotomy they have sought to transcend. Republican and liberal ideas are treated, sometimes explicitly but always implicitly, as distinct schools.[135] The Founders are said either to have selectively created syncretic combinations from preexisting sets of ideas or to have replaced one doctrine with the other (albeit with the persistence of elements drawn from their prior commitments).

Our argument is different. For Paine and Madison, the development of liberalism as a political and constitutional doctrine was an unplanned result of efforts to institutionalize a stable, well-functioning republic under the modern conditions of their time. As we have seen, they discovered that this achievement paradoxically would require that they set aside or make secondary features that had been central to the classical tradition, including civic religion, an objective and unitary concept of the public good, and the ideal of the virtuous citizen. In turn, other republican pillars of free governments, including the mixed regime, the rule of law, and popular participation were reformulated, even radically, to accommodate the specific challenges of modern politics and society, including value fragmentation and pluralism, the

133 Paul Eidelberg, *The Philosophy of the American Constitution: A Reinterpretation of the Intentions of the Founding Fathers*, New York: Free Press, 1968; Sunstein, "Beyond the Republican Revival," pp. 1561–1563, 1539–1571; McCoy, *The Last of the Fathers: James Madison and the Republican Legacy*, pp. xiv–xv; Colleen A. Sheehan, "The Politics of Public Opinion: James Madison's 'Notes on Government,'" *William and Mary Quarterly*, 49:4 (1992), pp. 609–627; Lance Banning, *The Sacred Fire of Liberty: James Madison and the Founding of the Federal Republic*, Ithaca, N.Y.: Cornell University Press, 1995, pp. 1–12, 396–402; Michael P. Zuckert, *The Natural Rights Republic: Studies in the Foundation of the American Political Tradition*, Notre Dame, Ind.: University of Notre Dame Press, pp. 1–8, 202–243; C. E. Merriam Jr., "Thomas Paine's Political Theories," *Political Science Quarterly*, 14:3 (1899), pp. 389–403.

134 Gary Kates, "From Liberalism to Radicalism: Tom Paine's Rights of Man," Journal of the History of Ideas, 50:4 (1989), pp. 569–587; Sheldon, *The Political Philosophy of James Madison*, pp. xi, xiv–xvi, 37, 65, 77–85, 98, 110–111, 125.

135 For example, see Lance Banning, "Jeffersonian Ideology Revised," *William and Mary Quarterly*, 43:1 (1986), pp. 11–12, 16–17.

enlarged boundaries of the political, and the individualism and self-interest associated with early capitalism. Further, Madison and Paine also enriched the republican tradition by introducing concepts and arguments that were most closely associated with Locke – the social contract, natural rights, universal freedoms, the centrality of legislative representation, and religious pluralism.

The result cannot be accurately described as a simple synthesis on a middle ground in between two contending traditions. Nor can it be designated sequentially as the story of replacement. Rather, Paine's and Madison's republic of the moderns was fashioned by the three processes of rejection, adaptation, and absorption. Starting with republican motivations, yet realizing the limits of the classical model for issues of social pluralism, political factionalism, order, and individual freedoms, both Paine and Madison innovated at the level of ideas and institutions. Seeking to refurbish republicanism, to make it modern, and to soothe fears about the corruption, instability, and decay that had been endemic to the history of free governments, they contributed to the development of a strand of political thought that had not previously existed.

As this intellectual achievement advanced central elements found much earlier in Locke's writings, it is tempting to treat it as a direct heir in a rather linear history of the unfolding of liberal thought. Yet, there was no straight line from *The Second Treatise* to *The Federalist* and *Rights of Man*. Paine's and Madison's political liberalism was not an institutional translation of Lockean principles (as it also was not a simple application of Machiavellian themes). Rather, they invented a liberalism attuned to concerns that Locke had not had to confront.

A similar process unfolded on the other side of the Atlantic where modern liberalism also emerged out of another effort to found a modern republic. But the character of the relationship was not quite the same. In the new United States, liberal beginnings had been associated with what both Paine and Madison thought to be a successful, although insufficient, republican revolution. In France, such leading thinkers as Germaine de Staël and Benjamin Constant reacted, by contrast, to what they believed to be republicanism's grave failures. It is to their responses that we now turn to discern key aspects of the beginnings of continental liberalism.

5

Embracing Liberalism

Germaine de Staël's Farewell to Republicanism

Recent studies in the history of modern political thought increasingly have been turning to the writings of Germaine de Staël.[1] Intriguingly, this revival of interest in a body of thought long neglected by students of political ideas has been marked by a stark dualism. For some, she helps reconsider the character of republicanism.[2] For others, her work

[1] Although she has been ignored for decades, there is now underway something of a Staël revival in political theory. For leading examples, see Madelyn Gutwirth, Avriel Goldberger, and Karyna Szmurlo, eds., *Germaine de Staël: Crossing the Borders*, New Brunswick, N.J.: Rutgers University Press, 1991; John Clairbone Isbell, *The Birth of European Romanticism: Truth and Propaganda in Staël's "De L'Allemagne," 1810–1813*, Cambridge: Cambridge University Press, 1994; Gretchen Rous Besser, *Germaine de Staël Revised*, New York: Twayne Publishers, 1994; Simone Balayé, *Madame de Staël et les Français*, Oxford: Clarendon Press, 1994; Lori Jo Marso, *(Un)Manly Citizens: Jean-Jacques Rousseau's and Germaine de Staël's Subversive Women*, Baltimore: Johns Hopkins University Press, 1999.

[2] Biancamaria Fontana, "The Thermidorian Republic and Its Principles," in *The Invention of the Modern Republic*, ed. Biancamaria Fontana, Cambridge: Cambridge University Press, 1994, pp. 118–138; André Jardin, *Histoire du libéralisme politique: de la crise de l'absolutisme à la Constitution de 1875*, Paris: Hachette Litterature, 1985, pp. 198–210; Michel Ganzin, "A l'aube de la symbiose République-nation: la république de Madame de Staël," in *Nation et République. Les éléments d'un débat*, ed. Philippe Seguin and Rene Monory, Aix-en-Provence: Presses Universitaires d'Aix-Marseille, 1995, pp. 204–237; and Mauro Barberis, "Constant, Mme de Staël et la constitution républicaine: un essaie d' interprétation," in *Le groupe de Coppet et le monde moderne: conceptions-images-débats*, ed. Françoise Tilkin, Geneva: Droz, 1998. It is interesting to note that in his work on French republicanism, published before the recent renewed interest in Staël's work, Claude Nicolet places her exclusively in the tradition of "liberal protestantism." See Claude Nicolet, *L' idée républicaine en France (1789–1924)*, Paris: Gallimard, 1982, pp. 111, 130, 476.

clarifies the birth of continental, especially French, liberalism.[3] Each version claims Staël as one of its canonical or foundational figures.

How might we come to terms with such different appraisals? Although her texts are both republican and liberal,[4] they appear so not at the same time but in a sequence characterized by an internal trajectory, a movement from an originally republican to, ultimately, a decidedly liberal stance. First a republican, she increasingly distanced herself from this tradition to become a liberal. It is this shift we seek to understand. The challenge is to appreciate when, why, and how she said farewell to republicanism and embraced liberalism. We do so by identifying a moment of inflection in Staël's orientation.

Unlike others who ask us to choose between a republican or a liberal Staël, Lucien Jaume and Marcel Gauchet also focus on her intellectual transition and political transformation. Our analysis, though, differs from theirs. Jaume's account attributes changes in Staël's thought to both biographical and theoretical causes. He identifies her disenchantment with Bonaparte, whose coup d'état revealed immanent authoritarian and despotic possibilities in the newborn republic. Jaume also imputes Staël's liberalism to her discovery of Kant when she was exiled in Germany.[5] Bypassing the centrality of the Revolution itself, and the institutional frailty of republican France, he effectively displaces the

[3] As early as 1818, *Gazette de France* published a book review of *Considérations* that described it as a "code des idées liberals." *Gazette de France*, 18, 20, and 22 May, 1818, cited in G. E. Gwynne, *Madame de Staël et la Révolution française. Politique, philosophie, littérature*, Paris: Éditions A-G Nizet, 1969, p. 274. Similarly, her biographer Albert Sorel labeled her the "muse of Restoration liberalism." Albert Sorel, *Madame de Staël*, Paris: Librairie Hachette, 1907, p. 197. For more recent depictions of Staël as a founder of French liberalism, see George A. Kelly, "Liberalism and Aristocracy in the French Restoration," *Journal of the History of Ideas*, 26:4 (1965), pp. 509–530; Louis Girard, *Les libéraux français 1814–1875*, Paris: Aubier, 1985, pp. 34–39; Susan Tenenbaum, "Staël: Liberal Political Thinker," in Gutwirth et al., *Crossing the Borders*, and "The Politics of History: Liberal and Conservative Perspectives on the French Revolution," *Annales Benjamin Constant*, 8–9 (1988), pp. 93–104; Beate Maeder-Metcalf, "La Révolution ou le 'Ce Temps incommensurable' selon Madame de Staël," *Annales Benjamin Constant*, 8–9 (1988), pp. 87–92; and Lucien Jaume, *L'individu effacé ou le paradoxe du liberalisme français*, Paris: Fayard, 1997, pp. 25–63.

[4] Marcel Gauchet, "Constant, Staël et la Révolution française," in *The French Revolution and the Creation of Modern Political Culture*, Vol.3, *The Transformation of Political Culture, 1789–1848*, ed. François Furet and Mona Ozouf, Oxford: Pergamon Press, 1989, pp. 166–172; and Jaume, *L'individu effacé*, pp. 26–27.

[5] Jaume, *L'individu effacé*, pp. 28, 29, 34, 39, 40, 45.

political dimensions of her thought in favor of biography. Staël thus emerges more as a moral philosopher concerned to ground individual freedom in particular metaphysical requisites than as a thinker struggling, as she was, with challenges associated with the founding of a modern regime based on a free constitution.[6]

Gauchet, by contrast, interprets the sequence of her writings by projecting from Staël's evolutionary theory of history, characterized by discrete stages. He argues that she abandoned republicanism because it was untimely. Moving too swiftly from absolutism to a free republic without the intermediate moment of a constitutional monarchy, the French Revolution had lapsed into terror as it imposed political solutions on an unready environment.[7] Gauchet is at his most persuasive in advancing a plausible interpretation of why Staël abandoned republicanism, but he leaves unaccounted her turn to liberalism.[8]

We proceed differently. Our point of departure is the critical juncture opened by the Revolution. Staël's thought reflected on its events and, in that sense, was constituted by them, especially by what she experienced as disappointing and catastrophic failures. An early fervent proponent of the Revolution, she was one of the first to offer a republican reading of this profound historical experience. As it was bringing about Europe's first fully authentic modern republic, she enthusiastically identified with revolutionary France. Her understanding of the Revolution as deeply republican never wavered. What changed was her evaluation. Though her views about the Revolution remained broadly sympathetic, they became tempered. Her rejection of republicanism, however, came to be drastic.

Staël's disillusionment with republicanism followed her despair at history's course. She came to think that republican ideas and institutions could not mediate between the pitfalls of the older arbitrary monarchical absolutism and an increasingly despotic, absolute democracy. In identifying too completely with the latter, republicanism had produced a permanent revolution that ushered in terror and instability and put individual lives at risk. Republicanism, she thus recognized, had become a recipe for revolution without end. Her liberalism

[6] Jaume, *L'individu effacé*, pp. 62–63.

[7] Gauchet, "Constant, Staël," pp. 168–169.

[8] Gauchet, "Constant, Staël," pp. 167, 171. His reading, moreover, flattens the differences that distinguish Staël's early from her late texts.

was the consequence of her search for a political center that could now hold, one that could succeed where republicanism had failed by reconciling freedom with order and popular sovereignty with legal authority.

The development and transformation of these ideas provide a privileged window from which to understand the limits of republicanism as it confronted the central political challenges of her age. The content of Staël's liberalism is of less interest than the process of its emergence and the motivations that impelled her to abandon 'pure' republicanism. What is telling, and what makes the study of her texts valuable, is the transparent visibility of her (self-)critical engagement with these difficulties. In attending to Staël's writings, we can trace her break with republicanism and better comprehend how her mature appeal to mobilize a "new generation of liberty's friends" became the rallying call for France's first proudly identified liberals.[9]

Staël's liberalism can be understood as the result of a struggle first within and then against the civic tradition. Initially "reformulated or resuscitated from within the sphere of republicanism," as Jaume argues, it developed more robustly by confronting republican legacies.[10] We trace this process in the history of her thought. We focus first on her early, political writings, most notably *Réflexions sur la paix, adressées à M. Pitt et aux Français* (1795), *Réflexions sur la paix intérieure* (1795),[11] and especially *Des circonstances actuelles qui peuvent terminer la Révolution et des principes qui doivent fonder la République en France* (1798–1799),[12] which, as Mauro Barberis has correctly noted, "is perhaps one of the most representative texts of republican constitutionalism."[13] These strongly antimonarchical writings, which also were deeply critical of democracy and its excesses,

[9] Staël, *Considérations sur la Révolution française*, ed. Jacques Godechot, Paris: Tallandier, 1983, p. 489.

[10] Jaume, *L' individu effacé*, p. 17.

[11] Both texts are reprinted in *Oeuvres completes de Mme. La Baronne de Staël, publiées par son fils*, Vol. 2, Paris: Chez Treuttel et Würtz, 1829.

[12] This text, unpublished in de Staël's lifetime, was edited by Lucia Omacini for Paris-Genève: Libraire Droz, 1979.

[13] Barberis, "Constant, Mme de Staël et la constitution républicaine: un essaie d' interprétation," p. 193. Similarly, Gengembre and Goldzink had argued that this text "is totally located under the lights of the republican creed." Gérard Gengembre and Jean Goldzink, "Une femme révolutionnée: le Thermidor de Madame de Staël," *Annales Benjamin Constant*, 8–9 (1988), p. 275.

aimed to develop a systematic, comprehensive, and "pure theory" of republican government by advancing a vision of a mixed representative constitution grounded in the pivotal values of equality, public spirit, the rule of law, patriotism, and civic religion.[14] Conspicuously absent, despite a rare reference to liberal principles, are individual rights and liberties.[15] In these texts, Staël also subordinates the separation of powers to a strong and independent executive representing the French nation in its entirety, which, at times, can take the form of a legal dictatorship.

This republicanism was motivated above all by the belief – a belief Staël never abandoned – that a center between the poles of royalist ultraconservatism and absolute democracy had to be discovered in order to procure stability and security for postrevolutionary France and to properly protect popular sovereignty. For the young Staël, republicanism offered the sole political impulse capable of achieving these ends. Again and again, she underscored that only republicanism can effectively occupy the center of the political spectrum.

She soon abandoned this 'pure' solution, all the while maintaining the quest for an encompassing middle position. Her later writings, *De l'Allemagne* (1810) and *Considérations sur la Révolution française* (1818), opened the modern era of French liberalism.[16] These two texts trace the gradual formation of Staël's distinct liberalism, incorporating individual rights and formal procedures grounded in the rule of law, the separation of powers, toleration, religious freedom, and a fear of undue executive command. Republicanism, she now maintained, could not perform its assigned role of mediating between the political extremes for the simple reason that its distance from Jacobinism had shrunk. Republicanism's fierce commitment to equality had bred terror; its search for virtue and public dedication had quashed guarantees of personal liberties; and its fascination with unity and homogeneity had proved inimical to civil diversity and religious pluralism. The liberalism

[14] Staël, *Des circonstances*, p. 40.

[15] Staël, *Sur la paix intérieure*, p. 162.

[16] Ganzin, "A l'aube de la symbiose République-nation: la république de Madame de Staël," p. 231. Unfortunately, although Ganzin distinguishes a republican from a liberal period in her work, he nonetheless fails to account for Staël's shift from republicanism to liberalism and, more broadly, tends to overlook the differences that separate the *Circonstances* from the *Considérations*.

her later writings announced, she believed, offered a more viable basis for achieving what republicanism could not: the ability to discern a political center in equilibrium.

I

Staël's early political project, to develop a "theory of the republican system," is marked by the turmoil and opportunities of the French Revolution and the sinister prospect of permanent insurrection.[17] By reconciling freedom and authority with autonomy and stability, she believed that only a republican constitution could salvage the gains and progress brought about by the Revolution, lay the foundation for a lasting free government in a large state, and put a definitive end to both anarchy and terror and to the ominous possibility of monarchical restoration.[18]

Staël advanced this claim by scrupulously crafting a series of tightly linked arguments demonstrating the superiority of republicanism against democracy and monarchy, its two main political rivals. Her point of departure was a vision of republican blamelessness, as not having been implicated in the horrors of the Revolution. She defended this innocence on two grounds. Opposing the reactionaries, she admiringly embraced the Revolution, praising its achievements as a "burning fermentation that produces a new world," "a novel creation," and an event that allows "society to restart, where man senses the entire force of man."[19] The Revolution not only facilitated public participation and political engagement of a previously excluded bourgeois stratum; it also was responsible for eradicating old privileges, entrenched hierarchies, inhuman inequalities, and the many injustices perpetrated by the *ancien régime*. History, she thus was persuaded, will remember the Revolution positively for having overthrown feudal bondage, for

[17] Staël, *Des circonstances*, pp. 9, 4, 40. Simone Balayé traces the origins of Staël's republicanism in 1793 as the result of the influence of the Count of Ribbing. By contrast, Gretchen Rous Besser dates Staël's shift one year later and attributes it to the influence of Benjamin Constant. Simone Balayé, *Madame de Staël. Lumières et liberté*, Paris: Éditions Klincksieck, 1979, p. 47; Besser, *Germaine de Staël Revisited*, pp. 38–39.

[18] Staël, *Sur la paix*, p. 113; Staël, *Des circonstances*, p. 5.

[19] Staël, *Sur la paix intérieure*, p. 120; Staël, *Des circonstances*, pp. 2, 33, 36, 128, 342.

fulfilling the philosophical promises of *les lumières*, and for realizing political equality.[20]

Simultaneously, opposing Jacobins and democrats, she attributed the excesses of the Revolution partly to them and partly to the uneducated poor masses.[21] With the radicals of the Left absorbing this responsibility, republicans were granted absolution. It is "the anarchists," the *démocrates babouvistes*, who, with their "revolutionary fury," their absolute notion of freedom, and their defiance of any form of authority and private property, have converted the Revolution by radicalizing it into a rule of fear.[22] Likewise, the sudden entry of dispossessed masses into the revolutionary process displaced its course. Anticipating Hannah Arendt's famous thesis about the "social question," Staël castigated the middle class, which made the Revolution, for arming the lowest social classes against the nobility.[23] This proved a dangerous alliance, as an unrestrained spirit of hate, greed, ignorance, and revenge deflected political elites from their noble revolutionary aims.

Staël did more than simply disentangle republicanism from the revolutionary crimes she imputed to extremists on each side of the political spectrum. She also shed comparative theoretical light on the broader, more abstractly considered, merits and vices of the three primary forms of government: monarchy, democracy, and republicanism. In these texts, Staël's republicanism was fervently antimonarchical. She categorically denounced plans to restore kingship in any form.[24] Absolute monarchy, she insisted, approaches national treason. Adopting Sieyès's expulsion of the nobility from the community of France,[25] Staël maintained that "the faction that sustains absolute power is completely outside of the French nation . . . they are foreigners, and must be fought

[20] Staël, *Des circonstances*, p. 128.

[21] Staël, *Des circonstances*, p. 5.

[22] Staël, *Sur la paix intérieure*, pp. 79, 78, 85; Staël, *Des circonstances*, p. 45.

[23] Hannah Arendt, *On Revolution*, New York: Penguin Books, 1990, pp. 59–114; Staël, *Des circonstances*, pp. 36–37. Of course, there are differences. Arendt emphasized the element of pity in the social question, whereas Staël underscored the presence of resentment.

[24] Staël, *Sur la paix intérieure*, p. 117.

[25] Emmanuel Sieyès, *Qu'est-ce que le Tiers état?*, Geneva: Librairie Droz, 1970, pp. 126, 132–133.

and treated as such."[26] Moreover, absolutism amounting to "ancient despotism" is incompatible with modern political equality and popular sovereignty, which she espoused cautiously.[27] Such hereditary monarchy belongs to the past. It also confronts a huge legitimation deficit, as it is not derived from "the spirit of its peoples" and does not rely on public opinion.[28] As an arbitrary and unaccountable form of personal rule, monarchy cannot be justified by reason. Its foundations dispose it to arbitrariness, and thus to despotism and tyranny.[29]

Staël equally dismissed limited monarchy, especially the English model. Against the moderate royalists who sought to temper the inevitability of revolutionary change with historical continuity by transplanting England's political institutions to France, she rejoined that it would be a mistake to neglect the vast differences in history, society, and politics distinguishing the two countries.[30] Institutions and laws, she cautioned, never operate in a vacuum. They are integral parts of broader cultural and historical configurations. Further, despite its similarities to the French, the English Revolution possessed a different point of departure and focused on a different set of vexing problems. In England, she stressed, revolution was initiated by "religious quarrels," was inspired by a "puritan faith," had a "religious dimension," and aimed to solve a sectarian schism.[31] In France, by contrast, revolution was predominantly political and certainly secular, pivoting on problems of sovereign power, its limits and its representation, as well as liberty and authority. She thus interpreted the English Restoration as the natural outcome of its religious dimension. Moreover, sectarianism, she observed, had limited reach, failing to inspirit English society as a whole. Further, and most important, she perceived limited monarchy to be ridden with a fundamental and irresolvable contradiction between national sovereignty and the sovereignty of the king. These normative and institutional principles she thought to be irreconcilable.[32] Mutually exclusive, they could not be accommodated

[26] Staël, *Sur la paix intérieure*, p. 101.
[27] Staël, *Des circonstances*, p. 57.
[28] Staël, *Des circonstances*, p. 195.
[29] Staël, *Des circonstances*, pp. 64–65.
[30] Staël, *Sur la paix intérieure*, p. 123.
[31] Staël, *Des circonstances*, pp. 68, 69.
[32] Staël, *Des circonstances*, p. 58.

one to the other. Attempts to bring them together necessarily would shatter one or the other, and efforts to imitate English government would fail to secure liberty or equality in France.[33]

This rejection of monarchy is accompanied by an equally critical, if more selective and nuanced, confrontation with what she labeled "pure democracy."[34] Although Staël acknowledged the democratic principle of popular sovereignty, welcomed the shift in the source of political authority from King to Nation, embraced Rousseau's theory of the general will, accepted the normative superiority of equal political rights over hereditary privileges, and recognized that a modern legitimate exercise of political power can be based only on democratic grounds, she nonetheless was dismissive of democracy.[35] Her manifold reasons direct attention to deeper tensions between republicanism and democracy.[36]

She believed democracy to have been responsible for the failure to end the Revolution. For Staël, this failure revealed two intrinsic democratic defects: negativity and lawlessness. Its spirit, she argued, essentially is destructive. Though perhaps necessary to initiate and sustain a revolution and to overturn instituted inequalities, democracy is incapable, even dangerous, in circumstances demanding the establishment of a new political and legal order. Lacking creative capacity, its sole power is negative – prone to sedition, factions, intolerance, and fanaticism, and thus inimical to authority, constancy, and constitutional self-limitation.[37] "Democracies know how to conquer; aristocracies how to conserve," Staël observed.[38] Reiterating a prevalent critique found in the writings of Montesquieu, Hume, and Madison, she blamed democracy for its inherent frailty, violent nature, and intrinsic agitation, all of which came to be manifested in Jacobin political terrorism.[39] Democracy also elevates popular will to absolute supreme law and is opposed to self-binding mechanisms considered external,

[33] Staël, *Des circonstances*, pp. 61, 67–69.
[34] Staël, *Des circonstances*, pp. 158–159.
[35] Staël, *Des circonstances*, pp. 20–24, 40–41. On Staël's ambivalent views on the general will, see Roland Mortier, "Comment terminer la Révolution et fonder la République," *Annales Benjamin Constant*, 8–9 (1988), pp. 296, 302.
[36] Staël, *Des circonstances*, pp. 169–171.
[37] Staël, *Sur la paix*, pp. 55, 79.
[38] Staël, *Des circonstances*, p. 164.
[39] Staël, *Sur la paix intérieure*, pp. 129–130; Staël, *Des circonstances*, p. 24.

restrictive, and antagonistic to the arbitrary wishes of the collective sovereign. Placing the sovereign outside the reaches of positive law, democracy is adverse to constitutionalism and prone to a "demagogic tyranny" of the majority.[40] Democracy's antiinstitutional bias thus amounts to anarchy.[41]

To strengthen this critique, Staël revisited and further developed the famous distinction between the ancients and the moderns.[42] Anticipating and influencing Benjamin Constant, she argued that pure democracy is anachronistic and unsuitable under modern conditions. The historical, geographical, and cultural changes in the habits, social practices, economic activities, and value systems of the moderns had undermined the conditions that had underpinned direct democracy in ancient Greek city-states.[43] Modern states were much larger in size.[44] Staël attended, moreover, to the rise of egoism and the proliferation of commercial activities, the shift to private considerations, the pervasiveness of self-interest, and the modern desire for security and wealth, which were displacing civic virtue, military glory, political excellence, and devotion to the greatness of one's city.[45]

Unlike Constant, who later stressed the lack of individual rights among the ancients and the development of such rights among the moderns, Staël emphasized the absence of constitutionalism, the excessive legal regulation of customs and manners, the want of an independent judiciary to control political power, and the relative disregard of private property as the main deficits of ancient democracies.[46] These discrepancies between Staël's and Constant's historicist rejections of democracy are not insignificant. They point to deeper differences that distinguish republican from liberal appraisals. For the early Staël, the

[40] Staël, *Sur la paix intérieure*, pp. 102–103; Staël, *Des circonstances*, p. 261.

[41] Staël, *Sur la paix*, p. 79.

[42] This familiar eighteenth-century distinction was announced anew by Condorcet a few years after the beginning of the Revolution and soon associated with the writings of Benjamin Constant. See Marquis de Condorcet, *Cinq mémoires sur l'instruction publique*, Paris: Flammarion, 1994, p. 86; Benjamin Constant, "The Liberty of the Ancients Compared with That of the Moderns," in *Constant: Political Writings*, ed. Biancamaria Fontana, Cambridge: Cambridge University Press, 1988, pp. 308–328.

[43] Staël, *Sur la paix intérieure*, p. 155.

[44] Staël, *Des circonstances*, pp. 109, 159–160.

[45] Staël, *Des circonstances*, pp. 110–111, 135, 165, 167.

[46] Staël, *Des circonstances*, pp. 375, 387, 423.

gap dividing ancient from modern times is not due primarily to the appearance of a new form of liberty, but rather to the neglect by the ancients of the unstable and self-destructive potentialities of political power organized solely on a popular basis. Although she mentioned that the moderns, contrary to the ancients, are inclined to favor private freedoms and individual independence,[47] she was intrigued far more by the contrast between the leveling egalitarianism of ancient democracies and the natural aristocracy of modern republics.[48] Whereas democracy takes political equality to its ultimate conclusions and monarchy institutionalizes hereditary inequalities based on birth, republicanism, to the contrary, establishes a "government of the bests," based on natural excellence.[49]

What distinguishes modern republics from ancient democracies is not new laws that recognize and protect individual rights, but how these aristocratic aspects are now embodied in the logic of representation and in the replacement of lottery by elections as the preferred method of selecting the most competent and enlightened citizens.[50] For Staël, political representation reconciles popular sovereignty with large advanced commercial societies by limiting access to political office to the most qualified and educated citizens. It also shields legislation from the pressure of private interests, enabling representatives to deliberate freely about the public good, the national interest, and the general will. Finally, via elections, representation salvages the principle of democratic legitimacy and secures public accountability while containing threats that are immanent in pure, direct democracy.[51] Staël stressed this point repeatedly. Only if partially disavowed can democracy be realized. Surprisingly, fully realized democracy produces its negation. Democracy is neither self-sufficient nor self-sustainable.

[47] Staël, *Des circonstances*, p. 111.

[48] Staël, *Sur la paix*, p. 50; Staël, *Sur la paix intérieure*, p. 125; Staël, *Des circonstances*, p. 12.

[49] Staël, *Des circonstances*, p. 12.

[50] Staël, *Des circonstances*, p. 20. For the most informed discussion on the distinction between election and lottery, see Bernard Manin, *The Principles of Representative Government*, Cambridge: Cambridge University Press, 1997.

[51] Curiously, Fontana misses the intrinsic relationship between modern republicanism and political representation. Thus, her claim that representation could have been combined with a limited monarchy lets pass Staël's point that this would amount to a contradiction that could lead to fundamental conflict between two forms of sovereignty. Fontana, "The Thermidorian Republic and Its Principles," p. 123.

When it aspires to self-sufficiency it undermines its own conditions of possibility; when it attempts to sustain itself with no external support it turns into a tyranny of the majority. Such realities, she believed, were understood only by the republicans, who "have finally discovered that democracy can destroy itself only by the principles of democracy."[52]

To approximate the results of pure democracy, a movement away from its forms thus is imperative.[53] Democracy is marked and sealed by a formidable paradox: its most important ends must be realized through nondemocratic means. Democracy can thrive only as, and through, the aristocratic principle of representation. As Staël puts the point, "by placing the democratic principles under the protection of aristocratic forms," representative government modernizes democracy.[54] For this reason, contrary to Michel Ganzin's claim that she urged republicans, as he put it, to "disassociate republicanism and democracy,"[55] she rather advised them, in her words, "to adopt some aristocratic ideas in order to firmly establish popular institutions."[56] The mixed government of a republican constitution adapts democracy to modern conditions by deploying nondemocratic institutions and mechanisms.[57] The directness and immediacy of democracy is sacrificed, but not its normative content.

Interestingly enough, in these early writings Staël's vision of a republican constitution hardly resembles today's liberal constitutionalism. References to fundamental individual rights, "which she never defined," are peripheral to her central arguments and undeniably subordinated to the higher status she accords political rights.[58] Individual liberty plays a secondary, instrumental role as a guarantee of political freedom. Violating the former leads to the violation of the latter. Individuals deprived of personal liberty will come to be deprived of

[52] Staël, *Des circonstances*, pp. 164, 44.

[53] Staël, *Des circonstances*, p. 24.

[54] Staël, *Des circonstances*, p. 174. This paradox of democracy is lost in Lori Marso's reading, which suggests that Staël endorsed democracy because it "encourage[s] diverse points of view, the conflict of values, and the challenge that erotic attachments and poetry entails for a set of moral orders." Lori J. Marso, "The Stories of Citizens: Rousseau, Montesquieu, and de Staël Challenge Enlightenment Reason," *Polity*, 33 (1998), p. 460.

[55] Ganzin, "A l'aube de la symbiose République-nation: la république de Madame de Staël," p. 210.

[56] Staël, *Des circumstances*, p. 164.

[57] Kelly, "Liberalism and Aristocracy in the French Restoration," pp. 515, 529.

[58] Gwynne, *Madame de Staël et la Révolution française*, p. 52.

political rights as well.[59] Thus, the protection of private autonomy is justified by the need to protect public autonomy. This reasoning, characteristic of the republican tradition, advances civil liberty through the overarching normative worth of civic liberty. After all, as Staël wrote, while "civil liberty can exist under a king, even under a despot," political rights can be secured only by a republican constitution.[60]

The priority Staël accorded to political freedom also informed a key aspect of her critique of the Revolution, one that took her beyond the familiar denunciation of terror and thus revealed the distinctively republican aspect of her thought. Rather than promote political freedom and participation, she claimed, the Revolution had destroyed them. Fanaticism, insecurity, and fear had led to the "annihilation of the public spirit," breeding privatization and passivity.[61] "The revolutionary measures," she added, "devour all public spirit" because "morals are depraved, patriotism is weakened, [and] distress spreads its devastation."[62] Depoliticization ironically had been produced by overpoliticization. Only constitutional guarantees and limitations on government can safeguard the public spirit and allow political liberty to flourish stably and predictably. Similarly, she denounced the separation of powers, another pillar of liberalism, as corrosive and divisive of political authority, which easily could harbor and reproduce entrenched social divisions between antagonistic particular interests, each representing a different order or class.[63] For Staël, echoing Rousseau, the doctrine of the separation of powers comes extremely close to a resuscitation of the *ancien régime*'s old estates.

Her republican constitution would frighten today's liberals.[64] Following the Roman tradition, she accepted the necessity of temporary

[59] Staël, *Des circonstances*, p. 202; Gwynne, *Madame de Staël et la Révolution française*, p. 64.

[60] Staël, *Des circonstances*, p. 418.

[61] Staël, *Des circonstances*, p. 327.

[62] Staël, *Des circonstances*, p. 330.

[63] Staël, *Des circonstances*, pp. 179, 181. Barberis prefers to describe Staël's stance toward the principle of the separation of powers not as one of rejection but rather as one of suspicion and distrust. Barbaris, "Constant, Mme de Staël et la constitution républicaine: un essaie d' interprétation," p. 199. On this point, also see François Furet, *La Révolution: 1770–1814*, Paris: Hachette, 1988, p. 363.

[64] As Jaume has correctly argued, "Staël's liberalism is far from being found in 1798." Jaume, *L'individue effacé*, p. 51.

legal dictatorship at exceptional moments of crisis. She allowed executive power to temporarily suspend the legal system in order to defend itself against internal and external enemies, provided that it remains simply a "dictatorship of institutions" within the limits of law rather than a dictatorship of persons.[65] She also supported suspending freedom of the press, treating it not as an inviolable or unconditional right but as subordinate both to considerations of public order and to the propagation of a republican ideology.[66] Importantly, she further opted for a strong executive – independent of the legislature – who could, as a direct instantiation of the nation, appeal directly to the people.[67]

Above all, her views on religion and patriotism separate Staël's early political theory from liberal thought. She argued that a republican government requires a state religion, what Gérard Gengembre and Jean Goldzink tellingly have described as the "republican religion" that best corresponds to building and securing a modern republic.[68] The rise of equality and liberty had corroded traditional forms of social solidarity and had disentangled the fabric of social integration and political authority. Echoing Rousseau's views on religion, Staël discovered state religion as a rejoinder to the disintegration of common bonds, the dissolution of a shared ethical life, and the laxity of modern

[65] Staël, *Des circonstances*, pp. 160, 177; and Ganzin, "A l'aube de la symbiose République-nation: la république de Madame de Staël," pp. 222–223. Carl Schmitt and Claude Nicolet trace the revival of dictatorship during the French Revolution back to the Roman tradition, of which the republicans were so fond. Carl Schmitt, *Die Diktatur*, Berlin: Duncker & Humblot, 1994, pp. 1–2; Nicolet, *L' idée républicaine en France (1789–1924)*, pp. 101–105. Staël, along with Constant, supported, in anticipation of a probable royalist victory in the elections of spring 1797, the republican coup d' état of the 18th of Fructidor. There is also ample evidence that she also participated in the coup d' état of the 18th of Brumaire that brought Bonaparte to power. For a detailed discussion of Staël's involvement in these events, see Gwynne, *Madame de Staël et la Révolution française*, pp. 39–43, 45–48.

[66] Staël, *Des circonstances*, pp. 114–117, 113, 277. Also see Simone Balayé, "Staël and Liberty: An Overview," in *Germaine de Staël: Crossing the Borders*, ed. Madelyn Gutwirth, Avriel Goldberger, and Karyna Szmurlo, New Brunswick, N.J.: Rutgers University Press, 1991, p. 17, and for a critical commentary that shows the distance of the young Staël from liberalism, see Mortier, "Comment terminer la Révolution et fonder le République," pp. 299–300.

[67] Staël, *Des circonstances*, p. 181.

[68] Gérard Gengembre and Jean Goldzink, "Madame de Staël ou pour une religion politique," *Annales Benjamin Constant*, 8–9, 1988, p. 211. Also, see Gwynne, *Madame de Staël et la Révolution française*, p. 150.

manners.[69] This solution appealed to Staël as a counterbalance to the centrifugal forces unleashed by the ascent of privatism, economic self-interest, and egoism. She was confident that state-sanctioned religion could re-create the symbolic preconditions of public morality and reestablish civic virtue in a large commercial society, thus retrofitting republicanism under modern conditions in order to secure its viability. As a result, she affirmed "it is up to the legislator to influence by all fair means, and consequently the only efficient ones, the progressive reduction of any dogmatic faith that fits badly with the nature of the government."[70] She added, further, that "the state will have in its hands all the power of influence over the cult it upholds, and this great power, one that interpreters of religious ideas always have had, will become a source of support for the republican government."[71]

This concern to restore the conditions for civic virtue and reconcile a changing world with ancient values also motivated her treatment of patriotism. If state religion can function as the cement of society, patriotism provides a new collective identity that can stir the body politic.[72] Like many other republican contemporaries, Staël was aware that procedures and abstract rules cannot function by themselves.[73] "The constitution," she cautioned, "... neither provides a real nor an imaginary guarantee."[74] Rather, the operation of institutions needs additional, more substantive, forms of identification, such as those provided by love of one's country. "In the republics," she claimed,

69 Staël, *Des circonstances*, pp. 222–237. As Nicolet correctly explains, the quest for a political morality, a republican morality, was at the center of the French republicans in their effort to find a modern equivalent to the ancient virtues. Nicolet, *L' idée républicaine en France*, pp. 492–499.

70 Staël, *Des circonstances*, pp. 226–227.

71 Staël, *Des circonstances*, p. 233. As Simone Balayé has observed, Staël's notion of state religion is deeply ambiguous, for it leaves unanswered the problem "of what will happen to other religions, to their believers and their priests," and more important to the notion of toleration that Staël seemed to have advocated. Balayé, *Madame de Staël. Lumières et liberté*, p. 72. Similarly, for Jaume, Staël's state religion "conforms badly with the liberal spirit." Jaume, *L' individu effacé*, p. 54.

72 Gengembre and Goldzink, "Madame de Staël ou pour une religion politique," p. 215.

73 Staël, *Des circonstances*, p. 276. For a similar point, see Biancamaria Fontana, "Madame de Staël, le gouvernement des passions et la Révolution française," *Annales Benjamin Constant*, 8–9, 1988, p. 181.

74 Staël, *Des circonstances*, p. 180.

"the love of one's homeland is considered as the first virtue" and "the first basis of a republic is national patriotism."[75] Only patriotism once again could unite French citizens, reinstate national and political unity against the inequalities of the *ancien régime*, and overcome the fractional politics of the democratic impulse. Patriotism inspires public dedication and civic excellence by inducing citizens to subordinate their partial personal interests to the general will.

The nation emerges in Staël's early writings not only as a surrogate to the king but as the ultimate ground for a stable and effective republic capable of sustaining the symbolic and moral motivational prerequisites for civic virtue and patriotic feeling.[76] A fusion of the people and the nation will guarantee that there is "one people that is only one, within which there is neither caste nor individual privilege."[77] Republican citizenship above all requires the nation to cultivate devotion to the public good. Precisely because public virtues are not given naturally, especially in a large commercial state, Staël supported a limited distribution of political rights. As duties of citizenship become more demanding in a modern republic, only a small number of enlightened individuals should have the privilege of political participation. "Political rights," she asserted, "must be considered as a tribute we pay to the homeland; it is to go on guard, it is to exercise the duties of the citizen."[78]

[75] Staël, *Des circonstances*, pp. 238, 321.

[76] For an informed discussion of Staël's understanding of the nation, see John Claiborne Isbell, *The Birth of European Romanticism*, Cambridge: Cambridge University Press, 2006, pp. 29–30, and Ganzin, "A l'aube de la symbiose République-nation: la république de Madame de Staël," pp. 229–230. For more general studies of the uses and misuses of the concept of nation in the French republican tradition, see Robert Derathe, "Patriotisme et nationalisme au xviii siècle," *Annales de philosophie politique*, 8 (1969), pp. 69–84; Jacques Godechot, "Nation, patrie, nationalisme, patriotisme en France au xviii siècle," *Annales historique de la Révolution française*, 206 (1971), 481–501; Michel-Henry Fabre, "L'emploi des mots Nation et Peuple dans le langage politique de la révolution française (1789–1799)," in *Nation et République. Les éléments d'un débat*, pp. 51–52; and Pierre Nora, "Nation," in *Dictionaire critique de la Révolution française: Idées*, ed. François Furet and Mona Ozouf, Paris: Flammarion,1992, pp. 339–357.

[77] Staël, *Des circonstances*, p. 170.

[78] Staël, *Sur la paix intérieure*, p. 153. At the same time, she contemplated the possibility that in the future, as patriotism would become more pervasive through civic religion and especially public education, politics would also become more accessible to broader segments of society. Staël, *Des circonstances*, pp. 276–277.

Staël's moderate republicanism was geared, above all, to mediate between the extremes of monarchy and democracy and thus occupy "le juste milieu," the empty center of politics that once had been defined by the majesty of the king located between the spirit of usurpation and that of factions.[79] "To end a revolution," she argued, "a center must be discovered, a common bond."[80] This, only republican doctrine could provide – not so much because of her "faith in fundamental human goodness... [one that] leads her to the ingenious conviction that she can persuade warring factions to unite in pursuit of equity and justice," as Gretchen Rous Besser argues, but because of Staël's confidence in republicanism's intrinsic political and institutional properties that made it best qualified to end the revolution and found a stable representative government.[81] Staël understood that while her demand directed at monarchists to sacrifice royalty for freedom and at democrats to sacrifice democracy for public order were impossible for them to implement, republicans alone could do so.[82]

Contrary to kingship that relinquishes liberty on the altar of unlimited public authority and opposed to democracy that renounces authority in the name of boundless liberty, republicanism combines these two principles, mediated by the aristocratic code of excellence. "Between the concentration [of power] that conduces despotism and its subdivision that encourages the emergence of armed factions, there is a reasonable combination that can produce political liberty. Likewise, institutions should be neither too compressed nor too extended."[83] This strategic formulation informs her call to republicans to forge alliances with the moderates of both extremes who can integrate and render harmless some of their central commitments.[84] To transform republicanism from a revolutionary force to a basis for constitutional governance, republicans also must modify their normative and instrumental

[79] On the notion of the 'juste milieu,' see Vincent Starzinger, *The Politics of the Center: The Juste Milieu in Theory and Practice, France and England, 1815–1848*, New Brunswick, N.J.: Transaction, 1991.

[80] Staël, *Sur la paix intérieure*, p. 155; Marcel Gauchet, *La révolution des pouvoirs. La souveraineté, le people et la représentation 1789–1799*, Paris: Gallimard, 1995, pp. 201–207.

[81] Besser, *Germaine de Staël Revisited*, p. 45.

[82] Staël, *Sur la paix intérieure*, pp. 155–156.

[83] Staël, *Des circonstances*, p. 187.

[84] Besser, *Germaine de Staël Revisited*, pp. 38–39, 40.

propensities.[85] No longer should they lean too hard in the direction of the democratic pole, for to do so would endanger the hegemonic aspirations of modern republicanism and thus undermine the prospects of "a constitutional peace."[86]

II

Within a decade, Staël's views changed markedly. As G. E. Gwynne observed, "the political situation in France and a certain evolution in Mme de Staël herself gave a totally new orientation to her thought that moved her considerably away from the opinions she professed in 1800."[87] But in what direction, and why? The elements of an answer first can be discerned by attending to *De l'Allemagne*, published in 1810. Here, we take note of a sporadic, far from complete, but nonetheless unmistakable turn toward liberalism, a shift accompanied by a symmetrical departure from her earlier devotion to republican doctrine.

In *De l'Allemagne* Staël focused on what she explicitly referred to as "the liberal impulse" sweeping Western Europe, without which, she argued, no grand political project could be achieved.[88] More important, she located this impulse within a broader progressive philosophy of history, which she divided into a succession of stages, each designating a higher level in relation to the preceding ones. This view of historical evolution, common to eighteenth- and nineteenth-century European historiography, and especially, as we have seen, in the Scottish Enlightenment, would be of no particular interest if not for the following reasons. First, Staël situated the liberal impulse, defined as a "love of liberty," at the apex of European political and cultural history and as the culmination of Western civilization, "whose history

85 For a detailed and informed discussion of Staël's distinction between "revolutionary republicans" and "moderate" or "reasonable" republicans, see Ganzin, "A l'aube de la symbiose République-nation: la république de Madame de Staël," p. 212.

86 Staël, *Des circonstances*, pp. 132, 152.

87 Gwynne, *Madame de Staël et la Révolution française*, p. 83. Jaume locates Staël's liberal turn in 1801 after the publication of *De la literature*, which still had some strong republican elements. Jaume, *L'individu effacé*, p. 54.

88 Staël, *De l'Allemagne*, ed. Simone Balayé, 2 Vols., Paris: Garnier-Flammarion, 1968, I, p. 73.

started during the period of the Reformation."[89] Here, modernity and liberalism appear as mutually constitutive.[90] She now had come to understand liberty predominantly in terms of individual freedom and personal independence from collective authority. In tracing its origins to the genesis of Protestantism, she tacitly revealed a preference for the liberty of the moderns. This proclivity later became explicit in *Considérations*' revised, and liberal, version of the distinction between the government of the ancients and that of the moderns.

Second, in *De l'Allemagne*, she relegated patriotism, an "enthusiasm for homeland," to classical antiquity – that is, to an outdated era.[91] Once a centerpiece of a republican constitution, patriotism had become a museum piece, a relic present only in the unrecoverable past located in the prehistory of the modern age. This historicist renunciation was entwined, first, with a wry understanding of current pitfalls, and then with a more emphatic critique in which Staël reproached patriotism for being "a pompous name, with which one could dream about one's personal interest."[92] Correspondingly, she also rejected any notion of a national or public interest as detrimental to such higher moral values as respect for individual liberty or personal autonomy.[93]

The critical text marking Staël's turn to liberalism followed some six years later. More than a ceremonial tribute to her father's deeds or a reassessment of the French Revolution from a privileged position provided by historical distance – two of the most common readings of *Considérations*[94] – this work is a pioneering effort to elaborate

[89] Staël, *De l'Allemagne*, I, p. 71.

[90] For this point, see Susan Tenenbaum, "Madame de Staël: Comparative Politics as Revolutionary Practice," in *The French Revolution of 1789 and Its Impact*, ed. Gail M. Schwab and John R. Jeanneney, Westport, Conn.: Greenwood Press, 1995, p. 63.

[91] Staël, *De l'Allemagne*, I, pp. 69–71.

[92] Staël, *De l'Allemagne*, II, p. 193.

[93] Staël, *De l'Allemagne*, II, p. 189. According to Tenenbaum, *De l'Allemagne*'s break with republicanism goes much deeper to reject the tenets of classicism that she equated with the ancient democracies, and which she had previously endorsed, in favor now of romanticism and liberalism. Tenenbaum, "Madame de Staël: Comparative Politics as Revolutionary Practice," p. 66.

[94] For the first interpretation, see Beatrice Fink, "Two Views of the *Considerations on the French Revolution*," in Gutwirth et al., *Germaine de Staël: Crossing the Borders*, p. 164, and for the second, see Michel Delon, "Germaine de Staël and Other Possible Scenarios of the Revolution," in Gutwirth et al., *Germaine de Staël: Crossing the Borders*, p. 26.

a systematic and comprehensive liberal interpretation of the Revolution and its aftermath, which, as Susan Tenenbaum argues, provides a "sweeping framework for the French Revolution which served as the foundation for the liberal school of Restoration historiographers."[95] There, Staël began to refer to the Declaration of the Rights of Man and Citizen as exemplifying "the liberal principles of the Revolution."[96] Concurrently, she praised the first phase of the Constituent Assembly for "its liberal institutions," which gave birth to "civil liberty for all" and introduced important legal changes protecting individual freedom against arbitrary state predation.[97] Further, Staël's critique of Napoleon condemned his militaristic and expansionist policy to the detriment of "a purely liberal politics" that she believed to be peaceful by nature. She thus accused him of lending support to "the enemies of any liberal idea."[98]

Are such references, however plentiful, sufficient to qualify Staël's posthumously published book on the French Revolution as liberal? Not if these are mere allusions unaccompanied by major substantive theoretical and political formulations. In fact, just such elements are present in this important text. Most fundamental is the predominant role she assigned to individual liberty, which emerges here as the guiding concept of her historical narrative. "The first basis of any liberty," Staël asserted, "is individual security."[99] This is the pivotal shift in her thought. On this basis, she completed her liberal revision of the distinction between the ancients and the moderns from the vantage of private individual freedom, which the ancients had lacked but the moderns fortunately had discovered.[100] Simultaneously, she embraced a discourse of unalienable individual rights. As constitutional essentials,

[95] Tenenbaum, "Staël: Liberal Political Thinker," pp. 162–163; Susan Tenenbaum, "The Politics of History: Liberal and Conservative Perspectives on the French Revolution," *Annales Benjamin Constant*, 8–9 (1988), pp. 93–104; Marina Valensine, "The French Constitution in Prerevolutionary Debate," *Journal of Modern History*, 60 (suppl.) (1988), p. 25.

[96] Staël, *Considérations*, p. 417.

[97] Staël, *Considérations*, pp. 403, 186, 183–185.

[98] Staël, *Considérations*, pp. 484, 497.

[99] Staël, *Considérations*, p. 531.

[100] Tenenbaum, "The Politics of History," p. 99; Claude Nicolet, "Les 'trois sources' de la doctrine républicaine en France," in Claude Nicolet, *Histoire, Nation, République*, Paris: Éditions Odile Jacob, 2000, pp. 46–54.

such rights are beyond the reach of majoritarian contests, legislative decisions, or electoral politics.[101]

Staël's support for English-style constitutional monarchy has long been the subject of quizzical inquiry and often has been seen as opportunism.[102] We believe this dismissal is both hasty and facile. Rather, her Anglophilia is best comprehended as a principled endorsement of individual rights. What is most praiseworthy in this model of government, she believed, is precisely the respect it accords to personal freedom, and the legal protection it offers to an individual sphere of action through the right of habeas corpus.[103] Therefore, Staël applauded the passage of a bill of rights by France's parliament in the aftermath of Napoleon's surrender. With this legislation, she considered her country to have been brought closer to the English liberal tradition of individual freedom.[104] She understood France's lag, moreover, as the product of its antiliberal aristocratic tradition. In contrast, England's aristocracy was decidedly "more liberal," even open to "the enlightened liberal party."[105] Fascinatingly, she now set the American example to the side as an inappropriate guide for France. Its republican constitution accommodating slavery, humankind's most illiberal institution, was antithetical to Staël's new commitments and sensibilities.[106]

This fundamental turn to individual rights went hand in hand with other important changes in her thinking. Staël became an ardent, even categorical, proponent of unconditional press freedom.[107] Avoiding reference to her previous positive view of censorship, she declared that any effort to limit such freedom amounts to an "annihilation" of representative government. "Freedom of the press," she insisted, "is

[101] Staël, *Considérations*, pp. 64, 200.

[102] For example, see Tenenbaum, "Madame de Staël: Comparative Politics as Revolutionary Practice," pp. 63, 65.

[103] Staël, *Considérations*, pp. 526, 535, 542, 518. As Joyce Appleby has thoroughly demonstrated, the debate between the *anglomanes* and the *américanistes* that dominated the constitutional deliberations in the National Assembly reflected a deeper dispute between two forms of government: a liberal constitutional monarchy and a modern republic. See Joyce Appleby, "America as a Model for the Radical French Reformers of 1789," *William and Mary Quarterly*, 28:2 (1971), pp. 267–286.

[104] Staël, *Considérations*, pp. 504–505.

[105] Staël, *Considérations*, pp. 68–69, 562.

[106] Staël, *Considérations*, p. 568.

[107] Staël, *Considérations*, p. 488.

the only right on which all the others depend."[108] Efforts to control the press had produced tyranny and terror. Freedom, she concluded, can be established not by state control, despotism, and oppression, but only by untrammeled free expression.[109]

Similarly, she distanced herself from her previous republican views on state religion. She now fervently favored religious freedom and freedom of conscience and advanced the separation of church and state.[110] Religion, she argued, "does not need the support of the state to maintain itself," and the state does not require religious support for its persistence.[111] Echoing John Locke, she treated religion as a strictly personal matter of faith and belief, shedding its political and public character. It strictly belongs to the realm of the inner self. In Staël's late political views, religious toleration displaces civic religion.[112] This displacement has been nicely captured by Gwynne, who has described Staël's new understanding of religion as "liberal christianism." For Staël, she notes, "Religion is . . . primarily a personal matter that takes a subtle form depending on the individual conscience and which remains closely tied to her intellectual development. This conception of religion is firmly and naturally allied to her political liberalism and her moral individualism."[113]

Staël's turn to individual rights also affected the balance between political and individual autonomy. In the past, she had approved the superiority of the former. Here, she attributed violations of civil liberty to its subordination to civic liberty.[114] Rather than praise civic virtue

[108] Staël, *Considérations*, p. 190.

[109] Staël, *Considérations*, p. 191. The only exception she permitted comes in situations defined by foreign occupation (p. 190).

[110] Staël, *Considérations*, p. 185.

[111] Staël, *Considérations*, p. 569.

[112] Staël, *Considérations*, pp. 568–569. Gwynne correctly describes Staël's views as undergoing a "radical change" between *Circonstances* and *Considérations* with respect to her previous endorsement of state religion. By contrast, we strongly disagree with Gengembre and Goldzink who have argued that there is no contradiction, break, or change in Staël's understanding of the relationship between religion and politics. Their claim that when Staël adopted the principle of the state-religion separation "she was following the same leading line and pursued the same objective" as when she advocated an official state-sanctioned religion flies in the face of all textual evidence. Gengembre and Goldzink, "Madame de Staël ou pour une réligion politique," pp. 220–221.

[113] Gwynne, *Madame de Staël et la Révolution française*, p. 159.

[114] Staël, *Considérations*, p. 249.

as she had before, Staël presently claimed that the French Revolution could have avoided terror and despotism if only it had respected and promoted "civil virtues."[115]

What, we might well ask, given the undeniably liberal character of these late writings, had become of her republicanism?[116] Staël herself eluded this question. Referring to the events of 1797, she wrote that "I surely would not have recommended, if I had been asked, the establishment of a republic in France."[117] But, in fact, she had recommended just such a republicanism.[118] This inaccurate disavowal is symptomatic of her tendency to distance herself from 'pure' republican theory the more liberal her views became. As she placed individual liberties and rights at the core of her mature political writings, she deserted the principles that had characterized her republicanism. First to have been affected in this manner was the normative ideal of equality so central to her earlier formulations.[119] At this juncture, liberty completely replaced equality. She dismissed equality, once an integral part and a condition of liberty, as a Jacobin legacy and blamed it for the Revolution's dangerous democratic surplus.[120]

[115] Staël, *Considérations*, p. 493.

[116] For Gengembre and Goldzink, *Considérations* "throws back into the shadows of a concluded past the republican program." See Gengembre and Goldzink, "Une femme révolutionnée: le Thermidor de Madame de Staël," p. 291.

[117] Staël, *Considérations*, p. 333.

[118] On the 3 May, 1795, *Nouvelles politiques, nationales et étrangères* published Staël's following open letter: "I sincerely wish the establishment of a French Republic on the bases of justice and humanity because it is proved to me that under the present circumstances only a republican government can procure calm and liberty for France." Cited in Gautier, "Le premier exil de Madame de Staël," *Revue des Deux-Mondes*, 15 July 1896, pp. 901–902. Although the sincerity of the letter has been disputed ever since, given the pressure exercised on Staël by the Committee of Public Safety, the content of her declaration summarizes the central argument she makes in *Circonstances* and in private correspondence. Moreover, even if we accept that Staël was able to deceive her alleged republican opponents, can we assume as well that she also misled her father, Jacques Necker, who wrote in a letter to a friend, dated 2 January 1797, that his daughter and the young Constant "are both wonderfully filled with republican ideas and hopes and a little too inclined to forgive the means employed by the present government in view of its aims"? Necker to Meister, cited in Henri Grange, *Les idées de Necker*, Paris: Klincksieck Librairie, 1974, p. 462.

[119] For the centrality of equality in Staël's work, see Gérard Gengembre and Jean Goldzink, "Une femme révolutionnée: le Thermidor de Madame de Staël," p. 285.

[120] Staël, *Considérations*, pp. 418, 214, 223, 245; Tenenbaum, "The Politics of History," p. 99.

Likewise, Staël replaced her previous preoccupation with the substantively ethical underpinnings of a republican society with a predominantly procedural and institutional approach based on interests. As we have seen, she now dismissed patriotic foundations. A resort to patriotism to facilitate public virtue and political participation, she warned, is "a kind of foolish self-deception" because "the people do not become free on account of their virtues."[121] Rather, only a felicitous and relatively thin institutional design produces freedom because of its capacity to envelop and appeal to the interests of all involved parties. "We must combine the institutions," she affirmed, "in such a way that each will have an interest in maintaining them."[122] The support of a liberal society can be found not in any unitary conception of the good but rather in legal and institutional arrangements that allow individuals to pursue their own conceptions of the good. Thus, quite diverse individuals and groups can come to possess an interest in the regime's stability and durability.

Similarly, she now abandoned her prior endorsement of dictatorship, her approval of a strong and independent executive, and her dislike of the separation of powers. These formulations all disappeared from her late writings. Instead, they were replaced by a fervent, even unconditional, embrace of abstract formal legality, an enduring rule of law, and the separation of powers.

III

Why did Staël, grappling with the legacies of Revolution and the exigencies of regime stability, repudiate, even deny, her republican past? Which flaws inherent in republicanism with respect to the problem of how to bring the revolutionary moment to a conclusion did she identify to warrant her turn toward liberal themes? Which advantages did liberalism offer to reconsider fundamental institutional and political challenges bequeathed by the collapse of the *ancien régime* that she previously had believed republicanism could successfully face up to? These questions direct us yet again to the complex relationship between liberalism and republicanism.

[121] Staël, *Considérations*, p. 243.
[122] Staël, *Considérations*, p. 243.

Central to Staël's critique was republicanism's failure to occupy the postmonarchical center of modern politics, a task she once had assigned to a version of this doctrine. This pursuit remained a constant in her writing. This preoccupation proved consistent, but republicanism, she came to think, could not offer a persuasive solution. More particularly, she attributed this inability to a series of distinct yet closely connected elements inherent in the theory.

Contrary to her earlier confidence, Staël realized that it had become impossible for a republic committed to virtue and a unitary public good to also secure and advance individual liberty. She once had hoped that republican rule could be inclusive within its own terms of political reference – that is, for virtuous citizens. Yet how was civic virtue to be discerned and implemented, and how were boundaries among members of the population to be drawn, under modern conditions in a large state where civil society no longer was homogeneous and where political preferences were diverse?

Even with the invention of representation, France could not make the leap from absolute monarchy to a free republic without resorting to state coercion. As republics require committed, active, and patriotic citizens ready to subordinate their private interests to the public good, only organized power, inherently coercive and intrusive, could secure this devotion. Such actions of imposition necessarily threaten the freedom and rights of individual citizens. Staël's sharp criticisms of Robespierre as an exemplar of republican theory and practice were shaped by just this concern.[123] In turn, however, should republicanism abjure the quest for virtue, even at the price of compulsion, it cannot realize its own enabling conditions, its sense of strong citizenship. That is, in this way, it loses a core feature and its distinctive identity.

Staël came to see that, in such circumstances, the Revolution had to resort to the only solutions it could offer, including the suspension of press freedom and religious liberty, adding up to a strategy of dictatorship, a remedy she once had accepted as a high republican thinker but now found abhorrent.[124] This is the basis for her evolving liberal turn. Once she recognized the need to combine representation with rights to safeguard persons against such unavoidable dictatorial infringements,

[123] Staël, *Considérations*, pp. 303–315.

[124] Staël, *Considérations*, pp. 240, 265–266, 272; Staël, *Des circonstances*, p. 132.

she entered into a liberal embrace. Liberalism can live with, and manage, the absence of unitary virtue and heterogeneous views by seeking to establish freedom through freedom – that is, through legality and the protection of the individual.[125]

With this insight, we can see Staël reaching into the core of the modern republican dilemma. She identified republicanism itself as the problem. To occupy the *juste milieu*, it would need to abandon its assertive endorsement of patriotism, civic virtue and the belief in a unitary common good, ethical homogeneity, and support for a strong executive. It also would have to distance itself from its own egalitarian impulses. In so doing, the doctrine would have no choice but to dissipate its singular specificity by moderating its defining claims. To mediate between absolute monarchy and democracy, republicanism could only surrender its distinct character.

In short, a republic either was unfeasible or could become practicable only at the price of coerced imposition by dictatorial force.[126] Staël thus pointed to an affinity between republicanism and terror. The excesses of the Revolution were not external to republicanism, she had come to believe. Even the abrupt rise of Bonaparte, she attributed to the legacy of republicanism's attempts to end the Revolution by deploying only its own means, thus unintentionally producing the reconcentration of power in the hands of a single person. For this reason, Staël backed away from her prior call for the exclusive control by republicans against their political rivals.[127] It was, after all, not the Jacobins, she recognized, but "the laws of terror and the military force created by a republican enthusiasm," as well as the recurrent recourse to coups d'état, that had prepared the ground for Napoleonic rule.[128]

The gap between Jacobinism and republicanism thus had blurred. Staël's new critique focused on their similarities. More precisely, she now argued that republicanism shared with Jacobinism a flirtation with extremism, a disdain for limitations and constraints, and an inability to generate stable institutions. Both orientations, in other words, faced the common problem not only of forced homogeneity but also

[125] Staël, *Considérations*, pp. 183–188.
[126] Staël, *Considérations*, pp. 272, 333.
[127] Staël, *Des circonstances*, p. 130.
[128] Staël, *Considérations*, p. 367.

of an institutional deficit. They were prone to promote revolution without end, and destruction without a new founding. This proximity annulled republicanism's claim to possess mediating and reconciling powers. Rather than being a force for moderation and balance between extremes, its obligatory pursuit of virtue and equality had eroded its noble postrevolutionary aspirations to rule a free society, leaving the political center vacant, a center Staël came to fill with liberal principles.[129] With this recognition, Staël came to desire a form of limited government, consisting of a separation of powers, abstract legality, and individual private liberties.

Having worked through these changes in Staël's writings, we have traced one lineage producing liberalism from within and against revolutionary French republicanism. This mapping permits two conclusions. We offer a solution to the largely unresolved paradox her writings have presented historians of political ideas. Neither a republican nor a liberal exclusively, Staël traversed the former only to arrive at the latter destination by searching without waver for a stable center of political gravity. Although her liberalism broke with republicanism, it continued to share a concern for a legitimate free constitution and expressed a parallel desire to avoid the perils of extremism.[130] Holding on to these aspirations, but disappointed with republicanism's ability to achieve them, Staël became far more attentive to problems of political power and its limits and sought to find means to protect individuals and enhance their personal freedom.

[129] We also are now in the position to revisit Judith Shklar's theory of the liberalism of fear in order to slightly amend it. We learn from Staël that fear of personal persecution caused by violations of individual freedom through the incursion of public power was first a republican rather than a liberal experience. There was, in fact, a republicanism of fear grounded in the failure to secure the political middle against extremes of the Right and the Left. It was this traumatic encounter with state-centered predation that instigated, from within republicanism, a transformation in the direction of liberalism. Confronting terror unleashed by the revolutionary process, republicans turned to individual rights to demarcate a sphere of personal autonomy against arbitrary and discretionary excesses of republican revolutionary foundings. By so doing, the central aspects of republican doctrine were modified in a manner that led to the crystallization of liberalism. From this vantage, it is at least as correct to understand liberalism to have been the product of republican fear as having confronted fears about statism directly. See Judith N. Shklar, "The Liberalism of Fear," in *Judith N. Shklar: Political Thought and Political Thinkers*, ed. Stanley Hoffman, Chicago: University of Chicago Press, 1998, pp. 3–20.

[130] For an argument along these lines, see Gengembre and Goldzink, "Une femme révolutionnée: le Thermidor de Madame de Staël," pp. 279, 284–291.

Second, we understand the process by which Staël qualified as the founder of French liberalism.[131] Seeking a stable and lasting constitution of liberty, her liberalism was geared to bring the Revolution to a political and institutional conclusion, while securing freedom from the predatory energies of the Right and the Left. Her work guides us in comprehending why, although republicanism had seemed well positioned to emerge as the main site of constitutional and popular common sense in the immediate aftermath of the demise of the French monarchy, these prospects were not realized. Rather, with Staël's encouragement, by the mid-nineteenth century republicanism had been discredited and liberalism was developing as a new force.

[131] Thibaudet, *Idées politiques de la France*, Paris: Stock, 1932, cited in Jardin, *Histoire du libéralisme politique*, p. 210.

6

On the Liberty of the Moderns

Benjamin Constant and the Discovery of an Immanent Liberalism

Reading Benjamin Constant provides a privileged access to the unfolding and gradual crystallization of modern continental liberal constitutionalism within and against a republican background. His experience parallels Germaine de Staël's, but because Constant was a more explicitly reflective and systematic political thinker, we can see this process develop in a more lucid manner. With Constant as our guide, we trace another political pathway for the emergence of postrevolutionary French liberalism. As we have seen, with the king deposed, monarchy's main doctrinal antagonist, republicanism, failed to fill the vacuum of authority and neutrality at the center of the state. This incapacity impelled a young generation of republicans, notably including Staël and Constant, to question their initial commitments and search for more effective political solutions. Encountering theories of rights, they produced a body of thought that gradually broke, though not completely, with its republican past, to become an independent and distinctive political doctrine.

Their liberalism faced two strong adversaries, each also competing to replace the deposed king. The political spectrum polarized between counterrevolutionaries and radical republicans. Satisfied with neither position, the generation of new liberals understood that substitution for the monarch demanded new instruments that could wear a magisterial mantle of neutrality. To this end, they designed a strategy of transcendence to supersede the radical and conservative extremes. They did so by raising the level of abstraction to constitute an impartial and objective point of view from which neutrality, detached from the person of the king, could reappear in the formal and procedural activities of the state's institutional ensemble.

But failing in their effort to identify a perfect analog to the king above and beyond politics, they shifted to another strategy. They climbed down abstraction's ladder, no longer seeking to transform neutrality into a 'view from nowhere.' Instead, neutrality was reconceptualized more syncretically as a force for integration at society's center, one they hoped would be capable, by mediating and reconciling the two extremes, to trump the other alternatives. The successful and full emergence of political liberalism as the predominant substantive alternative to royalty was advanced by this shift toward an immanent, contextual approach to neutrality.

Constant's writings clarify this tradition's genealogy, disclosing as an animating political objective the substitution of the neutral role of the monarch with an equivalent.[1] He pursued this objective, understanding it to be a quest to secure a modern concept of liberty. "Since we live in modern times, I want a liberty suited to modern times," he declaimed in his famous speech of 1819 on "The Liberty of the Ancients Compared with That of the Moderns."[2] No longer able to enjoy or practice the liberty of the ancients, humankind under modern conditions, he thought, must discover a novel solution to the problem of political order. Yet in practicing the liberty of the moderns, order itself had been profoundly brought into question. The particular conditions that had supported the democratic organization of liberty in classical times, which had closely entwined the will and participation of individuals with the exercise of sovereignty, no longer existed. The ties linking the individual and the collectivity of citizens were far more opaque. Modernity sharply poses challenges to democracy and authority as a result of commerce, social heterogeneity, religious pluralism, and individualism.

[1] See, for an interpretation that projects this as Constant's principal motivation, Roland Mortier, "Comment terminer la Révolution et fonder la République," *Annales Benjamin Constant*, 8–9 (1988), pp. 293–310.

[2] Benjamin Constant, "The Liberty of the Ancients Compared with that of the Moderns," in *Constant: Political Writings*, ed. Biancamaria Fontana, Cambridge: Cambridge University Press, 1988, p. 323.

While seeking the strategic goal of discovering an institutional surrogate for monarchical authority in democratic times, Constant explored divergent designs at different moments of his theoretical development. Working to secure this aim, each of his various explorations took an institutional form, resulting in sophisticated constitutional proposals.[3] As his thought matured, he moved from a primarily republican position, first to a purely liberal orientation and then, most interestingly, to a more synthetic hybrid we call immanent liberalism, encompassing three apparently opposed principles of legitimacy: democratic, liberal, and traditional.[4]

Our reading unfolds chronologically. We first show how excellent recent scholarship underscores only limited facets of Constant's overall project, thus forsaking the chance to persuasively argue for the contribution of his thought to the genealogy of liberalism. Taking his three major constitutional studies as points of reference, we treat the maturation of his intellectual evolution as exemplary of the development of liberal thought. To his perennial questions of how to organize a new political order and how to restrict but acknowledge democratic power without vitiating the prospects of an effective neutral government, his first systematic answer, *Fragments d'un ouvrage abandonné sur la possibilité d'une constitution républicaine dans un grand pays* (1800–1803), evinced the republican origins of his political thought, here centered on the principle of equality.[5] Later, his *Principes de politique applicables à tous les gouvernments* (1802–1806) took a sharp, confidently liberal turn.[6] Popular sovereignty, the axial principle in this text, is the main source of anxiety. Emphasizing the rule of law,

[3] Benjamin Constant, *Cours de politique constitutionnelle*, Geneva-Paris: Slatkine, 1982, p. LV. This collection was first published in 1861, but the version reproduced here was published in 1872.

[4] The complexity of Constant's third constitutional treatise has been recognized by Guy Howard Dodge, who refers to Constant at this moment as "traditional and conservative" rather than "abstract and radical"; and by Tzvetan Todorov who labels Constant the first French liberal democrat. Guy Howard Dodge, *Benjamin Constant's Philosophy of Liberalism: A Study in Politics and Religion*, Chapel Hill: University of North Carolina Press, 1980, p. 100; Tzvetan Todorov, *Benjamin Constant: la passion démocratique*, Paris: Hachette, 1997, p. 37.

[5] Benjamin Constant, *Fragments d'un ouvrage abandonné sur la possibilité d'une constitution républicaine dans un grand pays*, ed. Henri Grange, Paris: Aubier, 1991.

[6] Benjamin Constant, *Principes de politique applicables à tous les governments*, Geneva: Droz, 1980.

economic liberty, a bounded state, and distinctions between public and private, and the state and civil society, Constant here wrestled with liberal issues on liberal terms. Last, in his most complex constitutional statement, *Principes de politique applicables à tous les gouvernments représentatifs et particulièrement à la constitution actuelle de la France* (1815), he moderated this 'pure' liberalism to seek a more syncretic articulation of democratic, liberal, and monarchical thought.[7] Contrary to Constant's prior, more one-dimensional, efforts, this comprehensive theoretical statement constitutes an explicit effort to develop a liberalism rooted in the history and tradition of French society.

I

Of course, we are not alone in attending to these writings. Stephen Holmes's *Benjamin Constant and the Making of Modern Liberalism* thoughtfully intuits their significance for the origins and development of liberal theory.[8] We situate our discussion within his broader effort. Renewed attention to Constant, Holmes argued, can help recover a particular version of early liberal thought that is not adverse to democracy, that does not privilege a particular social class or interest, and which thus promotes a neutral state and creates a nonantagonistic relation between the right and the good.[9] Constant thus is treated as a model, a thinker whose work well exemplifies key features of liberal thought. Curiously, it is this welcome insight that we believe throws Holmes off course. What Holmes does is read backward to impute to Constant qualities found in liberal thought today. The result is a loss of the project his own title underscores: the relevance of Constant's writings for the *making* of modern liberalism.

This anachronism comes with a double price. First, by treating Constant as a late twentieth-century liberal, Holmes freezes the middle,

[7] Benjamin Constant, "Principles of Politics Applicable to All Representative Governments," in Fontana, *Constant*; Goyard-Fabre, "L'idée de souveraineté du peuple et le 'liberalisme pur' de Benjamin Constant," *Revue de Métaphysique et de Morale*, 71:3 (1976), pp. 289–327; K. Steven Vincent, "Benjamin Constant, the French Revolution, and the Origins of French Romantic Liberalism," *French Historical Studies*, 23:4 (2000), pp. 608–637.

[8] Stephen Holmes, *Benjamin Constant and the Making of Modern Liberalism*, New Haven: Yale University Press, 1984.

[9] Holmes, *Constant*, pp. 2, 9, 20, 22.

'pure' liberal, moment of Constant's intellectual development, making it representative of his corpus as a whole.[10] This approach simplifies the variety, nuance, and complexity of Constant's investigations and makes it impossible to account adequately for the development and transformation of his thought. Holmes recurrently treats Constant primarily as a tactician, thus regarding instances of change in his ideas as a kind of opportunism.[11]

Second, Holmes wrongly reconstructs Constant as a fevered critic of communal values.[12] In shifting from a strategy of transcendence to one of immanence, Constant offered an ambitious endeavor to have liberal and communal values constitute each other. Holmes's reading thus is partial. Constant, it is true, did appreciate tradition for stabilizing political authority.[13] What Holmes misses, however, is Constant's normative endorsement of collective experience, shared conceptions of the good, and common bonds. These 'communitarian' elements, he came to believe, generate resources for political legitimation. For this reason, he proposed a historicist account of individual rights as the pivot of modern Western societies, as distinct from the jurisprudential tradition of social contract liberalism from which he strongly dissented.[14] Both rights and the normative foundations of power never are created outside history, Constant underscored. Rather, his historicist and

[10] For comparable approaches, see George A. Kelly, "Liberalism and Aristocracy in the French Restoration," *Journal of the History of Ideas*, 26:4 (1965), p. 522; Philippe Raynaud, "Un romantique liberal Benjamin Constant," *Esprit*, 3 (March 1983), pp. 49–66.

[11] Holmes, *Constant*, pp. 15, 33, 36, 39, 100, 118, 187, 194, 210, 219. Holmes's reading underestimates the continuous doctrinal and theoretical seriousness of Constant's writings. From the start, Constant's political texts wrestled with a small number of key questions. His solutions, however, developed and evolved, but not, as Holmes has it, simply as situational and strategic responses to the ups and downs of French politics, but as a profound intellectual attempt to elaborate a consistent, comprehensive, and modern theoretical system able to confront political problems and provide valid institutional and doctrinal answers. Constant's thought did change over time, but not episodically. Rather, these shifts were geared to and motivated by an internal logic, a working out over time of vexing conceptual and practical dilemmas. As such, the body of work he produced is characterized both by deep continuities – hence it has a unified cast – and by stepwise shifts in which he experimented with fresh solutions to his central, consistent quests.

[12] Holmes, *Constant*, pp. 164–166.

[13] Holmes, *Constant*, p. 190.

[14] Marcel Gauchet, "Constant: le libéralisme entre le droit et l'histoire," in Marcel Gauchet, *La condition politique*, Paris: Gallimard, 2005, pp. 277–304.

contextual approach suggests an intimate relationship between modern liberalism and republicanism.

For Holmes, Constant's unity is substantive and continuous: always a liberal, always a thinker concerned with rights, always a principled antimonarchist. Against this reading, Biancamaria Fontana's *Benjamin Constant and the Post-Revolutionary Mind* proposes a radically dissimilar interpretation.[15] Her work portrays Constant as a republican thinker with strong democratic convictions, thus sensitizing us to otherwise neglected questions and issues that vexed Constant. His political thought, she observes, cannot be separated from modernity's most fundamental political challenge: that of reestablishing links between democracy and individuality within secular circumstances.[16]

Despite this contribution, Fontana's counterpoint, like that of Holmes, inflates only one dimension, the republican aspect of the young Constant, which she treats as defining. Reading Constant primarily from the perspective of his early, most republican work, she downplays his subsequent liberal development.[17] As such, she reproduces from the other side exactly the same interpretive structure as Holmes. She fails to account for the evolution and diversity of Constant's work and thus its significance within the lineage of liberalism. By asserting the republican singularity of his thought, she also reduces its multifarious qualities to mere tactical adjustments to political circumstances. Once again, Constant emerges as an opportunist.[18]

By contrast, we observe how Constant's political writings were steady only in their questions.[19] But the solutions altered: at times

[15] Biancamaria Fontana, *Benjamin Constant and the Post-Revolutionary Mind*, New Haven: Yale University Press, 1991.

[16] Fontana, *Constant*, pp. xv–xvii. In this respect, Constant sought the same resolution as Jean-Jacques Rousseau: to solve the dilemmas of modernity by political-institutional means. Where they differed, however, lay in the relationship each proposed between private and public autonomy. Instead of seeing Constant simply as opposed to Rousseau, he is better considered as a thinker who attempted to redirect Rousseau's project.

[17] Fontana, *Post-Revolutionary*, p. xvii.

[18] Fontana, *Post-Revolutionary*, pp. 60, 64, 66.

[19] Todorov likewise has made an effort to discover the central theme unifying all of Constant's writings, not just his political thought. However, he does little more than restate the now familiar view that Constant sought to reconcile political and individual autonomy. See Todorov, *Constant*, pp. 23, 24, 40, 48, 191. An earlier effort along these lines is Raynaud, "Un romantique liberal: Benjamin Constant," *Esprit*, 33 (1983), pp. 49–66.

republican, at times liberal, even at times traditional, and finally a combination of all three.[20]

II

Anticipating the central objective of his political thought, Constant described in an early essay the main task of political theory as the discovery, in the absence of the king, of how "to protect against arbitrariness... to bind to principles."[21] Writing in the aftermath of the French Revolution, during the years of rule of the Convention and the Directory, he argued for general and fixed principles to stabilize the new Republic against two opposed, but potentially dangerous, orientations: the conservative reaction of the *ancien régime* and the excessive impulses of the radical party.[22] Both, he remarked, echoing Staël, had failed to compensate for the lack of a stable, effective, modern counterpart to the fallen monarch. Despite their deep differences, they had converged to endorse a limitless political authority and arbitrary power prone to terror and violence.[23]

A preoccupation with this conundrum remained at the center of Constant's writing about constitutional politics.[24] Searching for "positive principles, of clear and precise laws: in a word, of the need of institutions so fixed as not to permit to tyranny any admission, to enslavement any excuse," he explored three constitutional models, differentiated by an understanding of arbitrary power, their principles of

20 Our interpretation is consistent with Constant's self-understanding: "Je dois cependant convenir avec franchise que le désir de perfectionner ce que je publiais, m'a engage souvent a y introduire des changements notables; mais ils ne portent jamais sur la base de mes théories. Ils consistent en developpements de ces théories, en preuves nouvelles, soit de raisonnement, soit de fair, et en inférences qu'autrefois j'avais ou moins clairement aperçues, ou moins soigneusement déduites." *Cours*, p. LV.

21 Benjamin Constant, *Ecrits et discours politiques*, Vol. 1, ed. O. Pozzo di Borgo, Paris: Chez Jean-Jacques Pauvert, 1964, p. 82.

22 Constant, *Ecrits*, pp. 27–31.

23 Constant, *Ecrits*, p. 77.

24 Constant defined arbitrariness "as the absence of rules, limits, definitions; in a word, the absence of everything that is precise.... And arbitrariness, being the absence of everything that is determined, everything that does not comply with." Constant, *Principes I*. He also defined a constitution as "the guarantee of the liberty of a people: consequently, whatever is conductive to this liberty is constitutional, and respectively, nothing is constitutional that is not conductive." Constant, *Ecrits*, pp. 72, 80. These two definitions did not change throughout his intellectual career.

government, and the identity of a postrevolutionary neutrality.[25] This quest generated distinct constitutional treatises, each of which reflected a desire to reconcile democratic legitimacy with stable authority.

Constant observed sadly that his contemporaries lacked a clear understanding of the nature and value of a constitution.[26] As a remedy, he announced a forthcoming study on constitutionalism to formulate and expose "the elementary principles of liberty... the fundamental ideas of a system."[27] That study, *Fragments d'un ouvrage abondonné sur la possibilité d'une constitution républicaine dans un grand pays*, is fixed firmly within the republican tradition.[28] It opens with a fierce attack on monarchy that mounts two criticisms. The first is based on historical observation. With the erosion of traditional legitimacy, monarchy faced an unprecedented crisis of legitimation. The cultural and social transformations wrought by the Enlightenment had dismantled and discredited the belief in divine right, sacred traditions, and shared identities.[29] The second exposes the normative deficits of monarchy. The existence of privilege and inequality had divided society into opposing classes, creating artificial conflicts and cleavages.[30] Consequently, kingship had become "a perpetual arbitrariness," unable to satisfy its historical neutrality.[31] It exclusively served the class interests of the nobility, thus violating the security of the citizenry and the common interest of society as a whole.[32] He concluded that the monarch no longer could represent the unity of a republican state.

What principle of legitimation might replace the old one? Constant quickly dismissed the two available solutions of an elected or a constitutional king of the English type. The former he thought to be

[25] Constant, *Ecrits*, p. 79.

[26] Constant, *Ecrits*, p. 80.

[27] Constant, *Ecrits*, p. 64.

[28] For a political biography of the young republican Constant, see Henri Grange, *Benjamin Constant. Amoureux et Républican 1795–1799*, Paris: Le Belles Letters, 2004.

[29] Constant clearly anticipates Weber's definition of traditional legitimacy. The latter defines traditional legitimate domination on similar grounds. Traditional authority, Weber argues, rests "on an established belief in the sanctity of immemorial traditions and the legitimacy of those exercising authority under them." See Constant, *Fragments*, pp. 137–39, 175, 178, 205, and Max Weber, *Economy and Society*, ed. Guenther Roth and Claus Wittich, Berkeley: University of California Press, 1978, pp. 215, 226–41.

[30] Constant, *Fragments*, p. 116.

[31] Constant, *Fragments*, p. 210.

[32] Constant, *Fragments*, pp. 141–143. See also pp. 133, 201–204, 209.

contradictory and inconsistent.[33] He initially praised the latter for its manifest qualities of stability, impartiality, and neutrality, but soon rejected this option as inappropriate to the particular needs and historical circumstances of France.[34] France is not England, he reminded partisans of the English monarchy; one must "look for liberty with means others than the ones of the British constitution."[35]

The collapse of social privilege and political inequality, Constant asserted in republican language, had been replaced by a "progression toward equality."[36] Building on the historical and political doctrines of the eighteenth century, he identified an irreversible trend culminating in the generation of a new principle of legitimation: popular election.[37] He never modified this commitment to the superiority of democracy.[38] "Only popular election by itself," he argued, "can invest national representation with a true force thus endowing it with strong roots in public opinion . . . the legitimate organs of the nation are the ones to express this sovereign will."[39]

If the displacement of the locus of political authority from the king to the people marked the perennial influence of republican thought for Constant, it did not exhaust his political project. Attentive to reactionary critics of the French Revolution, he integrated their fears about the tyranny of the majority. Combining both influences, Constant asked which normative principles, legal mechanisms, and institutional arrangements might circumscribe and delineate the proper contours of democratic power and eliminate the tendency for popular sovereignty to be exercised in an unrestricted manner. Such an unbridled force, he dreaded, would amount to a new, more pervasive, and fearful form of arbitrariness, the "tyranny of the people's elected representatives."[40]

Here we can discover the dynamic character of this early phase of his thought. Recognizing democracy as the indisputable principle of modern politics, he also acknowledged that "the republics suppress

[33] Constant, *Fragments*, p. 164.
[34] Constant, *Fragments*, pp. 188–193.
[35] Constant, *Fragments*, p. 193.
[36] Constant, *Fragments*, p. 226.
[37] Constant, *Fragments*, p. 300.
[38] Constant, *Fragments*, p. 151.
[39] Constant, *Fragments*, p. 300.
[40] Constant, *Fragments*, p. 295.

by popular movements with a rage and in masses that render their calamities more remarkable [than those of monarchy]."[41] To counter, he tried to adapt democracy to modern conditions by emplacing the "principle of representation" within a reconstructed republican theory of power that combines popular sovereignty with the general interests of the nation, thus overcoming the subordination of the common good to partial class interests.[42] But this insight is not much developed in this text and plays only a secondary role. Indeed, the three pages Constant devoted to it end with a gloomy comment on the antidemocratic and frail character of the representative system.[43]

What representation can only partially accomplish, a complex system of checks and balances and dividing powers is more likely to achieve. Relying on Montesquieu, Constant sought to translate the republican tradition of mixed government into institutions and mechanisms to guarantee that free government would be self-limiting. Lacking recourse to an independent principle with the capacity to circumscribe popular sovereignty from the outside, Constant proposed six specific institutional mechanisms that would induce the executive and legislative branches to check each other.[44]

Two further considerations bear emphasis. Within this constitutional scheme, individual rights are only peripheral. They are mentioned only three times, mainly toward the end of the book, and are not integrated into nor do they influence Constant's central argument.[45] Here, rights do not constitute an autonomous normative criterion and lack institutional expression. Thus, his first constitutional theory underplays the significance of rights, subordinating them to the overriding principle of equality. Likewise, this work neglects other key

41 Constant, *Fragments*, p. 217. See also pp. 152, 247, 256–257, 259, 260, 292, 304, 419–420.

42 Constant, *Fragments*, p. 263.

43 Constant, *Fragments*, p. 265. It is worth noticing that Constant was extremely ambivalent, as is the entire liberal tradition, about the scope and depth of democracy. On the one hand, he argued that parliament is not a mere talking shop but a "strong public sphere" that in addition to deliberation and discussion actively participates in the process of decision making. On the other hand, Constant opted for a bourgeois democracy characterized by restrictions on the franchise based on class and property. See *Fragments*, for the first claim, pp. 267–68, 271–272; for the second, see pp. 251–252, 260, 284, 297, 317–320.

44 Constant, *Fragments*, pp. 363, 267–272.

45 Constant, *Fragments*, pp. 298, 400–401, 436.

features that appear in his later, more liberal writings. These include the distinction between private and public, the separation of the state from civil society, economic liberalism, and the idea of a minimal state.[46]

Constant never separated his constitutional considerations, here or later, from the broader enabling factor of moral support. A constitution, he understood, is not simply a formal description of abstract and general principles. Constitutions of that kind are either transformed into dead letters or overthrown. Constant attributed the collapse of one constitution after another in France to the lack of public spirit.[47] Writing as a classical republican, he rhetorically asserted that anyone can draft a constitution, but not everywhere "is there the public spirit that will maintain it."[48] A republican state, he enjoined, "is solely supported by the sentiment of a public spirit.... Only when the citizens are animated by a vivid patriotic enthusiasm are public affairs working well.... And this patriotism originates when each citizen contributes to public matters."[49]

Attentive to the critique of the conservatives, Constant recognized that the institutional solutions he had proposed to remove arbitrary power had, in turn, created a new difficulty. Having sought to limit political authority by turning the executive against the legislative, the space of neutral authority the king had occupied now was empty. The state became weak.[50] How, he wished to understand, could limitations on arbitrariness proceed without damaging a strong and impartial government?

Constant's main expositors have neglected this aspect of his theory.[51] Constant's critique of monarchy announced an intention to

[46] The secondary and marginal role of individual rights is manifested in Constant's *Ecrits*. Here, the protection of individual rights ranks only third and last in the order of priorities a constitution should have. First, a republican constitution should guarantee the principle of popular legitimacy; second, it should guarantee governability; and, only third, should it protect the security of individuals. *Ecrits*, pp. 74–76.

[47] Constant, *Fragments*, p. 420.

[48] Constant, *Fragments*, p. 198.

[49] Constant, *Fragments*, p. 210.

[50] Constant, *Fragments*, pp. 182, 405.

[51] Constant's preoccupation with governability and stability contradicts Pierre Manent's interpretation that he is an "oppositional" and "critical" thinker who proposed a "negative" liberalism unable to rule effectively. By adopting and overimposing on Constant's texts Carl Schmitt's idiosyncratic and highly controversial approach to liberalism, Manent misses an entire aspect of Constant's thought. Pierre

avoid "vacillation" as well as "arbitrariness" by substituting a new collective institution for the monarch who had served as the traditional locus of neutrality. If arbitrariness threatens liberty, vacillation creates "dissolution."[52] Because he had avoided the first danger by juxtaposing the executive against the legislative, he confessed, having already rejected monarchy, that a "new inconvenience has arisen."[53] In the "extraordinary circumstances" of irreconcilable conflict between the two branches of the government, what authority could intervene?[54] A deadlock is a "state of crisis" that threatens the unity and existence of government.[55] Because the monarch no longer possesses supreme authority, no longer is there an institutional entity endowed with the right to decide in circumstances for which the constitution makes no provision, and conflict among the constitutional powers is not circumscribed.

To counteract these resulting centrifugal forces and fill the space vacated by the dethroned king, Constant sought to discover a new source of neutral power that, standing above conflicts and indecision, could defend the constitution and the unity of the state in the name of public interest.[56] Hence he proposed a new higher institution

Manent, *An Intellectual History of Liberalism*, Princeton, N.J.: Princeton University Press, 1994, pp. 91, 93. A similar, but less confident approach is expounded by Holmes. Paradoxically, although he rightly praises Constant for his institutional acuity and for a political liberalism capable of supplanting traditional monarchy as an effective instrument of governance, he scorns him for his excessive negative evaluation of power and for his obsession with the requisite limits to be placed on sovereign power and thus with the inability of his liberalism to rule and govern effectively. Holmes, *Constant*, pp. 128, 222, 259. Additionally, Mark Lilla reiterates the same misleading view characterizing Constant works as "mainly critical and oppositional, reacting to events of the day: the collapse of the Revolution into the Terror, the rise of Napoleanic despotism and empire." Mark Lilla, "The Legitimacy of the Liberal Age," in *New French Thought: Political Philosophy*, ed. Mark Lilla, Princeton, N.J.: Princeton University Press, 1994, p. 8. Marcel Gauchet, by contrast, attends to this aspect of Constant's thought and makes it a central pivot of his interpretive reading in his preface, "Benjamin Constant: l'illusion lucide du liberalisme," in *Benjamin Constant: écrits politiques*, ed. Marcel Gauchet, Paris: Le Livre de Poche, 1980, pp. 26, 38–39, 81–82.

52 Constant, *Fragments*, p. 211.

53 Constant, *Fragments*, p. 259.

54 Constant, *Fragments*, p. 370.

55 Constant, *Fragments*, pp. 389, 370.

56 Paul Bastid, *Benjamin Constant et sa doctrine*, Vol. 1, Paris: Librairie Armand Colin, 1966, p. 110.

equipped with extraordinary, almost dictatorial, powers.[57] It must, in fact, be a "discretionary" power located above existing constitutional arrangements, securing its capacity by the absence of "constitutional guarantees against it.[58] "We cannot give a guarantee in the guarantee itself."[59] Constant called this *pouvoir neutre* the *pouvoir preservateur*.[60] It would speak the name of the public interest and protect the constitution by its monopoly to decide how a crisis among the ordinary branches of government should be resolved. Endowed with the capacity to dissolve both the legislature and the executive, it would remain neutral, as the king once was, in the service of French citizens.[61] In one formulation, Constant went so far as to assume that the *pouvoir preservateur* represents the *pouvoir constituent* (even if he remained highly ambivalent and uncertain about this issue).[62] On the other side, he dismissed the option of granting this "third power" to the judiciary for the simple reason that it must be placed outside any formal legal restriction, free from existing norms.[63]

In subsequent writings, Constant repudiated this republican institutional design that incorporated dictatorial powers. But he did not renounce the search for a neutral force.[64] His political ideas remained faithful to the double challenge laid down in this primarily republican constitutional discussion, asking how to limit popular power and executive prerogatives without threatening the unity, coherence, and impartiality of authority.

57 Constant, *Fragments*, pp. 380, 398, 403; Bastid, *Benjamin Constant et sa doctrine*, Vol. 1, pp. 117–136; Eugène Asse, "Benjamin Constant et le Directoire," *Revue de la Révolution*, 15 (1889), pp. 337–356; Vincent, "Benjamin Constant, the French Revolution, and the Origins of French Romantic Liberalism," p. 623.

58 Constant, *Fragments*, pp. 451–452.

59 Constant, *Fragments*, p. 451.

60 Constant, *Fragments*, p. 374; see chap. 14, pp. 436–439, and 448.

61 Constant, *Fragments*, pp. 387, 442.

62 Constant, *Fragments*, p. 442. For a detailed account of young, republican Constant's endorsement of emergency powers, see Grange, *Amoureux et républicain*, pp. 156–174.

63 Constant, Fragments, pp. 369, 381–82, 390; Gauchet, La revolution des pouvoirs. La souveraineté, le people et la représentation 1789–1799, pp. 238–255.

64 Bastid, *Benjamin Constant et sa doctrine*, Vol. 1, p. 134. For two different interpretations of this transition, see Annelien de Dijn, "Aristocratic Liberalism in Post-Revolutionary France," *Historical Journal*, 48:3 (2005), p. 663; Vincent, "Benjamin Constant, the French Revolution, and the Origins of French Romantic Liberalism."

III

Constant began his second major constitutional text, *Principes de politique applicables à tous les governments*, in a self-critical tone. Dissatisfied with the republican tilt of his prior constitutional proposal and aware of its historical and institutional limitations, he came to realize that internal checks are insufficient to counterbalance excesses of popular sovereignty and executive power, asserting that "by dividing power one is not erecting limits against the competence of the law."[65] Popular rule, he implied, cannot limit itself. On its own, democratic legitimation "does not increase the sum of the liberty of the individuals; and if we do not resort to different principles for determining the scope of... authority, liberty can be lost, in spite of the principle of popular sovereignty or even because of it."[66]

This realization propelled Constant to test a liberal orientation that might successfully reconcile state sovereignty with nonarbitrary rule while avoiding the dictatorial temptations of republican power.[67] An independent principle must be found to bind the will of the people and of the executive office from the outside. Liberalism matured as a compelling political doctrine through this search, the result of which was Constant's famous discovery and defense of individual freedom. Given the insufficiency of intrinsic restraints, Constant asked, referring to democratic authority, "is it still possible to limit it? Is there any force which can prevent it from crossing the barriers that have been erected? We can, one will say, limit power by dividing it with ingenious combinations. We can oppose and balance its different powers. But by what means can we ensure that its total sum is not unlimited? How is it possible to restrict power without power?"[68]

[65] Constant, *Principes I*, p. 55. This acknowledgment is accompanied by Constant's critique of Montesquieu. His theory of the division of powers, Constant accuses him, fails to provide adequate limits to democratic authority. Constant, *Principes I*, p. 27. For an informed biographical approach to Constant's turning away from republicanism, see Grange, *Amoureux et républican*, pp. 208–270, 329.

[66] Constant, *Principes I*, p. 28. It is this aspect of Constant's thought to which Fontana insufficiently attends. Instead, her republican reading reduces these substantive explorations to tactical moves.

[67] Vincent, "Benjamin Constant, the French Revolution, and the Origins of French Romantic Liberalism," pp. 618, 622, 625–632; Thierry Chopin, *Benjamin Constant: le libéralisme inquiet*, Paris: Éditions Michalon, 2002, pp. 69–114.

[68] Constant, *Principes I*, pp. 55.

Constant's search for an external, independent principle to accomplish this task was associated with an important revision to his theory of modernity. Previously, he had associated modern times primarily with the rise of equality and the collapse of traditional hierarchy and privilege. Now, he extended his vision to include "civil liberty."[69] His distinguishing definition of the "liberty of the moderns" – "whatever guarantees the independence of the citizens against power" – became crucial for his second constitutional design, a proposal that replaced his previous republican one.[70] Contrary to past historical experiences of political freedom, he argued, modern liberty consists primarily in private enjoyment. Influenced by William Goldwin's treatise, *Inquiry Concerning Political Justice and Its Influence on General Virtue and Happiness*, and anticipating Isaiah Berlin's distinction between positive and negative liberty, Constant redefined the terms of the relationship between political and private autonomy.

The confident, assertive liberal tone of *Principes I* contrasts with the more timid, tentative quality of *Fragments*. This shift, we believe, was motivated by Constant's discovery of individual rights at a moment of growing disillusionment with republicanism for its dictatorial deviations and abusive uses of power. Nowhere in his earlier writings did he elucidate the normative or political significance of such rights. Here, with a sense of excitement, he placed rights at the very center, rights he understood to be a set of prepolitical, presocial perquisites that no human collective authority can eliminate or threaten without losing legitimacy.[71] Crucially, such individual rights are not instruments of power but means of protection. Rather than authorize persons to make claims, rights, for Constant, impede the state from intervening in clearly demarcated areas of life. Rights are preventative, not permissive.[72]

[69] Constant, *Principes I*, p. 432. This shift is missed by Beatrice Fink's two essays, which view equality as the central principle of Constant's political thought. Beatrice Fink, "Benjamin Constant on Equality," *Journal of the History of Ideas*, 33 (1972), pp. 307–314; Beatrice Fink, "Benjamin Constant and the Enlightenment," *Studies in 18th Century Culture*, 3 (1973), pp. 67–81.

[70] Constant, *Principes I*, p. 432.

[71] Constant, *Principes I*, 29.

[72] This distinction has been elaborated by W. N. Hohfeld. He distinguished between an affirmative paucital right and a negative multilal right. Wesley Newcomb Hohfeld, *Fundamental Legal Conceptions as Applied in Judicial Reasoning*, New Haven: Yale University Press, 1966 [1919], pp. 73–74.

Constant depicted rights as "a shield," independent of politics.[73] He sought to secure rights from political conflict and games of power and, in particular, from the arbitrary and discretionary potentialities of the executive. By naturalizing individual rights, he elevated them into absolute, "immutable principles" and "eternal rules."[74] Understanding the state to be the main site of domination, he sought to provide conceptual resources to institutionally delineate and normatively circumscribe the realm of politics, thus protecting the private sphere of intimacy, pleasure, and individual freedom from being overwhelmed.[75]

Constant's justification of individual rights can be distinguished from utilitarianism and social contract theory. Utilitarianism, he believed, fails to take rights seriously. Individual freedoms must not be subordinated to utility or subjugated "to the everyday interests."[76] The attempt to derive right from utility leaves individuals unprotected. Rights are prior and superior to aggregate utility.[77] Concurrently, he criticized contractarian theories for deriving rights from a natural state.[78] Already in the nineteenth century, the existence of such an original condition had lost its plausibility in the face of the crisis of natural-law theories and the rise of historicist ideas. Rejecting transhistorical notions of human nature, Constant dismissed universal natural rights as too intangible to be politically useful. By contrast, Constant's liberalism pioneered in embedding individuals within social relations. His human agents are not located outside time and space. They are not asocial.

In this way, Constant developed a historicist and contextual justification for individual rights.[79] The modern age, he noted with melancholy, had experienced the collapse of absolute foundations, had witnessed the rise of skepticism, and had lost its capacity for strong beliefs.

[73] Constant, *Principes I*, pp. 461, 29.

[74] Constant, *Principes I*, pp. 52, 60.

[75] Constant, *Principes I*, pp. 29, 52, 58. Also see Gauchet, "Constant: l'illusion lucide du liberalisme," pp. 67–70.

[76] Constant, *Principes I*, p. 60. Despite his rejection of utilitarian justifications of rights, he occasionally refers to their utility as the basis of their legitimacy. Constant, *Principes I*, p. 129.

[77] Constant, *Principes I*, pp. 58–61. Constant's critique has been adopted by John Rawls in his rejection of utilitarianism as an appropriate theory of justice. See Rawls's *A Theory of Justice*, Cambridge, Mass.: Harvard University Press, 1973, pp. 28–33.

[78] Constant, *Principes I*, p. 202.

[79] Gauchet, "Constant: le libéralisme entre le droit et l'histoire," pp. 285–288.

The post-Galilean world was decentered, lacking a unitary worldview to keep the value spheres together. Religious proliferation and secular pluralism had transformed the way individuals relate to social reality and to themselves.[80] Privatization, individualism, and hedonism, together with liberty and equality, had formed a new historical constellation.[81] These new cultural and social transformations made claims for individual rights both possible and meaningful. In such circumstances, he cautioned, should modern politics neglect the new value of "private happiness," the price would be arbitrary power and oppression.[82] As they most conform to the conditions of modern society, individual rights and private autonomy become liberal norms that can form an independent basis for political legitimation.

This historical justification provided Constant with the resources to design a constitution that explicitly could embody and codify "liberal principles."[83] "A constitution," he forcefully asserted, "is the guarantee of these liberties. Consequently, whatever is related to these principles is constitutional, and subsequently nothing is constitutional that is not related to them."[84] To strengthen this point, he also spelled out the substantive content of a liberal constitution as consisting of "those rights of the human existence, of individual liberty, liberty of opinion, those of the laws, those of the courts."[85]

This institutionalization of rights to guard against arbitrary power sparked several substantive changes in Constant's political theory. Departing from his earlier republican orientation, he introduced an argument favoring a minimal night-watchman state, whose main tasks are to protect private property and secure the conditions required to generate profit for the capitalist class.[86] He strongly embraced Adam Smith's idea of the "invisible hand," devoting several chapters to free market transactions and economic liberalism.[87] Additionally,

[80] Constant, *Principes I*, pp. 30–31, 163–168, 173, 386, 430–432.

[81] Constant, *Principes I*, pp. 435, 444, 443, 432–436.

[82] Constant, *Principes I*, p. 435.

[83] Constant, *Principes I*, p. 144.

[84] Constant, *Principes I*, p. 115.

[85] Constant, *Principes I*, p. 119.

[86] Constant, *Principes I*, pp. 384, 261, 308, 297. In a strikingly modern chapter on the multiplicity of laws, Constant envisions what later will be called the 'juridification' thesis. The more laws the state creates, the more scope it gives for the regulation and control of the private life of the individuals. Constant, *Principes I*, book IV.

[87] Constant, *Principes I*, pp. 276–280, 285, 313–314.

Constant underscored the centrality of the judiciary, seeing procedural justice and the formal rule of law as the new face of neutrality.[88]

In this purely liberal position, Constant radically modified two themes that previously had been central to his thought. First, his discourse became more class conscious, speaking directly and openly in the name of bourgeois interests, in favor of a "government of the proprietors."[89] While acknowledging new forms of inequality, he nonetheless placed a higher value on private property and private autonomy. For this reason he rejected universal suffrage, which, he realistically observed, can threaten existing structures of power and interest.[90] The "goal of the propertyless is to achieve property. All the means that one will give them, they will use for that end. If with the liberty of their faculties and the industry that one owes them, you were to give them political rights which you do not owe them, these rights, in the hands of the greater number, will be used invariably to invade property."[91] If, in *Fragments*, Constant identified arbitrary power mainly with the monarch, in this *Principes* he identified arbitrary power with the laboring class, betraying an uneasiness when liberalism is confronted with the possibility of an inclusive democracy.

Second, Constant entirely dropped the argument for a *pouvoir preservateur*, declaring there is no higher authority than legality and the rule of law. He rejected recourse to discretionary powers even in cases of extraordinary urgency caused by a conflict between the instituted powers, and he condemned any temporary suspension of the constitution for its potential to unleash arbitrary power in the form

[88] Constant, *Principes I*, pp. 181, 184–186.

[89] Constant, *Principes I*, pp. 220, 222. Here Constant speaks as an 'organic' intellectual of the bourgeoisie whose aim is to unite the different, conflicting fractions of his class under a liberal constitution. Constant, *Principes I*, p. 223.

[90] Dodge, Holmes, and Fontana have overlooked this aspect of his political thought, arguing that he unimaginatively reproduced middle-class bias regarding the lack of education and political immaturity of the working class. Holmes, for example, adopts this interpretation even if he appears hesitant and ambivalent. Thus, he elevates Constant as a thinker who did not ground his liberalism in class interests and private property to criticize him for being oblivious to new forms of economic exploitation. Dodge, *Constant*, p. 112; Holmes, *Constant*, pp. 21, 25, 43, 54, 70, 75–77, 85, 153, 260. Fontana is rather more prepared to excuse Constant because, otherwise, her 'republican' interpretation will be shaken. Fontana, *Post-Revolutionary*, p. 77.

[91] Constant, *Principes I*, pp. 205–206. In this text, Constant appears to treat a liberal constitution as a weapon in the hands of the bourgeoisie enmeshed in class conflict, juxtaposing the "liberty and justice" of a constitutional regime against the force of numbers.

of executive prerogatives.[92] He did not stop searching for a neutral power, however, now suggesting a neutral state. This *pouvoir neutre* is divested of personal characteristics. In this impersonal state, rules and practices take up this task. In so doing, the state does not privilege any substantive concept of the good. To fill the gap left by the absence of a king as the source of impartiality and neutrality, the state must abstain from representing particular beliefs and specific parts of the social order.[93]

In an original move, Constant's liberal theory presents neutrality as an empty space. In a monarchy, neutrality is attached to the figure of the king. In modern society, it is symbolized by no particular person. Neutrality is a vacant topos that does not contain any specific configuration of the political community. It does not specify substantive values that should govern society, nor does it reflect any future collective goal of a good society toward which everyone should strive.

What characterizes Constant's liberal moment is this sustained and principled pursuit of a neutral power. Aspiring to succeed the monarch, his liberalism, itself the product of this quest, located a middle ground between radical and reactionary poles. Like the king, he conceived liberal neutrality as a force of transcendence with no particular interests, representing no particular values, and acting as an exterior instrument of regulation insulated from substantive perspectives. This neutrality is an external norm that can regulate interaction among competing ideologies and political doctrines.

Constant's liberalism was underpinned, however, by a gnawing sense of incompleteness. Although he was confident that his constitutional theory offered a bulwark against arbitrary power, his continuing republican sensibilities directed him to the possibility that privatization, self-interest, the pursuit of economic profit, and the "corruption of the superior classes" might generate new forms of oligarchy.[94] Further, formal political rights might generate political passivity, permitting a minority to seize power for its own benefit, thus violating political autonomy and the principle of democratic legitimacy.[95]

92 Constant, *Principes I*, pp. 105–115.
93 Constant, *Principes I*, p. 378.
94 Constant, *Principes I*, p. 170.
95 Constant, *Principes I*, p. 464.

He worried that his liberalism would be uncomfortably helpless against these dangers. Finding no solution, he returned to the republican tradition. Warning against the lack of a common morality, he defended himself from the charge of being oblivious to the substantive content of institutions.[96] "Independently of their immediate advantages," he argued, institutions "also create and sustain a public spirit. This public spirit," he asserted, "is the only effective guarantee."[97] But just this guarantee he could not find inside his own liberal turn.

Constant also remained attuned to the most persuasive elements of the counterrevolutionary critique.[98] He never renounced his project to combine the organization of stable political authority with a liberal constitution to guarantee individual freedom. He exhorted his readers that "when we limit the competence of the authority, it must be done scrupulously."[99] A frail government, he cautioned, can create new sources of arbitrary power. In this text, Constant failed to resolve this tension. His arguments concerning the contested boundaries between the executive and the judiciary as well as between the executive and the legislative are unconvincingly vague. He either implausibly claimed that exactly those principles which limit power account also for the state's strength or confessed that "it is not the object of our investigations to decide from which of the two inconveniences we have to resign. It is a question that must be solved differently according to the circumstances of each country."[100]

An implicit paradox haunts this text. Constant sought to resolve the problem of neutrality in modern society by postulating it as an external force. At the same time, he understood that liberal values and principles constitute and represent the most valuable political doctrine. Thus, it does not stand on the same plane as its competitors. Here lies the paradox: as Constant's liberalism strove to reestablish a neutral power, it could not divest itself from its own partisan and substantive character. His attempt to grapple with this paradox initiated his third, and most fertile, if also problematic, approach. Combining three

[96] Constant, *Principes I*, pp. 170–171.

[97] Constant, *Principes I*, pp. 347, 170–171, 397.

[98] Gauchet, "Benjamin Constant. L'illusion lucide du liberalisme," in *Benjamin Constant: écrits politiques*, p. 25.

[99] Constant, *Principes I*, p. 462.

[100] Constant, *Principes I*, pp. 195, 346, 462–463.

principles of legitimacy, this orientation is characterized by a strategy of immanence instead of transcendence.

IV

Increasingly uneasy with his previous identification of neutrality with a transcendental version of impartiality, and less confident about liberalism's inherent capacity to govern in a postrevolutionary situation, Constant gradually became critical of a purely liberal constitution. Restless to discover the conditions and norms for the preservation of individual liberty and the stabilization of democratic power, he moderated his liberalism and continued to explore the relations among alternative political traditions in yet another constitutional treatise, *Principes de politique, applicable à tous les gouvernements représentatifs et particulièrement à la constitution actuelle de la France.*[101]

There can be no doubt that individual rights, the rule of law, and political representation continued to lie at the center of Constant's political thought. Yet these liberal elements were incomplete. Even when he rhetorically continued to describe them as eternal and sacred, his motivation was primarily instrumental. He assessed their utility by their capacity, whether alone, or now in combination with other principles, to solve the core dilemmas of modern politics.

In *Principes II*, his most accomplished, comprehensive, and synthetic constitutional work, he joined together, in a complex composition, republican, liberal, and monarchical strands. Eluding familiar ideological categories, this text has been either ignored or harshly criticized; its rich potentiality has been missed.[102] Here, Constant attempted to reconcile and integrate France's political adversaries – the king and the people, authority and freedom, rights and sovereignty. Aware of the limitations of his previous constitutional attempts, and

[101] This shift was announced one year before by the publication of Constant's *Réflexions sur les constitutions et les garanties*, in *Cours*; originally published in 1814 as *Réflexions sur les constitutions, la distribution de pouvoirs et les garanties dans une monarchie constitutionelle*. This text marks the first appearance in his work of arguments on behalf of constitutional monarchy.

[102] Charles Augustin Sainte-Beuve, "Benjamin Constant et Belle de Charrière, Lettres Inédites," *Revue des deux Mondes*, 14, n.s., 6 (April 1944), pp. 193–264; Jacqueline de la Lombardière, *Les idées politiques de Benjamin Constant*, thèse de droit, Paris, 1926.

those of others, Constant sought to incorporate conservative and republican insights into a broader, syncretic but still predominantly liberal framework.

By probing this third and last elaboration, we can gain privileged entry into the process by which French liberalism came to define the political center as society's integrating political force. With the failure of the radical and reactionary contenders, and with republicanism's inability to fill the vacuum created by the absence of a king, liberalism, Constant believed, but only if properly combined with other strands of political thought, had the chance to protect individual rights by reconciling democratic legitimacy, neutrality, and governability. By attending to *Principes II*, we can apprehend how Constant's liberalism, by shifting strategies, deepened its capacities and broadened its appeal.

"The vice of almost all constitutions has been to fail to create a neutral power."[103] Responding, he now endorsed constitutional monarchy despite his former harsh criticism of monarchy as anachronistic and his previous confidence in the neutral capacities of a minimal liberal state. To the "will of the people" he added the "will of the prince."[104] This shift understandably has been puzzling. How might we account for this decision?[105] Our explanation centers mainly on the internal

[103] Constant, *Principes II*, p. 185. Alone among major interpreters of Constant, Dodge has understood this aspect of his thought. See Dodge, *Constant*, pp. 82–84, 86, 91. Gauchet has also pointed out that "For Constant himself things are perfectly clear: his idea of a neutral power, he said since 1802, is an idea of monarchical origin." Gauchet, "Benjamin Constant. L'illusion lucide du libéralisme," p. 87.

[104] Constant, *Principes I*, p. 200.

[105] Two main interpretations try to answer this question. According to the first, Constant's mature constitutional scheme demonstrates, in fact, it is characteristic of the dilemma of political liberalism in the face of social tension and class conflict. When the threat to social unity came and capitalism itself was jeopardized, Constant was only too ready to turn in the search for a strong institution incarnated in the figure of the king. According to this view, his political shifts are the integral part of the liberal tradition itself, which ever since the arrival of an organized labor movement and the immanence of universal suffrage has seen the rights of property and the independence of individuals threatened by active popular movements. Constant's theory of constitutional monarchy is, according to this reading, a forerunner of this tradition. Therefore, the tensions and contradictions were not unique to Constant. They were a characteristic feature of a bourgeois political standpoint searching for external support and risking an alliance with conservative forces in the uncertain circumstances of the development of liberal regimes. See Jacques Droz, *Histoire des doctrines politiques en France*, Paris: Presses Universitaires de France, 1948,

logic of Constant's project and his mature understanding of the role he hoped liberalism could seize.

Constant's prior solution, one that was more abstract and procedural, had proved unable to elicit the effective support of the contending parties or to truly reconcile deep social conflicts. His continuing search for neutrality, impartiality, and governability, however, brought him to a reevaluation of kingship. Suitably constrained, he now argued, the crown provides the best available symbolic and institutional embodiment of neutral power.

A parliamentary system of representation, he came to believe, in tilting toward freedom risks a new form of despotism. Even as he thought it to be indispensable, Constant expressed the republican concern that political representation can help create a new elective elite that appropriates political power by depoliticizing large sections of the population.[106] The citizens of a liberal regime "absorbed in the enjoyment of... [their] private independence, and in the pursuit of... [their] particular interests," Constant warned forcefully, "should surrender... [their] rights to share in political power too easily," especially when the "holders of authority are only too anxious to encourage... [them] to do so. They are so ready to spare... [them] all sort of troubles, except those of obeying and paying."[107] He went so far as to assert, returning to a position he once had announced in *Fragments*, that representative democracy is potentially more dangerous and more susceptible to arbitrary power than direct democracy. Unlike the *demos* that acts on its behalf and can limit itself, elected representatives tend to be unconstrained by their constituencies,

pp. 69–73. Against this interpretation, a new generation of scholars, like Holmes and Fontana, have juxtaposed a different reading aiming at relativizing Constant's changes. By reducing them to tactical and strategic accommodations reflective of the political battles in which he was involved, this approach hopes to save Constant from the pitfalls of a class thinker representing the narrow interests and values of a particular social group. Yet, by proposing an occasionalist Constant, it equally reduces and impoverishes his thought and contributions. For a third, less significant, interpretation that accounts for this shift by reference to Constant's moral theory, see Ephraim Harpaz, "Benjamin Constant entre la Republique et la Monarchie," *Annales Benjamin Constant*, 12 (1991), pp. 43–52.

106 This critique of representative government first was formulated in *Réflexions*, pp. 187–189.

107 Constant, "The Liberty of the Ancients Compared with that of the Moderns," p. 326.

"forming a class apart, separated from the rest of the people," developing "an *esprit de corps*" with its own particular interests.[108] Not only is the common good threatened, but neutrality itself is violated. Severing all ties to public opinion, Constant concluded, an unconstrained legislature can become "unlimited ... more dangerous than the people."[109]

Additionally, he drew from the reactionary tradition the fear that the absence of a king would render the state either impotent or arbitrary. This second major "vice" of representative government, most apparent at times of crisis, is its "indecision" and "exhaustion."[110] Composed of different parties, views, and sectional interests, representative assemblies are unable to act effectively as collective bodies. Although Constant valued a strategic model of bargaining and compromise among particular wills as an alternative to Rousseau's general will, he acknowledged the inability of legislative assemblies to grapple with ungovernability at extraordinary moments.[111] Even in more ordinary times, he worried that representative government can fail to embody neutrality sufficiently. Compromises are situational, the result of contingent relations of power among actors. Neutrality, by contrast, implies a critical distance from such relations.

Reiterating his old argument that cautioned against tendencies for conflict between the three branches of a representative government, Constant brought face to face the most viable elements of republican and conservative thought. He resurrected a traditional solution – find an external force to counterbalance these centrifugal tendencies.[112] The division of powers fragments political authority between antagonistic entities, which, "disturbed in their functions, cross, clash with, and hinder one another." Thus, "you need a power that can restore them to their proper place. This force cannot reside within one of these three competences.... It must be external to it, and it must be in a sense neutral."[113] This is the role for royal power, a fourth force charged

[108] Constant, *Principes II*, p. 209.
[109] Constant, *Principes II*, p. 196.
[110] Constant, *Principes II*, p. 196.
[111] Constant, *Principes II*, pp. 205, 206–207.
[112] "Le pouvoir royal est, en quelque sorte le pouvoir judiciaire des autres pouvoirs," *Réflexions*, p. 181.
[113] Constant, *Principes II*, p. 184.

with the responsibility to coordinate, harmonize, and stabilize political authority.[114]

This institutional restoration was oriented to remedy the deficiencies of an exclusively liberal design, which itself had been invoked to solve the shortcomings of a pure republic. "It is indeed the masterpiece of political organization, to have created, amid those dissensions, an inviolable sphere of security, majesty, impartiality, which leaves those dissensions to develop without danger."[115] The choice of a constitutional monarch, though anachronistic, was principled, not opportunistic or tactical. "Constitutional monarchy creates this neutral power in the person of the head of state," displacing the *pouvoir preservateur* of his first constitutional treatise and the neutral, procedural state of his second.[116] Located above partial interests, political agitations, partisan divisions, and ideological conflicts, the king possesses the motivation and the strength to protect the constitution and the unity of the state and to produce security, impartiality, and neutrality. "He floats, so to speak, above human anxieties," intervening in politics only "as soon as some danger becomes evident" where there are irreconcilable collisions and deadlocks, which he "terminates . . . by legal constitutional means, without any trace of arbitrariness."[117]

This synthesis signifies a decisive turn in the history of liberalism from transcendence to immanence. Constant inserted republican ideas and an appreciation for tradition under the leading authority of individual rights. His mature liberalism returned to the contested field of politics and history, aiming to play a convening and mediating force as the central organizational principle of a postrevolutionary society. The king returned, but in a radically reinvented role. In spite of obvious similarities, there is a crucial difference between this formulation and Constant's republican constitutional proposal for a "pouvoir preservateur." In *Principes II*, the king never oversteps the constitution. His interventions remain within limits delineated by constitutional norms

[114] For a discussion of stability, see *Réflexions*, pp. 174, 175. Here, Constant quests for order and governability.

[115] Constant, *Principes II*, p. 187.

[116] Constant, *Principes II*, p. 184; Constant, *Fragments*, p. 373. On the concept of neutral power in Constant, see Bastid, *Benjamin Constant et sa doctrine*, Vol. 2, pp. 917–927.

[117] Constant, *Principes II*, p. 187.

and provisions, without extraordinary monarchical prerogatives.[118] Rather than a source of neutrality, even less of sovereignty, he is a magisterial, symbolic, and purely ceremonial figure.[119]

What, however, can guarantee the king will not exploit his exalted position to become again an arbitrary power? In asserting that the "hereditary monarch can and must be answerable to no one. He is a being apart at the summit of the pyramid," does Constant not reproduce here the very formulation that earlier had compelled him to abandon the theory of the *pouvoir preservateur*?[120] What distinguishes this text is how the king is constrained by tradition, rather than by rules and formal norms. In this manner, Constant breaks with the familiar view that liberalism is juxtaposed to the authority of tradition, indeed that liberalism as an antitraditional ideology finds its enemy in the validity of the past. Instead, by embedding monarchy in common values and shared practices, the institution is both constrained and assertive – enclosed by history, yet a producer of these very constraints. "I admit two sorts of legitimacy: one positive, which derives from free election, the other tacit, which rests upon heredity; and I shall add that heredity is legitimate because the habits it generates and the advantages it grants render it the national will."[121]

How did this insertion of tradition in Constant's late liberalism shape a new understanding of neutrality? Because the monarch's power is "sacred," he can be counted on to symbolically represent the unity of the state and the nation.[122] Insulated from the petty interests of sectional groups, the legitimacy of royal authority rests on the "spirit" with which the nation "subjects itself to its laws and obeys them." Laws seem to derive from "a sacred source, the legacy of generations whose ghosts it venerates; then they fuse themselves intimately with its morality, they ennoble its character, and even when they are faulty, they produce greater virtue, and consequently greater happiness, than

118 Constant, *The Spirit of Conquest and Usurpation and Their Relation to European Civilization*, in *Benjamin Constant: Political Writings*, pp. 118–120. Also see Benjamin Constant, *Réflexions*, pp. 373–381.

119 Constant, *Principes II*, pp. 292, 301; Constant, *Usurpation*, p. 136. Constant personalized neutrality by the physical presence of a king but did not desert his prior argument favoring legality and procedures.

120 Constant, *Principes II*, p. 180; Constant, *Réflexions*, p. 195.

121 Constant, *Usurpation*, p. 158.

122 Constant, *Principes II*, p. 180.

would better laws that rested only on the orders of authority."[123] Monarchy with its deep roots in the history of a particular society, acquired through its lineage, ancestors, and family patrimony, subordinates and bounds the will of the king to the "quasi-mysterious tradition" and the "work of circumstances."[124] Rather than act as a concrete person, the monarch represents neutrality by incarnating the history and collective identity of the nation as such.

This synthesis is enriched by two additional aspects. The first is a deep concern about the potential for a rampant individualism that he distinguished in social contract approaches. "For men to unite together in face of their destiny," Constant argued, "they need something more than mere self-interest; they need beliefs; they need morality. Self-interest tends to isolate them, because it offers to each individual the chance to be more successful or more skillful on his own."[125] Shared dispositions, attachments, and sentiments provide a countercurrent against the dislocating and alienating effects of market competition. A "heritage of traditions, usages, and habits," of "the attachment to local customs," and of "mutual affections" generates ethical resources to counterbalance the radical individualism found in commercial societies.[126] Emphasizing this feature of Constant's immanent liberalism – a liberalism rooted in the histories of Western societies and appealing to the constitutive shared values of individuals – Tzvetan Todorov persuasively labeled it "allocentrique," distinct from a liberalism based on egocentric, abstract, and disembedded individuals.[127]

By deploying tradition in this manner, Constant addressed lacunae in his second, most liberal, constitutional proposal. He now understood the effectiveness of political rights to depend on the existence of prior communal bonds and ethical understandings, especially the "love of one's birthplace" and an attachment to "those places which offer them memories and habits" that induce the necessary motivational sentiments for a public spirit and a dedication to common affairs.[128] For Constant, the reconciliation of political with individual autonomy

[123] Constant, *Usurpation*, p. 75.
[124] Constant, *Usurpation*, p. 92.
[125] Constant, *Usurpation*, p. 58.
[126] Constant, *Principes II*, pp. 94, 76, 253.
[127] Todorov, *Constant*, p. 127; a comparable discussion can be found in Dodge, *Constant*, pp. 146–147.
[128] Constant, *Principes II*, p. 254.

is advanced by the cultivation of "communal honour" and "local customs and institutions."[129] Shared beliefs and practices can invigorate a democratic political culture by making citizens more prone to participate and more respectful of law.

His republican commitments also resurfaced. "Multiply, multiply the bonds that unite men," he implored. "Make the fatherland a part of everything, reflected in your local institutions as in so many faithful mirrors."[130] This also is the cause motivating Constant's attack on industrial capital in favor of the most traditional landed property. As Nadia Urbinati has observed, this argument betrays the clear influence of Aristotle and Cicero.[131] In combating these two economic groups, Constant stressed shared traditions, patriotism, and collective memories. Industrial property fragments, disconnects, and destroys the symbolic realm that sustains the belief in the sacredness of tradition.[132] Thus, Constant's historicism equipped him to resist the abstract construction of rights as universal. Rather than derive individual rights from natural law, he extracted them from historical experience and forms of life. Rights are the direct outcome of "the changes brought by two thousand years in the dispositions of mankind."[133] They do not hover above and before history as permanent fixtures. Rather, they are fully attached to past and present circumstances, commitments, and collective projects of particular cultures that embed individuals in specific traditions and situations.

This liberalism possesses an immanent character. Eclectic and heterogeneous, it combines republican-democratic, liberal, and traditional principles of legitimacy. With the democratic principle, first proposed in *Fragments*, and associated with a republican standpoint, he argued that we can distinguish "two sorts of power in the world: one, illegitimate, is force; the other, legitimate, is the general will."[134] The "supremacy" and absolute priority of the democratic principle that

[129] Constant, *Principes I*, p. 253.

[130] Constant, *Principes II*, p. 255.

[131] Nadia Urbinati, *Individualismo Democratico. Emerson, Dewey e la cultura politica americana*, Rome: Donzeli Editore, 1997, pp. 44–45.

[132] Constant, *Principes II*, p. 217–219. The same concern informs Constant's positive evaluation of religious feelings. What he rejected was the institution of the Catholic Church rather than religion as such.

[133] Constant, "The Liberty of the Ancients Compared with that of the Moderns," p. 317.

[134] Constant, *Principes II*, p. 175.

defines the nature of political power, is indisputable. "Indeed," he wrote, "this principle cannot be contested."[135]

But alone it is insufficient. It must be restricted by an external principle, a liberal one, that can demarcate the proper scope of popular sovereignty. These "legitimate liberties,"[136] introduced in *Principes I*, which provide normative criteria for distinguishing justified from arbitrary uses of political authority, are individual rights that citizens possess "independently of all social and political authority, and any authority that violates these rights becomes illegitimate."[137] While Constant's first republican constitution was based on the single principle of democratic legitimacy, the second constitution was endowed additionally with liberal legitimacy.

His final constitutional proposal, the one that he called "constitutional monarchy," asserts a third principle of legitimacy that is drawn from France's conservative legacy but fused with popular sovereignty, individual rights, and common virtues and bonds. This rich constellation emplaced liberalism within a spacious range of political traditions and values. Yet it is not his specific combination, or his introduction of a monarchical element, that compels us to appreciate this plan, but rather Constant's underlying motivation, a relentless search for an inclusive, integrative, free polity.

V

Our rereading contests predominant views of Constant as exemplified in the valuable works of Holmes and Fontana. It also enriches our understanding of the origins and amplification of modern continental liberalism. Against prevalent considerations of Constant, which, by reducing the complexity of his intellectual evolution to a single aspect, conclude by treating him as unsystematic and tactical, our reconstruction restores the full coherence and continuity of his political project. Against attempts to render Constant as either a pure liberal or a pure republican, we reestablish the complex interplay of these, and other, ideological elements in his writings. Finally, against the portrayal of

135 Constant, *Principes II*, p. 175.
136 Constant, *Principes II*, p. 181.
137 Constant, *Principes II*, p. 180.

Constant as a critical, oppositional thinker, we underscore his continuing concern for governability, stability, constitutionalism, and effective legitimacy.

Our intellectual history, further, suggests, perhaps even facilitates, an additional hypothesis about the sources and strategies of liberalism. With Constant, we witness the formation of a new political doctrine from within the broader intellectual and political space defined by republicanism. Able to break with its insufficient progenitor, Constant's liberalism, now newly autonomous, searched for the appropriate means to supplant competitors in the struggle to replace the king. After experimentations and failures, it incorporated other tendencies broadly on its own terms, thus marginalizing them and depriving them of their claims to represent neutrality as such. In this way, Constant's liberalism sought to become an inclusive center, discrediting or integrating its opponents. Deeply committed to liberty for the moderns, Constant came to see that an effective, legitimate, and stable liberal solution must not be pure or freestanding but needs the underpinning of the liberty of the ancients. As he concluded in his famous address of 1819, echoing Adam Ferguson's own project to reconcile civic virtue and individual interest, "far from renouncing either of the two sorts of freedom which I have described to you, it is necessary, as I have shown, to learn to combine the two together."[138]

[138] Constant, "The Liberty of the Ancients Compared with that of the Moderns," p. 327.

7

After Republicanism

A Coda

Thus, a new political liberalism was born, as three generations of seminal thinkers transformed the world of political ideas. Despite their continuing, if uneven, faithfulness to the founding principles of republicanism, their innovative writings brought its distinctive intellectual and political identity to an end.[1]

Of course, this dynamic movement in political philosophy had diverse features and took a variety of paths. Our primary goal, notwithstanding, has been to understand how Smith, Ferguson, Paine, Madison, Staël, and Constant partook in a common project. Crossing national, linguistic, and regional boundaries, as well as philosophical and political borders, they shared a way of thinking, reasoning, and imagining about politics for modern times. They drew from within on republican resources, and, aware of the limitations of these ideas in dealing with novel conditions, also were receptive to currents that presently are associated with the long history of liberal development.

Their method was predominantly historical. Rather than think abstractly in the manner of social contract philosophers, who begin with hypothetical circumstances of nature outside of time and place,

[1] This is a reversal of the formulation offered by Maurizio Viroli, who, in advocating a republican revival today admonishes that "republicanism must keep its distinctive intellectual and political identity and remain faithful to its founding principles." Maurizio Viroli, *Republicanism*, New York: Hill and Wang, 2002, p. 103.

and rather than contemplate transcendentally in the manner of natural-law theorists, who wish to establish on earth norms that hover outside and prior to human experience, they emplaced their ideas in a concrete lineage and sequence of time. As social analysts, they wished to identify arrangements, mechanisms, and causes that were specific to the circumstances they observed and analyzed, and within which they wrestled.

Smith and Ferguson famously were historicists of a particular kind. Thinking of human history as characterized by progressive stages, each corresponding to a particular form of government, they considered the status of republican political ideas in relationship to the demands of a new moment, that of commercial society. Similarly, Staël and Constant explicitly adopted such a view of historical development, but in terms of forms of liberty and rights rather than types of regime. This historicism is an aspect of their influential critique of ideas concerning states of nature. Such constructions seemed rather too constant, abstract, and remote from the reality with which they were engaged. By contrast, inflections of such thinking can be found in the writings of Paine and Madison, but their treatment of both the state of nature and the emergence from it by means of a social contract was subordinated to the pressing, immediate task of creating a tangible republic. They climbed down the ladder of abstraction and moved from normative justification to constitutional founding and institutional design.

All these thinkers also refused to sharply partition reason and sentiment. Their comprehensive philosophical anthropology composed an integrated portrait of agents that did not emphasize the capacity for reason at the expense of passion, emotion, or belief. This sensitivity to the full range of motivation, moreover, was primarily an account of the inexorable embeddedness of individuals within networks of human relationships and webs of meaning. In this way, their writings presented a singular conception of individuality that is relational and social, a situated individuality that can be comprehended only in context. These works offer a portrayal that, for sure, values reason – in markets, in civil society, in political life – but their sense of rationality is not reified or disassociated from the full range of human experience. Interestingly, the primacy of communal association thus grounds a variety of arguments favoring the worth of individuals and individuality.

In Smith, the desire for moral approbation and social recognition drives individual behavior in the marketplace. There is no contradiction between validating the self and acknowledging its constitution in ethical relations with others. Ferguson, by contrast, underscored the centrality of action and conflict in shaping and motivating modern subjectivity. A passionate identification with political life, he believed, promotes the development of persons who can think, judge, and choose as autonomous moral persons. Madison also recognized the power of human passions. But he neither gave them primacy nor celebrated their presence, but sought to find means to control their expression in political factions. Paine was himself an exemplar of the linkage of emotion and reason in political argument, as he used rhetorical tropes to mobilize citizens on an extrarational basis. Of the group, Staël is most noted, especially by literary critics, for a romantic sensibility. Her political reasoning narrated the political events of her time not by tracking failures to a lack of rationality by the major actors, but through unforgettable psychological portraits of their feelings and emotions. Constant likewise understood political fanaticism, the enemy of liberty, in just these terms.

These understandings informed their theories of politics. They superseded philosophical justifications of authority, obligation, and rights. Much as in Locke's writings on toleration, their practical reason aimed to propose specific institutional arrangements designed explicitly to reorganize political life in the here and now.

These interventions were characterized by a quest to design and promote actual, achievable institutions and norms to advance the political end – liberty for the moderns – they most desired. Their range was considerable. They explored appropriate rules and means that polities could deploy to govern a world marked by the rise of capitalism, nascent civil society, imperial expansion, religious fragmentation, and, most important, centralized political power in large territorial states and their crises of sovereignty and legitimacy.

Ferguson's quest was for relatively neutral institutional arrangements within which bargaining and political compromise could tame conflict and antagonism, channeling militaristic impulses into competitive negotiation. Markets as institutional sites, for Smith, provide just such regulated competition that can generate and sustain social order despite starkly diverging interests. Paine and Madison, Staël and Constant took the pursuit of appropriate institutions to the level of constitutional design. Face to face with the problem of how to form a proper republic after the demise of monarchy, each contributed directly, with pens, voices, and deeds, within the political fray to constitutional politics and institutional architecture.

Working with these orientations, proclivities, and tools, these thinkers and actors powerfully transformed republicanism into political liberalism but did so distinctively. Their pathways to a common outcome were not identical. The formation and crystallization of political liberalism was not the result of a single line of development. Nor can its origins be identified with a seminal thinker, or even with one lineage or sheer acts of substitution. Even in the case of Staël's shift from republican to liberal commitments, there was no defeat of the republican doctrine by a liberal rival. There was, rather, a republican failure to identify and secure a stable and enduring political center in the space between radical Jacobinism and reactionary monarchism. This disappointment prompted her liberal inventions. It was her dissatisfaction with French republicanism's violence, fanaticism, and dictatorship, as well as her fears that republicans could not end the Revolution, that impelled her to explore such new political formulations. Republican traumas, in short, motivated Staël's liberalism.

For the others we have considered, the road to liberalism was more elaborate, less direct, not as willful. More republican fragments survived the journey. In Madison and Paine, republican language and sensibilities continued to characterize and sustain their political thought. Retrofitting republicanism, each built a novel liberalism step by step. To make their republican dreams real, they equipped it with new features that transformed it into something else. With Smith, republicanism survived primarily as a theory of purpose and offered the ethical underpinnings of seemingly amoral market exchange. Yet another course was followed by Ferguson and Constant. Starting from strong republican loyalties, they ended, after inventions that were pristinely liberal, with proposals that combined civic, civil, and royal features.

These various paths converged. At their terminus, constitutional liberalism existed; republicanism no longer was a freestanding alternative, but it did not disappear. Republican values, sensibilities, and orientations have survived as deposits that fused with, and became integral to, liberal politics. In light of this history, some of the most familiar, and often pejorative, dichotomies in today's political thought, including the right and the good, interest and virtue, individual and community, make little sense. These oppositions are new fabrications that do not accurately capture the rich historical and conceptual relations between the two traditions. They contradict the most prominent aspects of liberal beginnings.

Further, both republican nostalgia and liberal purity are revealed to be false alternatives. In the late eighteenth and early nineteenth centuries, it became apparent that the republican model was radically deficient. So it is worse than ironic that some leading thinkers today counsel a resurrection of what even leading republicans two centuries ago transformed and superseded, and for good reasons. It is respectively discomfiting that a good many liberal advocates have distanced themselves from the lessons taught by key founders. By contrast with often abstract and philosophical exercises, the thick and sturdy liberalism fashioned within and against republicanism was open and syncretic, not closed and exclusive.

It goes without saying that this body of ideas was crafted for particular moments, circumstances, and pressures at some distance from our own. Read separately, one author at a time, or together, as a unified strand of political thought, that period's liberalism is not a portable or an ideal model. As a guide, however, it directs us to a particular mode of reflection, thought, and practical reasoning. Above all, by occupying space between the abstract and the concrete, the normative and the descriptive, the universal and the particular, it puts forward principled political judgments that can shape and constrain thought and action in particular situations. Its reasoning took shape not prior to but in the act of confronting especially vexing problems grounded in large-scale social and political change. It demonstrated a taste for sustained, contested, and self-critical political argument tempered by an appreciation of complexity and contradiction. It understood that normative ambitions are realized only within concrete settings, and thus that rigorous reasoning about politics requires a political sociology of existing and possible institutions.[2] It delimited and inspired a

[2] For an earlier discussion of the attractive character of liberal reasoning, see Ira Katznelson, "A Properly Defended Liberalism: On John Gray and the Filling of Political Space," *Social Research*, 61 (Fall 1994), pp. 611–630.

range of both permissible and possible forms of action, including political endeavors permeated by ethical commitments across a range that included social recognition and individual rights, agonistic participation and private independence, civic identity and religious pluralism, virtues and interests. And it especially utilized a political imagination to craft designs for a republic devoted to freedom. It thus identified a range of prospects to both empower and canalize liberty.

History has moved on; contexts have changed. But this mode of liberal reasoning – its historicity, methods, and playful combinations – remains germane. Forged within a historical crucible, and intended to confront pressing questions, that type of thinking is badly needed today. There is no shortage of challenges that resonate simultaneously as matters of theoretical reflection and practical politics. Living at a turbulent and radically uncertain time of perpetual violence, threats of annihilation, spheres of lawlessness and exception, deepening global inequalities, and often ugly forms of exclusiveness and protection, we also require new forms of consideration, understanding, and judgment.

These must transcend moral indignation, refuse to find too facile refuge in high universal principles, and resist the manipulation of fear. Rather, today's tests call out for the type of institutional resourcefulness, situated reasoning, and political invention that once characterized the cutting edge of liberal thought.

Index